T0097893

TURKEY INTERRUPTED

TURKEY INTERRUPTED

DERAILING DEMOCRACY

Abdullah Bozkurt

NEW JERSEY • LONDON • FRANKFURT • CAIRO

BLUE DOME

Copyright © 2015 by Blue Dome Press

18 17 16 15   2 3 4 5

All rights reserved. No part of this book may be reproduced or transmitted in any form or by any means, electronic or mechanical, including photocopying, recording or by any information storage and retrieval system without permission in writing from the Publisher.

Published by Blue Dome Press
335 Clifton Avenue, Clifton
New Jersey 07011, USA

www.bluedomepress.com

Library of Congress Cataloging-in-Publication Data Available

ISBN: 978-1-935295-69-3

Printed by
Çağlayan A.Ş., İzmir - Turkey

Contents

Introduction

The main reason for the confusion among many observers of Turkish politics—who try to make sense of what has been happening in Turkey based on conventional thinking—stems from their failure to grasp the real motives and petty interests to which political actors subscribe. In other words, more often than not, today's leading political figures in Turkey pursue a subtle agenda that serves the interests of a few, diverging from what is required of them: promoting the interests of their country and its people.

It is true that both classical and modern political science theories have ample tools to provide a comprehensive understanding of Turkish politics, on both the domestic and foreign policy fronts. Yet such analyses remain incomplete or insufficient when these templates fail to take into account parochial group interests and the personal ambitions of greedy politicians who shape or influence the policy decision making process to a varying degree.

My past experiences as a journalist both in the US capital covering Washington's beltway politics, special interest groups, and lobbyists and in New York covering the United Nations where supranational actors make their sales pitches help me here in the Turkish capital to identify the interests of factions, key players, and groups who may very well defy a common sense approach simply because they have a completely different agenda than many people think Turkey should pursue.

I've certainly been wrong a fair amount in the past and would never claim that my analyses—published at regular intervals in Turkey's best-selling English daily, *Today's Zaman*, and that are now collected in this book—are immune from criticism.

To my credit, however, I think I have gathered a reasonable amount of insight into key actors in a gossipy town like Ankara, where there is no shortage of access into Parliament, the higher judiciary, the government, and the diplomatic community. Sorting out facts from the myths and rumors that are abundantly available is not easy. Without knowing the background of political actors and their often complicated and latent web of linkages among businesspeople, technocrats, and bureaucrats, it would simply not be possible to comprehend the political behavior of the Turkish government or to pass a sound judgment on what the government is up to.

Only after mapping out this murky and shadowy web of the politicians do I believe one can better explain Turkey's troubled foreign policy in its neighborhood and the reasons behind the government's insistence on continuing to make similar mistakes, most of which defy logic.

Only after understanding this complicated web can one make sense of why leaders—who are supposed to reach out and embrace their citizens—deliberately divide and polarize their constituents. Without knowing the political players and their personal and ideological drives, the following questions cannot be answered in any satisfactory way: Why did the elections fail to put an end to the hateful discourse employed by President Recep Tayyip Erdoğan and his gang who continue to escalate tensions and marginalize large swaths of Turks? Why has the government been skating dangerously close to the slippery slope of a total collapse of the country's fragile social fabric?

I think the massive graft scheme that was exposed by anti-corruption investigators on Dec. 17 and Dec. 25, 2013, and that incriminated Erdoğan, his family members, and his close business and political associates, laid bare a major dichotomy in Turkish politics: the interests of Erdoğan and his band of political Islamists no longer matches with the interests of the nation that has been anchored strongly to the Western alliance for many years. The dragnet investigators were able to decipher revealed the illegal and illicit network of ties Erdoğan has used to involve himself with many regional pariahs. The alleged practices of money laundering, financing terror, and investing in highly controversial proxies in the region have been quite unprecedented; they can only be explained by objectives pursued for special interest groups rather than in the national interest.

There is no doubt that the way Erdoğan, the chief political Islamist in Turkey, waged his battle against the damaging corruption scandals has shaken the country's democratic institutions and damaged the trust citizens have in their government. The extent to which he has relentlessly kept pushing his artificially-constructed war against a "global conspiracy" after ruling the nation for 12 years is a testament to the great fallacy and poor reasoning on the part of his leadership.

Erdoğan suddenly invented the so called "parallel structure" that he alleges has been trying to topple his government under the cover of a legal investigation. He has done this in order to scapegoat his troubles to others. Erdoğan and his loyalists have blatantly accused the US, the EU, Egypt, Gulf countries, and Israel for being foreign conspirators in this conspiracy, which was allegedly been helped out by the opposition parties in Turkey as well as business interest groups, including the wealthiest club in Turkey, TÜSİAD, and the largest trade advocacy group in Turkey, TUSKON. It was further assisted allegedly by a critical and independent media, the vast majority of Alevis, and Fethullah Gülen, a 76-year old Islamic scholar who has inspired Hizmet, a worldwide social movement that is active in education and interfaith and intercultural dialogue.

The smear campaign against many in the country followed the effective suspension of the rule of law through revenge operations conducted against anti-corruption investigators in sham trials. These were done in order to intimidate Erdoğan's critics and opponents. The pressure on the press has been increased tremendously while businesses are subjected to harassment via targeted auditing, administrative fines, and license revocations. The flagrant abuse of the criminal justice system has reached a new peak (or valley!) with the government rendering the Parliament into a law factory that has produced a series of unconstitutional and undemocratic pieces of legislation. To the dismay of many observers, the democratic achievements of the nation over the last decade have been rolled back in a very short period of time.

The critical question at this juncture becomes why would Erdoğan risk a Turkish economy that is largely dependent on foreign cash to finance the country's chronic current account deficit? Why would he jeopardize critical access to foreign markets that Turkish manufacturers and producers rely on in order to maintain their exports? Why scare investors—foreign or domestic—away from the Turkish market by shaking the precious trust of the Turkish economy? Why does Erdoğan antagonize and alienate NATO partners that Turkey has been depending on for the last sixty years for its security in a tumultuous neighborhood?

The simple answer to these questions is because Erdoğan and his band of brothers have huge legal troubles and they need to stall, derail, and hush-up legal investigations that they know will eventually catch up with them. In short, there is no longer an overlap between their personal interests and the interest of the nation any more.

When you add ideological and ethnic interests of the small group of people that hijacked power in the ruling party and now dominate the political decision making process in the Turkish government, it becomes clear why certain policies have been pursued to the detriment of Turkey's national security. For one, there is a strong pro-Iranian lobby in the government, some perhaps working as covert Iranian agents that shape the nation's policies according to the Mullah-regime's interests. This is the result of a long-term investment by Iran in political Islamists who have now penetrated into the leadership of the country. Secondly, there is a larger group of political Islamists who think along the lines of the Muslim Brotherhood type of ideology in expanding Turkey's interests through religious adventurism.

Former Interior Minister İdris Naim Şahin, who parted ways with Erdoğan after working with him for some 30 years, described these groups as an "oligarchic cadre," whose intentions are questionable at best. They have seized power in the ruling party and the government.

The question of whether this oligarchic group can actually succeed in turning Turkey's regime into an authoritarian style of government with rampant corruption and highly ideological tendencies becomes very relevant for today's Turkey. To me, there is simply no chance of this happening. Turkey, a country that is anchored to European and Transatlantic institutions, cannot sustain the Erdoğan regime for much longer. The vibrant and dynamic Turkish society, with a huge youth population, won't allow Erdoğan and his sorts to turn the clock backwards in a progressive country like Turkey.

The fact that the judiciary, the military, and the opposition parties reject Erdoğan's utopian vision for Turkey, and that the business community, independent media, and civil society have not completely yielded to the terror of fear that is perpetuated by political Islamists, are strong signs that Turkey will certainly move forward on its democratic voyage, albeit with some turbulence in the short run. The centuries-long tradition of Sufism—which is strongly embedded to the nation's culture and which is amplified by the powerful narrative maintained by today's modern scholars, like Gülen—has always served as a bulwark against extremist ideologies taking hold in these lands, whether they come from the Iranian version of an extremist political Shiite ideology or the Saudi version of an ultra-orthodox Sunni Wahhabi ideology.

Surely Turks will experience some setbacks and sustain some damage on this long journey. Things may very well get worse before they get better. Perhaps that is a bitter lesson Turkey needs to learn in order to overhaul its democratic institutions to better reflect accountability and transparency, with strong check and balances, among its state institutions. The most important lesson would be to not let anybody or any group consolidate so much power in the government. I have no doubt whatsoever that Turks will eventually bury this political Islamist experiment—which has nothing to with Islam itself and is in fact an aberration on the true teachings of the Islamic Prophet by exploiting religion and delegating Islam to mere symbolism rather than focusing on its substance—into the dustbins of history, just as they did to the ultra-secular, militarist Kemalist ideology in recent past.

Chapter 1

How Erdoğan Governs Turkey

Scare, Divide, and Rule[1]

I n a very polarized society, it appears that Turkey's powerful prime minister, Recep Tayyip Erdoğan, and his popular Justice and Development Party (AKP) have set the election campaign on fear and divisions, rather than a conciliatory tone. Erdoğan's people are determined to run a partisan campaign, hoping this will prevent defectors from peeling away from the ranks. In the aftermath of the May-June anti-government rallies as part of the Gezi Park protests, the AKP was in fact able to gain some points it had lost since the last elections of 2011, when voters were scared off by the violence that erupted amid protests. This was a temporary spike, however, and the AKP could not hold onto gains when the tension was diffused.

That is the primary reason why Erdoğan thinks he needs to invent straw men to attack in a bid to channel voters' disillusionment with his government. Out of the blue, he comes up with issues that nobody has been discussing in society and in fact no mainstream political party was even proposing. Then he holds these up as if they are real issues that matter to voters. He played around with abortion, coed housing, capital punishment, the interest lobby, and private prep schools to steer the national debate away from substantive issues that might damage his rule. Erdoğan is now pinning his hopes for election victory on sharpening divisions with artificially inflated issues.

---

[1]   First appeared in *Today's Zaman* daily on Nov. 15, 2013

When Erdoğan was fighting against nosy military generals and over-zealous judges and prosecutors, who were sworn to protect state interests against individual rights and liberties, he was getting big support from Turkish people who felt the brunt of this overbearance in their daily lives. This time around, however, he is picking battles with made-up enemies that are not on the radar for Turks. When he touted the idea of an "interest lobby," a murky and ambiguous term, as being behind the Gezi Park protests, Erdoğan was unsuccessful in creating a solid and formidable enemy to fight in the eyes of voters.

The AKP may very well survive a bruising victory in the local elections in March of 2014, with Erdoğan's popularity taking a hit. It may win the next national elections in 2015. However, in the medium term, the AKP is vulnerable to challengers. First, the public is not buying the artificial issues thrown at them by the AKP leadership and voters are not afraid of straw men dressed up by Erdoğan as villains. Second, the opposition has smartened up and is no longer taking the bait. When the AKP pushed the headscarf issue for women deputies in Parliament with the hope of scoring some points from the escalation of the crisis, the main opposition Republican People's Party (CHP) balked at the idea of mounting a fierce opposition to that change. The same tactic also paid off for the CHP when it did not endorse the controversial coed housing for students. The governing party felt like it had the rug pulled from underneath when it was stripped of the ability to play with controversial issues.

Moreover, Erdoğan's strategy of consolidating his own troops with deepening divisions seems to have backfired. Rather, the troops on the opposite side of the line seem to be strengthening and solidifying their positions in the face of relentless stigmatizing and marginalizing attacks by the government on various groups. The constant playback of harsh rhetoric by Erdoğan and his men emboldens anti-AKP groups into digging their heels deeper into the trenches. As if adding further fuel to the fire, the governing party has alienated enough groups that supported the government in tough times. This includes liberals, independents, social democrats, moderates, and conservative groups that are turned off by increasingly assertive political Islamist ideology on the government's agenda.

At the crux of the problem lies the ownership issue with which AKP does not seem to be comfortable. Erdoğan's "my way or the highway attitude," which has driven the national agenda without actually consulting all the stakeholders on a given issue, has unnecessarily increased tension in Turkish society. When the government proposed some legal amendments to improve press freedom as part of judicial reform packages, we, as media professionals who are on the frontline, were not even consulted! Instead, the government came up with its own version and rushed it through Parliament, keeping the sword hanging over our heads. The result is that press freedom woes still linger in Turkey.

On the fast-tracked education bill that was adopted in March 2013, the government did not ask for input from the teachers' union, professional organizations, academia, or parent-teacher groups. The law, popularly known as the "4+4+4" education law, included some good changes. Yet the hastily arranged reforms caught the education system unprepared with a lack of teachers and facilities, while leaving parents bewildered about what to do. Hence, the reform received much criticism from everybody, just as has been the case for many ensuing changes in the education system, most of which the government abruptly announced at the last minute.

To suppress public debate on important issues, the government often resorted to back-door politics to circumvent established rules in holding a wider discussion in Parliament and the media. Draft bills, usually prepared by the relevant ministries with input from stakeholders, have been penned in the Prime Ministry's Office with a small cadre of advisors and dropped on the Parliament's floor with last-minute motions. Therefore, no discussion was held in parliamentary commissions. Even Cabinet members whose portfolios were impacted were kept out of the loop. For example, in July of last year, the government rushed an amendment through a motion on the floor to abolish specially authorized courts that were dealing with crimes against constitutional order, organized crime, terror, and drug trafficking. The Justice Ministry was not even aware of the motion, even though it had to deal with the ramifications of the amendment.

In April 2013, the AKP resorted to another bypass to amend the law on the Court of Accounts in order to significantly trim the court's powers to audit and review government expenditures. Instead of sending the draft through a government-sponsored bill, the AKP asked some deputies to co-sponsor the bill and submit the draft to Parliament. The draft will revise the 2010 law on the Court of Accounts, which was hailed as a breakthrough by the EU on improving transparency and accountability in government spending. The draft comes after the AKP's botched attempt to change the law by burying an amendment in an omnibus law that was appended at the last minute on the floor in the summer of 2012. Thankfully, the change was later cancelled by the Constitutional Court on an appeal by the opposition.

In June of 2013, the *Taraf* daily reported that the government was secretly preparing a draft bill to give overarching and broad powers to Turkey's intelligence agency. The draft, obtained by the newspaper, indicated that the National Intelligence Organization (MİT) can prey on the privacy of Turkish citizens by profiling and collecting a massive amount of data while obtaining sweeping powers to conduct domestic operations and psychological warfare, and arrest people without a judge's order. The draft came a year later when the Turkish government pushed an amendment through Parliament in February 2012 to require prosecutors to receive special permission from the prime minister when taking legal action against or questioning intelligence officials.

The last straw by Erdoğan came this week, when a draft version of a law seeking the closure of all kinds of privately established prep schools (*dershanes*) leaked to the media. The bill is so drastic that even private tutoring for kids at homes by parents is banned. The intrusive move is seen as a huge blow to free enterprise and the right to education, prompting concerns that the closure of these schools will block upward mobility in Turkish society. Many saw this as Erdoğan's attempt to pressure the Gülen Movement, which runs one-third of prep schools, into silencing criticism of the government on the eve of elections. The movement is critical of the government on corruption, weakened transparency and accountability, loss of enthusiasm for the EU process, and a lack of bold democratic reforms to address the country's chronic woes, including the Alevi and Kurdish problems. The banning of prep schools curtails the free market credentials of the AKP government while potentially scaring international investors into shying away from the Turkish market.

All in all, Erdoğan's new way of ruling Turkey has dealt a big blow to his credibility as well as to the trustworthiness of the AKP's election program, which promised better accountability, increased transparency and better protection of privacy in government while boosting the free market economy and limiting the role of government. It will be difficult to convince voters on new pledges in the next election when the AKP has already reneged on past promises.

Shadow Cabinet of Advisors[2]

Turkey's ruling Justice and Development Party (AKP) insiders draw a bleak picture of the small inner circle around powerful Prime Minister and AKP leader Recep Tayyip Erdoğan; this circle acts as a "shadow government" which governs the country. While the official Cabinet members become a lightning rod for the government on issues that draw criticism from the public, most of Erdoğan's advisors work "in the shadows," playing a significant role in shaping the tone, views, and policies of the government.

That is why Education Minister Nabi Avcı was seen as contradicting himself in his public remarks on the government's controversial plan to ban all privately run prep schools in Turkey: he was kept out of the loop most of the time. When the phone rang in the early hours of the morning, on the day a major story about the draft bill on the ban was exposed by Turkey's largest daily, *Zaman*, Avcı said to the caller, an AKP heavyweight, that he did not have a clue about the issue. He had to rush to the ministry to get briefed before making comments publicly. The fact that Avcı's remarks have created more confusion than clar-

---

[2]   First appeared in *Today's Zaman* daily on Nov. 22, 2013

ity with conflicting and even incorrect statements has led other officials to take the podium to explain what the government is up to.

This small team of advisors appears to project more powers than
Cabinet members and elected members of the AKP in Parliament. They
are reportedly administering the government through "point persons"
(undersecretaries, deputy undersecretaries, or deputy ministers), bypassing the established rules of bureaucracy and overriding standard oper-
ating procedures. At the same time, they connect to other groups of
advisors at the AKP headquarters, shaping the party's public face and
drawing upon state resources to help the party. For example, a chief
coordinator of the AKP's social media drive sent instructions to ministries and government agencies on Monday, suggesting to civil servants
what to post on Twitter related to the prep school row. The opposition,
claiming that the move is against both laws and the principle of separation of powers, submitted an inquiry motion to Parliament.

Since Erdoğan's advisors have an impact on policy decisions in
practically every field, ranging from economy to foreign policy, from
social policies to education, their profiles and characteristics obviously matter a great deal for observers of Turkish politics. It is fair to say
that most come from a politically charged Islamist background with
strong traits from the anti-Western National View ideology, the hallmark of the late Necmettin Erbakan, who had championed a very nar-
row-minded political Islam in Turkey. Hence, it should not come as a
surprise that some of these advisors strongly uphold anti-US and anti-
West views, with some clearly anti-Semitic strains. For example, just
this week, one of Erdoğan's chief advisors publicly accused advocates
of prep schools against the government ban as "Israel's servants" in his
Twitter feed and stood by his statement when confronted with accusations of anti-Semitism.

Through this team, Erdoğan micromanages the government and
interferes in jurisdictions that normally fall into ministers' portfolios.
This has created uneasiness not only among Cabinet members but also
within the AKP, primarily because, unlike elected officials who have to
take the concerns of their constituencies into account, these advisors
have a strong personal loyalty to Erdoğan and their allegiance only lies

with him. After all, it was Erdoğan who offered them these positions and ultimately it will be him to decide whether to keep them on payroll or fire them.

This team of advisors makes sure Erdoğan enjoys unimpeded control over executive and legislative branches of the government. The consolidation of power at the hands of Erdoğan is achieved through means such as controlling legislative agenda, public procurement, government purchases, licensing, and approvals. For example, an advisor to Erdoğan who looks into government permits and licensing has more to say on a given subject matter than a minister whose portfolio covers the area that involves that licensing. The reason why so many applications for authorizations, permits, and licensing for business ventures, both from domestic and foreign investors, have piled up on the prime minister's desk is because of this bottleneck created around Erdoğan's advisors.

According to many government insiders, most of these advisors are in their 30s or 40s, much younger than the 59-year-old Erdoğan, who sort of fosters a personality cult requiring adulation and approval. They say his approach is more patronizing and controlling than consultative and participative. Coupled with that, Erdoğan's intolerance for what he perceives as criticism, especially from the foreign media, does not give any encouragement to his advisors to confront the root causes of the perception problem for Erdoğan in the media. They are afraid to speak candidly and even bluntly in addressing what and how Erdoğan should communicate his message to the audience. Instead, the advisors take the easy way out, shifting the blame to the media for Erdoğan's blunders, which reinforces their boss's own thinking.

There is one tactic the prime minister's team of advisors consistently sticks to when they face a crisis they want to weather. Although Erdoğan wields almost unchecked control over state resources, his advisors always try to paint him as the "underdog" who is ready to take on domestic and foreign enemies at all times. They often like to recall Erdoğan's brief jail time and forceful removal from his position as mayor of Istanbul after a court verdict more than a decade ago and play that to the public as a constant reminder of his victimization phenomena.

This serves well in rallying people around Erdoğan in crunch time, especially when the government faces an uphill battle. It also helps muzzle criticism within the party. For example, Erdoğan was depicted by his advisors as the underdog fighting for the Turkish people against unidentified or vaguely defined enemies like the "interest lobby" during the Gezi Park protests in May and June of 2013.

Erdoğan's desire to be an important leader in the Muslim world and even in the world at large plays well among his advisors, who pick up on his desire to be recognized as a revered personality who will have a lasting legacy in history. It must be like music to Erdoğan's ears when one top advisor, who used to be ultra-nationalist and a harsh critic of Erdoğan before converting and becoming his chief aide, said on TV that there are only two-and-a-half leaders in the world—and Erdoğan is one of them.

"The world has a leadership problem. Today there are two-and-a-half leaders in the world. One is Recep Tayyip Erdoğan, the second is [Russian President Vladimir] Putin and the other half is [US President Barack] Obama," he said, adding that lobbyists in the US had reduced Obama to a "half-leader." The same advisor also claimed that powerful groups, possibly both inside and outside the country, were trying to kill Erdoğan—with telepathic attacks—because of his struggle against the interest-rate lobby. He floated these claims after the Gezi protests without offering a shred of evidence to support this claim. As an expression of his admiration for the prime minister, he even went so far as to say he was ready to die for Erdoğan if need be.

These advisors enjoy a network, both inside and outside the government, which communicates well among their own inner circle, and which draws its strength from a shared past and a shared political Islamist ideology. Some in this network are sympathizers of the Iranian revolution and adore Ayatollah Khomeini's teachings. As such, their views are propagated through government agencies, with the resulting impact not only on policy decisions but also on the tone the government line adopts. Some unusual tweaks in foreign policy issues, channeling of development funds, networking with Turkish expats abroad, cooperation among academia and think tanks, and outreach activities in religious and charity work can be partially explained with the input coming from this tight ship of networks the Erdoğan advisors run.

The concerted smear campaign run against government critics by some circles in Turkey, and the fact that they are supported to some extent by some of Erdoğan's close aides (who tap into the social media and Internet to spread these rumors), fuels suspicions that a government-sanctioned secret campaign is going on. It also gives rise to speculation that the government, using intelligence assets, is eavesdropping on its own critics, intruding into the private lives of journalists. It was exposed last year that the National Intelligence Organization (MİT) tapped the phones of several journalists using court orders in which the journalists were only mentioned by their foreign codenames. When a suit was brought against MİT for privacy violation and communication interception in breach of the law, MİT chief Hakan Fidan asked Erdoğan to halt proceedings by not granting permission for the case to move forward. Erdoğan granted that wish in May of 2013, protecting MİT from legal troubles.

If rumors and claims about this small network of advisors are true, Turkey has a long way to go to get rid of a highly centralized and authoritarian political landscape that nurtures this undemocratic culture in the state.

Predictability No More[3]

The most significant damage beleaguered Prime Minister Recep Tayyip Erdoğan has inflicted on Turkey in a frantic effort to rescue himself, his children, and close associates from legal troubles amid massive corruption and money laundering, and illegal land-zoning deals, was a blow to the "credibility" of Turkey and the "predictability" in its political and economic environment. Unfortunately, he has plundered state institutions with the unprecedented displacement of thousands of well-qualified and experienced law enforcement personnel, and hundreds of independent judges and prosecutors. He has exposed the nation to huge security risks amid terror, organized crime, and separatist threats in an unsta-

---

[3]   First appeared in *Today's Zaman* daily on Feb. 21, 2014

ble part of the world. He has pushed controversial—in all likelihood unconstitutional, as well—bills through Parliament, such as the Internet censorship legislation and amendments to the judicial council and penal codes, ostensibly in the name of reform, but in what actually turned out to be a steps in the wrong direction.

Now the Erdoğan government has submitted another bill to Parliament that gives the notorious intelligence agency sweeping powers with no accountability and no judicial review. If it becomes law, the agency will be able to collect all kinds of data on private citizens, as well as companies. The education bill, which would ban all privately funded prep schools, will also terminate the jobs of almost 100,000 principals in public schools across the nation, paving the way for a reconstruction of the educational system based on political Islamist ideology. The haste in adopting these controversial laws, without much public discussion, indicates the government is in panic mode. Erdoğan, who made it abundantly clear that he has no interest whatsoever in a balance of power among state institutions, has been eroding checks and balances while trying to muzzle the critical press.

Erdoğan's attempts cast a long shadow on the credibility of Turkey, a NATO member and important partner in most trans-Atlantic and European institutions. Questions are now being raised on the reliability of Turkey as an staunch ally in these circles after the Erdoğan government effectively suspended the rule of law, curbed fundamental human rights and freedoms, including the right to privacy and the rights to free speech and assembly, and tainted democratic credentials in a once-shining country in a turbulent region. Erdoğan is fighting a losing battle, and he just does not realize that the game is over. He was left with only one arm to fight for his survival, and that is the ballot box. That is why he is constantly reminding his supporters to make an appearance at the March 30th local elections.

This great nation got rid of past authoritarian regimes even in difficult times in the aftermath of military coups, when circumstances were even worse than today. Turks have always shown their disdain for autocratic governments; when they've gotten the chance, they've gotten rid of them, ever since 1950, a year when the country made the transition to a multi-party system for the first time since the establishment of the republic. Even during interim periods, when the military interrupted the functioning of the democratically elected governments, the political engineering and social design by the military rulers fell apart quickly. Therefore, no matter how hard Erdoğan tries, in all likelihood, voters will remove him from power as well—although it may take some time, as the functioning of a democratic system moves slowly but surely. Erdoğan's attempt to obtain absolute power is just a futile one and will backfire on him when the opposition is further emboldened against the encroachment into democratic structures.

In the meantime, however, the predictability of Turkey's business climate, at least in the short run, will take a blow, impacting trade, investment, and business. Perhaps long-term investors will work with what they have got in Turkey at the moment and do their best to map out their business plans under the circumstances. Yet many will recalibrate their policies and may even defer their investments until the dust settles in Turkey. Considering that this country desperately needs external financing because of its low savings rate and dependency on foreign energy resources, navigating through troubles under unpredictable times will be a big challenge. That was one of the talking points US President Barack Obama raised with Erdoğan on the phone on Wednesday night, when Obama highlighted "the importance of sound policies rooted in the rule of law to reassure the financial markets, nurture a predictable investment environment, strengthen bilateral ties, and benefit the future of Turkey."

The critical question to ask at this juncture, however, is whether Erdoğan gives a hoot about what Obama, or anybody else, for that matter, says or thinks. Swamped with personal legal troubles, I do not think Erdoğan cares about issues of credibility and predictability in Turkey at all. He is pressed with the immediate challenge of surviving local elections first and foremost, with an outcome that he can claim relatively as a success. He already set the bar at 38.8 percent, at the same level the party got in the 2009 local elections, but way below the 50 percent Erdoğan garnered in the 2011 national elections. He has already acknowledged a more than 10 percent loss, and polling data indicates he is fighting to stay above 35 percent. Depending on new revelations of scandals involving his government, Erdoğan's ruling party may even go into the low 30s and lose the landmark municipalities of Istanbul and Ankara. This doesn't factor into account the possibility for electoral fraud, either.

The economic outlook will not get worse before the local elections, so he does not have to worry about shoring up predictability for investors for the moment. The only thing that matters to him is to buy enough time so that he can figure out what to do next. He can call snap elections to get a fresh mandate before the economy takes further blows due to the US Federal Reserve's tapering off policy and the big need to finance the current account deficit with hot money which becomes scarcer. The corruption scandal has exposed how Erdoğan was able to create a pool of funds in exchange for favors in contracts, tenders, and influence-peddling. Hence, he must have amassed enough cash on the sidelines as a war chest to wage a costly election campaign without engaging in too much populist spending from the budget.

The road markers pointing out that Erdoğan simply brushed aside valuable advice provided by Obama on Wednesday night were detectable in Erdoğan's speech, delivered at a pro-government union meeting less than 24 hours later in Ankara. He rehashed old arguments of a global conspiracy, lumping the opposition parties, media, business groups, and Hizmet Movement all into one basket, labeling them "traitors." He even called them, for the first time, "bloodsucking vampires," because he alleged they all opposed the settlement process with the terrorist Kurdistan Workers' Party (PKK). Erdoğan's escalation of rhetoric by a couple of notches in every speech is a clear indication that he is failing to gain traction on his agenda of distracting the Turkish people from the corruption scandal.

His relentless campaign to further polarize and divide Turkish society along ethnic, religious, and ideological lines makes Erdoğan the most dangerous and biggest liability for Turkey at the moment. He knows he needs a major enemy to fight his epic battle and survive the elections. Targeting Hizmet, the most peaceful faith-inspired civic movement in Turkey, did not fit the profile of an enemy description he desperately needs, despite his slanderous accusations. He tried to pick a proxy fight with the US by publicly threatening to expel its envoy in Ankara and orchestrated a smear campaign in the pro-government media attacking the US ambassador with fabricated stories. The US, knowing full well that Erdoğan tried to elicit a harsh Hugo Chavez-type public rebuke from Washington, decided to convey the message privately. Erdoğan had to back down when US Secretary of State John Kerry dressed down his Turkish counterpart, Ahmet Davutoğlu, and warned about the serious consequences if targeting the US and its envoy continued.

Despite the fact that all the terms of agreement are in place for a compensation deal with Israel over the 2010 flotilla incident, Erdoğan has not given the political approval to go ahead with the normalization with Israel ahead of the local elections. This is because he needs to demonize Israel and bash the Jewish state while accusing the opposition in Turkey of working for Israeli interests and the Jewish lobby in a conspiracy, despite having offered no evidence to that effect. Perhaps Syria remains the only avenue for Erdoğan to create an enemy, a big enough threat that the Turkish people will stop paying attention to the wrongdoings of the government and overlook corruption scandals in the face of an impending threat from its southern neighbor. The scenario that Erdoğan may pick a fight with Syria must raise alarm bells in Brussels as war with a neighbor may also pull NATO into the conflict as well. If we see an incident like the Reyhanlı bombing, which killed 53 people in May of 2013 in Hatay province and with the blame put on regime elements in Damascus, Erdoğan may find a pretext for war and immediately seize that opportunity.

Breaking news on Thursday night has clearly shown how far Erdoğan is willing to take his fight to distract the public. In a blistering statement, Hasan Palaz, former head of the Scientific and Technological Research Council of Turkey's (TÜBİTAK) Research Center for Advanced Technologies on Informatics and Information Security (BİLGEM), revealed that he was forced to tamper with key evidence in a scientific report that was prepared as part of a criminal investigation into the installation of bugging devices at Erdoğan's office in 2012. Two years after the inquiry, Palaz said he was asked to change the date when the bugging device started functioning, perhaps as part of an attempt to implicate

Hizmet, because Erdoğan claimed the bugging device found was placed there by individuals close to the Hizmet Movement. Palaz, who refused to falsify the original report, was sacked by the government.

It is clear that the Erdoğan government will not hesitate in plotting false-flag operations to blame others in order to change the public discourse and to benefit politically in the meantime. With an intelligence agency that has full immunity, sweeping powers, and a broad mandate to stage secret operations tasked by government at home and abroad at his disposal, Erdoğan can manage his dirty biddings and dealings. There is no judicial, parliamentary, or independent oversight to monitor, check, and hold him accountable for any of this if Erdoğan completes his plan to subordinate the whole judiciary to his rule.

A Psychological Profile of Erdoğan[4]

Beleaguered Turkish Prime Minister Recep Tayyip Erdoğan's increasingly erratic and miscalculated – but not irrational—behavior does not fit into any sound political science theories and as such makes it difficult to provide future projections for analysts and observers of Turkey, who use a conventional wisdom approach. Perhaps Professor Mümtaz'er Tüköne was right in his comments in an op-ed piece he wrote for the daily *Zaman* on Sunday, in which he said that Erdoğan's behavior can no longer be subject to political analysis. He said the prime minister is experiencing a "panic attack" which can only be analyzed by psychologists. "The prime minister has no strategy, but simply follows his inner instincts," he wrote.

My analysis, however, differs somewhat from this. I believe that Erdoğan is not unpredictable, given his background, how he sees the world, and how he has become increasingly authoritarian in his leadership. Surely Erdoğan's characteristics differ from those of other leaders the nation has seen in recent times. Rather, he represents a throwback to an older period when authoritative leaders ruled the nation, in the late Ottoman times or the early years of the Republican era. This was a successful trait for him when he confronted the once-powerful

---

[4] First appeared in *Today's Zaman* daily on Mar. 24, 2014

generals who mistook him for just another politician who could be easily cowed under pressure. But that characteristic has now turned into a major liability.

Coming from a poor neighborhood in Istanbul's Kasımpaşa district, where his family migrated from an unforgiving life in the northeastern province of Rize—a place where the limited availability of land was a constant source of friction and fights among residents—Erdoğan's principal goal was probably to enrich himself and his family while leaving a legacy of an underdog who turned himself into a national hero. The corruption probe has allegedly unearthed his massive newfound wealth with allegations of huge amounts of cash and luxurious mansions he and his family members purportedly possess. Yet, he continues to successfully play the victimization card at every opportunity, citing powerful internal and external enemies, naming groups or interests as major obstacles thwarting his ambitious plans for the country.

Erdoğan's political ideology was nurtured at an *imam-hatip*, or religious vocational, high school. The schools are known as hotbeds of the political Islamist ideology known as Milli Görüş (National View), even though both religious and scientific education is offered under the same roof. Seeing this ideology as a threat, every military coup administration in Turkey tried to curb the growing number of imam-hatip schools through severe limitations and restrictions, albeit in an undemocratic manner. Erdoğan took this issue to heart and not only rectified the wrongdoing of past governments that instituted discriminatory practices towards these schools, but went overboard by channeling huge amounts of resources to imam-hatip schools in contrast to other public schools.

His government provided ample employment opportunities for graduates of these schools. What is more, the Erdoğan administration allocated land belonging to the Treasury for the building of new imam-hatip schools, while businesspeople close to the government are encouraged to finance their construction in exchange for favorable deals in government contracts and tenders. Erdoğan hopes that imam-hatip graduates will be able to provide the human resources needed to fill positions in the government in order to sustain his rule, while the schools nourish the culture of political Islamist ideology to which Erdoğan wants wider Turkish society to subscribe. That is why at practically every public rally address, he makes references to these schools, and his party supporters transport imam-hatip students to rallies en masse.

In Erdoğan's mind, loyalty matters a lot but is subject to changing circumstances. He can easily drop those who have been working with him for a long time. Some of the leading figures who were present during the establishment years of the ruling Justice and Development Party (AKP) have become distant figures over time. In contrast, some of the people who used to be fierce critics of Erdoğan have now turned into loyal supporters of his policies. Erdoğan offers favors, positions, and money to purchase loyalty and involves so many of those around him in corruption and graft that they are afraid of exposure if they defect. Erdoğan's inner circle is mobilized by fear of losing their positions rather than strong agreement with his policies. For Erdoğan, there is no gray area. He let his arch enemies—the Ergenekon suspects—walk free from jail, under a government-endorsed law, to enlist fresh helping hands against anti-corruption drives. He is ready to work with anyone on a tactical basis, but he stands alone on strategic calculations.

There is little doubt that Erdoğan loathes the West, especially the US, and this has been on display in his public discourse and frequent outbursts. Although his dislike of the West does not seem to translate into actual policy decisions most of the time, nevertheless, forceful rhetoric and bitter words take a toll on Turkey's relations with its long-time partners and allies. Although Erdoğan appreciated the US support for his government in the past, Washington is always a convenient scapegoat for him when his back is against the wall. All the same, he tried to exploit his first phone conversation with US President Barack Obama after a six-month hiatus in his battle against his opponents. Erdoğan's deliberate distortion of the content of the phone talk prompted an unusual rebuke from the White House. But, given the chance, Erdoğan would hop on a plane to meet Obama in Washington. He definitely values his international credibility and reputation, and showed his love for the spotlight during the Arab Spring revolutions. However, he would sacrifice global political capital to win few points at home.

Any group or individual who Erdoğan sees as an obstacle thwarting his ambitions is automatically designated a threat that needs to be dealt with. He does not care much whether the individual or group supported him in the past. He sees himself as a leader struggling not only for the Turkish people, but also for the cause of all Muslims worldwide. The oft-mentioned places named in his public addresses, such as Damascus, Cairo, Myanmar, and Bosnia, reflect this self-image in Erdoğan's mind. When he goes abroad, especially in Muslim and Arab nations, he is able to achieve his craving for praise and exalted self-worth; Erdoğan's public relations campaign managers reportedly organize supportive rallies using cash to attract crowds around the hotel he is staying in.

The standard behavior for Erdoğan when he faces an obstacle is to fight and continue his course. He believes in the infallibility of his judgment and at such times will push even harder to make his point. But he is also capable of reversing his course of action, not directly, but with more subtle approaches. The problem about the recent corruption cases, however, is that he is left with no exit strategy. He is facing insurmountable challenges, both legal and political, and it is impossibly difficult to map out a trajectory for Erdoğan to save himself and his family members. He has no course left to reverse the present path of antagonism and polarization. As he did during Gezi Park events, he will deliberately push for street violence by trying to provoke Alevis, nationalists, and even members of the Hizmet Movement inspired by Islamic scholar Fethullah Gülen. The good news is that the opposition is aware of Erdoğan's highly dangerous strategy and has repeatedly called for calm and common sense.

Erdoğan's inner circle is staffed entirely by yes-men who are afraid to contradict him. Since he is not receptive to criticism and takes dissenting views as a sign of disloyalty and rebellion, all of them parrot exactly what he would like to hear, and he therefore suffers from poor counseling. For Erdoğan, communicating with him means agreeing unquestionably with his point of view. His micromanaging style of ruling leaves his advisors—and, by default, his ministers and senior officials—with a lack of courage to take risks and initiatives. In turn, the wheels of the government bureaucracy sometimes come to a grinding halt until Erdoğan comes out and provides directions.

On top of that, the behind-the-scenes Cabinet that helps Erdoğan run the country is infiltrated with advisors who have ties to Iran and feel sympathy for the Iranian revolution. Erdoğan does not seem to mind that and probably encourages the pro-Iranian tilt in the government, given that he himself feels the same way about the Iranian revolution and former Supreme Leader Ayatollah Ruhollah Khomeini. He even called Iran his second home during a recent visit to Tehran. Erdoğan, who strongly criticized the West for its lack of involvement in the Syrian conflict, has never openly criticized Tehran for its unwavering support for the Syrian regime.

Intimidation and threats are also part of the pattern in Erdoğan's governing style. His vehement attacks on the press and his harsh rhetoric and tone in public speeches are all bullying tactics to get what he wants. He uses and abuses power to come after opponents, employing an army of tax inspectors to punish selected individuals and corporations. On the election campaign trail, he openly issued threats to companies that supported the Gezi protests and the Hizmet Movement.

Faced with huge troubles with the law stemming from corruption, influence-peddling, money laundering and tender-rigging, Erdoğan relentlessly pursues immunity by extracting new laws from Parliament, which he controls. By doing so, he threatens the rule of law, the independence of the judiciary, and institutional stability in Turkey. He even ordered a complete ban on access to Twitter in Turkey (though this ban was lifted in spring 2014, the government has now increasingly been muzzling the twitter users), despite the fact that there is not a single court judgment ordering such a blanket ban, and he has threatened to deal with YouTube and Facebook before long. The opposition even claims he is ready to set the country ablaze by provoking a conflict with Syria in order to shift the debate away from corruption. That would not be surprising, given that Erdoğan deliberately stirred up street protests in the Gezi Park events to present himself as victorious in the fight against mass demonstrations he accused of being orchestrated by international conspirators in cooperation with domestic collaborators. That is his way of solving problems and gaining acceptance for his leadership in Turkey.

Perhaps the Turkish Medical Association's (TBB) warning last week that they are worried about the emotional well-being of Erdoğan must be taken seriously. The TBB described themselves as being "very worried," adding that they are "concerned about him, his family and the entire country."

Bad Crisis Management: The Soma Disaster[5]

Turkey's angry man, Prime Minister Recep Tayyip Erdoğan, has added more insult to the national tragedy of a mining disaster with his frequent public outbursts. Instead of offering some solace and comfort to his fellow citizens and rallying the nation with his leadership during a time of grief, this man is enraged and has taken a defensive posture. He compared the massive losses in the coal-mining town of Soma in western Turkey to the number of casualties from 19th-century mining accidents in the US and the UK. To the shock of the nation, Erdoğan even described this heartbreaking incident as "common," a jaw-dropping reaction in the eyes of a grieving nation.

As if the hurtful words were not enough, Turkey's prime minister even resorted to physical assault and slapped the face of a bystander who happened to be in the wrong place at the wrong time when a crowd booed the visiting Erdoğan. Rumor in the Turkish capital has it that he has, in fact, slapped his own ministers on more than one occasion when he was furious, although no Cabinet member has come forward to confirm or deny these rumors. Wednesday's incident in Soma was the first public exposure of that violent side.

This pattern of behavior confirms my earlier assessments that he has been on a destructive path for the last couple of years. While he displays a more authoritarian streak with strident emotional outbursts, Erdoğan's behavior also signals that he is very frustrated about not being able to control unfolding events as he would like to. The Gezi Park protests that swept the nation in May-June of 2013—perhaps the first sig-

---

[5] First appeared in *Today's Zaman* daily on May 16, 2014

nificant anti-government protests to threaten his rule—threw him off balance. But instead of reaching out to these people and listening to their grievances, he immediately mobilized his own supporters with public rallies to prove that he was the man who can command the street.

Then the explosive graft investigations revealed on Dec. 17, 2013, destroyed his image as a corruption-free politician because of the overwhelming evidence incriminating him, his family members, and his close associates in politics and the business community. Not only did his political reputation take a beating, but he has also become immersed in deep legal trouble that will catch up with him eventually. By reshuffling more than 40,000 civil servants—mostly in the police force and the judiciary—and rushing bills through Parliament giving him more power, Erdoğan only bought himself some precious time.

We knew that Erdoğan's increasingly hateful speech, which amounts to a hate crime at times, stigmatizing various segments in Turkey, including the media, businesses and civic groups, had unfortunately inflicted damage on the social peace and harmony in Turkey by stoking division and polarization. But his behavior during the national calamity of the mining disaster has also unveiled how much psychological damage he can inflict on a nation in mourning. Perhaps Erdoğan, all by himself, has rendered the government's psychosocial support for the victims of the accident, in particular the women and children left behind, completely ineffective by downplaying the significance of the tragedy and calling it not unusual.

This accident also showed in stark terms that Erdoğan, the power-hungry politician, does not understand the principle that when you've been entrusted with power, you are accountable for how you use it. He simply does not want the miserable performance record on mining safety and security to be examined by the public, even though he personally consolidated all the licensing, leasing, and sale of state properties, including mines, into his hands in 2012. Local and regional authorities' real decision-making and administrative powers were stripped away, and without accountability, power brought out the worst in Erdoğan; he has started to display behavior that is more and more tyrannical in public places.

Now, Turkey is confronted with a serious problem: Erdoğan is undermining the trust the state has built over time with its citizens. His erratic behavior and his government's policies that have separated power from responsibility and accountability have dealt a serious blow to the predictability and clarity that people expect, which risks eventually eroding the precious trust and social contract between citizens and the state. Erdoğan's leadership style, which allows him to take all the credit when there is a success and blame everyone else when things go wrong without absorbing even some of the responsibility, actually eats away at this trust very rapidly.

Erdoğan and his loyalist yes-men that surround him, kicking and screaming, do not seem to realize the broad impact of this mining disaster, which is receiving significant national and international press coverage. Social science studies of traumatic events indicate that while tragedies have the greatest impact on those directly involved, they can also have a profound effect on those not present at the event, especially those who can identify with the victims. Feelings of being very upset, irritable, and angry are common symptoms among citizens during a tragic event and its aftermath. Perhaps the most vulnerable group is children, who may be exposed to a greater risk of post-traumatic stress disorder, even if they live outside the disaster area.

To cope with these symptoms, the leadership ought to reassure the uneasy public, provide a sense of purpose for the future and guide citizens through a complex grieving process. Erdoğan could have told people it was OK to cry and perhaps even wept himself with the giving relatives. Erdoğan has not done so. He broke into tears on a program aired live on pro-government TV in August when senior Muslim Brotherhood politician Mohammad al-Beltagy's letter to his daughter Asma, killed by Egyptian security forces in a crackdown in Cairo on Aug. 14, 2013, was read. He did not, however, shed a tear for some 300 fellow citizens, many of whom were young, who suffocated to death in the mine shafts.

Instead, he tried to minimize the disaster, insulting people's intelligence and shattering their already weakened confidence. He looked like a politician who is always eager to hear his own voice. Perhaps it was an effort to increase his popularity and garner votes for the upcoming presidential elections, but this ill-advised tactic backfired when Erdoğan tried to deliver an impromptu speech in front of the city hall building in Soma. He was booed and the crowd called for him and his government to resign. Instead of taking in this reaction with empathy, Erdoğan went haywire and called the protesters ill-mannered and immoral people. Recalling his party's March 30th local elections victory, he claimed that voters had given the appropriate response to these protesters, as if past elections have anything to do with a national disaster.

A video of the incident shared on the popular video-sharing platform YouTube shows Erdoğan daring one protester, "Come up to me and boo me to my face," and then walking up to the man in a store. At one point in the video, Erdoğan grabs the protester and slaps him in the face. This is then followed up with a beating from Erdoğan's bodyguards. This is completely unbecoming of a man who is supposed to lead the nation in a time of great tragedy. He exacerbated the already tense situation. We knew Erdoğan had a bad temper, but he has contained his anger most of the time, at least in public. However, his recent frequent flare-ups may be indicative of a worrying pattern of disconnect from the people and perhaps even disassociation from reality.

He could have been griever-in-chief in the face of this massive tragedy, yet he managed to further polarize the nation and widen the opposition front against him. Frankly, I think Erdoğan no longer needs an opponent to fight. He is his own worst enemy. Given time, he will wear himself down and his once-shining political beacon will burn out.

Specter of a Totalitarian Regime[6]

Top Turkish political Islamist Prime Minster Recep Tayyip Erdoğan's increasingly assertive and authoritarian policies, which are doomed to eventually fail given the vibrancy and dynamism of Turkish society, will nevertheless inflict significant damage on Turkish democracy. These policies seem to have been designed to turn Turkey into a totalitarian

---

[6]   First appeared in *Today's Zaman* daily on Jun. 06, 2014

regime. As such, the Erdoğan government's highly controversial efforts represent a direct threat to the very foundations of modern Turkey.

The different manifestations of the revival of authoritarian tendencies in both discourse and policy, coupled with the justification and glorification of extremist political Islamist ideology, indicate that a joint effort is required to battle this creeping authoritarianism in Turkish society, one that ought to draw support from various stakeholders. Such a showdown is already in the works, with groups hoping to stop the advance of the Erdoğan government in curbing fundamental rights, freedoms, democratic principles and the rule of law. These groups include civil society, the media, and business groups, as well as the military and high judiciary.

As Erdoğan tries to strengthen his grip on the institutions of the state, the economy, and society, he knows that he needs to dismantle democratic structures so that a totalitarian and/or authoritarian system of governance based on political Islamist ideology may be established in its place. In other words, he is trying to establish a totalitarian country in a democratic society where citizens enjoy rights and freedoms. Erdoğan knows that this is simply not possible in a country like Turkey, which has a strong tradition of bouncing back to democratic regimes even after bloody military coups. Turks have always loved their military, but they despise its interference into politics. This is why they have never accepted the military's pressure on the government, just as they won't do so for political Islamists who, for all intents and purposes, are trying to turn the system of governance into a totalitarian one.

Therefore, Erdoğan's ultimate game plan focuses on creating a state of limbo, a power vacuum or even a sort of anarchy that wreaks havoc among state institutions, divides and polarizes Turkish society, and undermines citizens' fundamental rights and freedoms. He hopes to accomplish this through provoking a clash between his authoritarian polices and the democratic values and principles this nation loves dearly. As growing chaos rules in the country, with the balance of power unsettled, checks and balances eroded, and hatred and hostility unleashed, Erdoğan is buying some time to survive politically. The public will pay less attention to the prime minister's personal troubles with the law in relation to corruption and other major wrongdoings when it is being challenged by an imminent and serious danger.

Here are the road markers for this tactical game plan: First, Erdoğan has somewhat undermined the democratic political system by amassing huge power in the hands of the ruling Justice and Development Party (AKP), which abuses the influence of the state in swaying the electorate to its favor. There is simply no equality in resources between the ruling party and opposition parties during election campaigns, which hampers free and fair competition for votes. When you add allegations of massive election fraud and irregularities orchestrated by the governing party in the March 30, 2014, local elections, the odds have grown against the opposition. That naturally undermines voters' confidence in the democratic political system.

Second, Erdoğan effectively suspended the rule of law with a series of political and legislative measures so that he could derail the corruption investigations that incriminated him, his family members, and his close associates. The lead graft prosecutors and police chiefs were reassigned, some even arbitrarily fired, and the persecution of civil servants who have simply fulfilled their duties according to the law has gone unabated. He has pushed for the adoption of a series of flawed laws, especially regarding the criminal code, the code on criminal procedure, the civil code, and electoral laws. In the meantime, the independence of the judiciary received a fatal blow at the hands of Erdoğan.

Third, Erdoğan knew he needed to muzzle the media and create a press favorable to the government in order to feed biased and wrong information to the electorate so that their right to make informed decisions on election days would be undermined. He has partially succeeded in that, especially in the broadcast media and the print and digital press. The same has also occurred at universities, research centers, and think tanks. A recent circular by the government-controlled Higher Education Board (YÖK) even barred professors from providing quotes to the media on their field of expertise without prior permission from university administration. Erdoğan and his team of advisors have turned many independent think tanks into mouthpieces of the ruling party and have co-opted critics as supporters using cash and the promise of prestigious positions in government.

Central to this attempted totalitarian overhaul is pressuring civil society groups to yield in despair and to no longer be critical of government policies. To make this happen, Erdoğan's government picked on innocent people and groups, and persecuted them. He subjected them to smear campaigns, something that is not acceptable in normal democratic societies, in order to intimidate others. Turkey's liberals, social democrats, nationalists, Alevis, and moderate conservative groups, including members of the Fethullah Gülen-inspired Hizmet Movement, are opposed to the exploitation of Islam in the name of politics and have all felt the brunt of Erdoğan's repressive and harsh tactics. Thus, Erdoğan strove to destroy the very hallmarks of democracy—respecting the right to dissent, and the toleration of different opinions and viewpoints.

His government brutally quashed peaceful protests held by disenchanted and disillusioned citizens exercising their right to freedom of assembly, as guaranteed under the Turkish Constitution. The police showdown in Taksim Square on the anniversary of the Gezi Park events and the blockade of the town of Soma—where Turkey's worst mining accident took place, killing 301 miners—in order to suppress angry backlash and protests against the government are indications that the Erdoğan administration is gradually turning Turkey into a sort of police state. On top of that, the Erdoğan government violated the basic legal principle that groups or people cannot be punished collectively, since guilt of a crime must be proved individually in a court of law, with protections on the right to defense and the presumption of innocence.

Fourth, Erdoğan upset the rules and regulations of the liberal market economy, creating a unique type of crony capitalism in which democracy is abused to gain wealth and power for a select few. In this system, the government provides lucrative government deals and contracts to its supporters in the business world, while those who are not loyal to the regime get audited and left outside of government tenders, and their business licenses run the risk of being revoked. Moreover, those well-qualified people working at government agencies dealing with the economy and finance were sacked with no regard to procedures, rules, or laws in order to open positions up to Erdoğan's cronies and loyalists. All this has led to unfair competition among businesses while bringing the advent of reforms and the management of the economy to a grinding halt.

Fifth, the Erdoğan government is trying to engineer a revision of the education system to change values to reflect the political Islamist ideology. The reconstruction of history, changing school curriculums, the reassigning of some 100,000 school principals with a single piece of legislation, and supporting religious foundations close to Erdoğan with government grants and incentives are all part of the objective to raise an army of political Islamists in Turkey. The AKP government also perpetuates discrimination and hatred in order to harden the young generation and widen the rifts in Turkish society.

All these drastic measures are desperate attempts on the part of Erdoğan to create bigger troubles for the nation so that he can have a freer hand in the government. The main opposition Republican People's Party's (CHP) fresh claim that Erdoğan wanted to escalate tension with Syria ahead of the presidential election and that he had to postpone the incursion into Syria when the Soma mining accident happened bears the footprints of the same flawed logic of creating a bigger problem. Under a lingering atmosphere of fear, Erdoğan's tactics will pay off only in the short run. It will only be a matter of a time before he stumbles over his own feet while moving down his path to turn Turkey into a totalitarian regime.

Political Fundamentalism[7]

With increasingly aggressive and intolerant posturing, Turkey's controversial prime minister, Recep Tayyip Erdoğan, has been rapidly transforming what used to be a successful progressive party, the ruling Justice and Development Party (AKP), into an organization that mainly features the characteristics of political fundamentalism in this predominantly Muslim nation.

---

[7]   First appeared in *Today's Zaman* daily on Jun. 16, 2014

To the extent he makes use of, or rather abuse of, religion to defend his own personal interests, Erdoğan's political authority rapidly moved to rest on extremist ideology, one that can shake the very fundamentals of the Turkish Republic if not checked. In fact, both the narrative and policies employed by the Turkish prime minister display most of the features one can find in an extremist ideology, latent if not manifest, such as a blind conviction by followers that the leader is always right in what he says. The hostile discourse he sometimes employs in public rallies against the opposition, media, business, and civic groups certainly borders on hate speech, if not openly within the scope of hate crime laws.

The footprints of the religious intolerant fanaticism that exalts Erdoğan and makes no distinction between the individual spiritual sphere and public authority can easily be seen in the remarks attributed to his associates. For example, İsmail Hakkı Eser, chairman of the local party branch of the ruling AKP in the western province of Aydın said, on Feb. 3, 2010, that "to us, our prime minister is a second prophet."

"A two-rakat thank-you prayer should be performed for Erdoğan every day," said Oktay Saral, a former mayor who now serves as an AKP Istanbul deputy, on Feb. 6, 2010.

"I recognize Erdoğan as a righteous caliph and pay him homage," pro-government journalist and Erdoğan's supporter Atılgan Bayar said on Aug. 23, 2013.

The former EU affairs minister and chief negotiator, Egemen Bağış, who was forced to resign after the corruption scandal, said on Feb. 10, 2013, that "Rize, Istanbul, and Siirt are sacred places." Rize is Erdoğan's hometown, Istanbul is the city where Erdoğan started his political career, and Siirt is where his wife was born and where Erdoğan was first elected deputy. "Believe me, even touching our dear prime minister is a sacred prayer," said AKP Bursa deputy Hüseyin Şahin on July 21, 2011. Erdoğan never contradicted these remarks. In a way, with his silence over glorifying religious references among party loyalists, he encouraged the creation of a sort of sub-culture called Erdoğanism.

Moreover, the worrying pattern that fuels the extremism in Turkey under Erdoğan's rule includes perhaps the deliberate failure on the part of government to address discrimination against AKP opponents. The manifestation of rampant discrimination has recently been seen in access to government employment, public services, contracts, and tenders.

Last year, investigative reporter Mehmet Baransu exposed the widespread profiling of unsuspecting citizens by this government based on their ethnic, religious, ideological, or political affiliations. Since he exposed the government's dirty laundry, which served the public interest, he should have been rewarded for this; yet an Istanbul prosecutor is now seeking 52 years in prison for this journalist, under charges of "exposing state secrets" after a government complaint.

Another indication that the Erdoğan government has little or no interest in dealing with extremism is that there is a lack of emphasis on civic education. Rather, a special focus has been made on religious education in imam-hatip schools, the kind of school from which Erdoğan also graduated, with special dispensation made for these schools. Erdoğan's relentless attacks against the Hizmet Movement, inspired by Islamic scholar Fethullah Gülen, who has been a pioneer in Turkey on intercultural and inter-religious dialogue efforts, strengthens the hands of extremists in Turkey. By demonizing Mr. Gülen in public rallies with derogatory remarks, Erdoğan also stigmatizes millions who have a deep respect for the valuable contribution Gülen has made in moderating extremism and preventing Turkish youth from slipping into radicalism.

No doubt that extremism can also reach its worst when it condones or even promotes violence. Erdoğan defended the way the Turkish police dealt with the weeks-long demonstrations that began as a peaceful protest against government plans to demolish a green park in Istanbul's central Taksim Square last year. Although the police have been heavily criticized for their use of brutal force in the crackdown on the protests, Erdoğan said police displayed an "unprecedented democratic stance and successfully passed the test of democracy." On the anniversary of Gezi in 2014, Erdoğan also once again encouraged the police to clamp down on protesters. He even expressed surprise at how "tolerant" the Turkish police were against the demonstrators. His blamed the so-called "interest lobby," a veiled reference to Jewish financiers, as being behind Gezi, a claim that raised the specter of anti-Semitism in Erdoğan's narrative.

Since Turkish democracy is not yet consolidated and still in a transition phase with many political reforms placed on the waiting list, the risks of extremism in this country are elevated. The institutions of democracy, especially the judiciary, which were supposed to fight any extremism, have been weakened by Erdoğan in his quest to save himself, his family members, and his close associates from serious legal troubles that originated from a massive corruption scandal.

The tension and polarization in Turkish society, instigated by Erdoğan's exclusionary discourse, also makes it difficult to cope with extremism that requires a broad-based social consensus for the battle to be effective. Unfortunately, the political culture is poisoned, society is divided, people are confused, and institutions have been weakened with the lack of accountability and transparency.

Erdoğan's militant wording that feeds fictitious issues as if they were real to the Turkish people and his frequent use of demagogy make it very difficult to move forward in addressing pressing challenges. He often invokes a global conspiracy theory, one that is allegedly supported by the US, the EU, and Israel, organized to weaken Turkey. He openly accuses the opposition, media, businesses, and civil society organizations with treachery. When he was confronted with a corruption probe last December, all of a sudden he devised the so-called "parallel state," a reference to the Hizmet Movement, to obstruct the investigation and distract Turks from discussing real issues that matter to them.

The current crisis in Turkey's domestic political landscape represents a fight against virulent extremism, one that has little respect for the rule of law, democracy, and fundamental human rights and liberties. What makes it more troubling for Turkey is that the competent authority that is supposed to combat extremism—Erdoğan's ruling AKP—is in fact perpetuating it.

Spin Machine and Propaganda[8]

Perhaps drawing on an example set by Iran's authoritarian and highly intrusive regime, Turkey's beleaguered prime minister and the presump-

---

[8] First appeared in *Today's Zaman* daily on Jun. 27, 2014

tive nominee for the presidency, Recep Tayyip Erdoğan, who called Iran his second home, has built a potent propaganda machine to communicate his message to the masses, to wage a smear campaign in order to discredit opponents and to manipulate people's views on various issues with half-truths, lies, and disinformation.

It appears the spin machine is operated primarily by teams located mainly in two different centers: One was set up in the Prime Minister's Office and the other in the spy agency, the National Intelligence Organization (MİT), run by Erdoğan's close confidante Hakan Fidan. Both teams coordinate closely to feed information to traditional print and broadcast outlets as well to online portals, including social media. The smear campaign plastering outgoing US Ambassador Frank Ricciardone's picture on the front pages of five dailies on the same day in December of last year with a headline alleging that the US was somehow behind Turkish prosecutors' corruption investigations that incriminated Erdoğan, his family members, and close associates was likely co-produced by these teams.

The modus operandi of this propaganda is that once the fabricated story makes the pages, the prime minister and his associates pick up on that in public speeches and keep repeating the same narrative over and over to amplify the message. That is how it happened when Erdoğan publicly threatened the US ambassador with expulsion in a public rally in Samsun province on the day the conspiracy theory made the headlines in the pro-government dailies. The same smear campaign was deployed against other opponents, including Islamic scholar Fethullah Gülen, who is critical of corruption in the Erdoğan government. All kinds of manipulative stories were published in pro-government dailies while Erdoğan tried to spin the corruption probe as a coup and to pin his misconduct on others.

The leaked audio files earlier in year 2014 and wide coverage in the independent media on this subject have in fact unmasked these propagandists in Erdoğan's team. One leak in March revealed that one of the key players who control the media on behalf of the government is Yalçın Akdoğan, chief political advisor to the prime minister and a regular contributor as a columnist in two different pro-government dailies, *Star* and *Yenişafak*. According to a conversation uploaded onto YouTube, Fatih Saraç, deputy chairman of the Ciner Media Group, which includes the *Habertürk* daily and the *Habertürk* news channel, informs Akdoğan how he fired the three journalists responsible for negative reporting that drew the ire of the prime minister. He also appears to be an influential figure in deciding who will show up as a commentator on government mouthpiece TV stations.

Another participant in the propaganda machine is Mustafa Varank, whose name was implicated in multiple smear campaigns to advance the political goals of his boss, Erdoğan. Varank was alleged to be the key conduit in disseminating the video footage of former main opposition Republic People's Party (CHP) leader Deniz Baykal's adultery, though he acted under the orders of Erdoğan. A leaked audio revealed how Erdoğan was allegedly conspiring to manipulate the sex tape intrigue, which compelled Baykal to resign in 2010 and helped Erdoğan to get rid of his archrival on the political stage. The leak reportedly came from the email account of Varank, hinting that the recording was somehow coordinated by the prime minister's own consultant. The CHP believes Erdoğan orchestrated the trap to remove Baykal from his position using the intelligence branch. CHP leader Kemal Kılıçdaroğlu described the incident as "yet another version of the US Watergate scandal."

Varank is reportedly in charge of fake Twitter accounts, manned by thousands of hired users by the ruling Justice and Development Party (AKP), to advance any campaign that benefits Erdoğan in the social media. Various leaks indicate that he is involved in schemes such as getting people fired from media outlets, denying opposition placement of ads on billboards, coordinating a suspicious shipment to Nigeria, and forcing representatives of civil society groups to sign a declaration in support of Erdoğan. The prime minister's son Bilal, daughter Sümeyye, and his son-in law Serhat Albayrak all seemed to have played some sort of role in this propaganda campaign as well. His daughter worked with Varank in directing social media users, while his son and son-in law have played crucial roles in deciding the layout of the front-page stories attacking government opponents in the so-called pool media in the *Sabah* and *Takvim* dailies, financed by kickbacks from contracts and tenders.

On the intelligence side, Fidan directed resources of the spy agency to feed content for the propaganda war on behalf of his boss, Erdoğan. The CHP believes Fidan has been doing the dirty work of Erdoğan, who effectively turned the spy agency into his private intelligence branch with sweeping immunities granted by the AKP government. Former Interior Minister İdris Naim Şahin, who resigned from the AKP in protest of what he called a "narrow oligarchic group" that seized the party administration and dictated government policies that he viewed as contradictory to national interests, accused the AKP of engaging in efforts to produce fake sex tapes that implicate a number of deputies who recently parted ways with the ruling party.

When Erdoğan hinted publicly for the first time that Turkish President Abdullah Gül and Chief of General Staff Gen. Necdet Özel were all secretly eavesdropped on, the CHP spokesperson Haluk Koç questioned how Erdoğan knew all about this, accusing him of accumulating a collection of tapes in order to design a political map in his favor. He said a cache of tapes has been maintained with the approval of Erdoğan and leaked when needed with his orders. "The main actor in this dirty political era is Recep Tayyip Erdoğan," Koç said. Even the judges who rendered rulings that irked Erdoğan were accused of being blackmailed with secret tapes that reveal them in uncompromising situations.

Nuh Yılmaz, former director of the Washington branch of the Foundation for Political, Economic and Social Research (SETA), a government think tank charged with the task of whitewashing what Erdoğan does, is the main coordinator in the intelligence organization in running an intel-related network with journalists and media groups that are funded by the government, directly or otherwise. He worked in the pro-government media before moving to the agency to lead the press office last year. According to claims raised on the *MedyaAnaliz* news portal, Yılmaz works very closely with about a dozen journalists and op-ed editors in order to broadcast the agency's views to the public with manipulative information. He also coordinates a propaganda campaign directly with top editors of pro-government dailies and TV stations. Several web portals allegedly set up by MİT to plant fabricated stories and to run a smear campaign against opponents to disparage their reputations are also directed by him. It appears Yılmaz works closely with Varank to counter critical reporting in the independent media as well. The tapped phone call between Varank and Yılmaz that was uploaded onto YouTube in March reveals how both engaged in joint efforts to support the government's denial of the illegal profiling claims published by the *Taraf* daily in December of 2013.

The third part of the spin machine, although not as influential as the one at the intel and prime minister's offices, lies at the Foreign Ministry and works closely with SETA, a think tank that also acts as the main thoroughfare for Foreign Minister Ahmet Davutoğlu to place his loyalists in government agencies. This part of the spin machine produces newsbytes to promote Davutoğlu as well as supplying information that needs to be shared with the public but can't be attributed to the Foreign Ministry in any way. The point man is Durmuş Ali Sarıkaya, who has been working with Davutoğlu for about 20 years in various capacities. Although he has the title of advisor to the foreign minister and the prime minister, he joins in key high-level meetings and never leaves Davutoğlu's side. He built an extensive network with like-minded people in government agencies, including spymaster Hakan Fidan, whose family members were even taken as guests on Davutoğlu's plane for foreign trips.

The list goes on, as there are other government propagandists working as consultants, advisors, and party officials to put a spin on things and events and to perpetuate disinformation. Fabricated news bytes also create a pretext for the government to justify reshuffling, reassigning, and even purging civil servants from their positions with politically engineered investigations. It also helps the government orchestrate sham legal proceedings in kangaroo court settings to obtain an outcome that is essentially decided in advance. In other words, Erdoğan's spin machine is not just working to shape the perception but also generating show trials to put opponents behind bars and intimidate others in the meantime.

The end result is that in Erdoğan's Turkey, the citizens' right to be informed has been grossly violated with manipulation, lies, half-truths, and disinformation, dealing a blow to democratic governance and shaking people's trust in the government. The fabricated fable parroted by the partisan media has unfortunately led to further polarization and tension in Turkish society, making it difficult to sustain social peace.

The incessant campaign of disinformation and systematic propaganda on behalf of the government shamefully places Turkey on par with the experience of former communist regimes where the media were under strict control and under constant manipulation. The overarching propaganda machine might have helped those regimes survive for some time but never succeeded in convincing people to believe in lies. The gap between the truth and lies eventually widened. What is more, as opposed to the communist regimes, Turkey still has a formidable independent media to expose lies, and there is no shortage of patriotic whistleblowers to reveal what Erdoğan propagandists have been doing in the shadows.

Chapter 2

Massive Corruption in Government

Tip of the Iceberg[9]

I f the massive corruption investigation of Dec. 17, 2013, perhaps the biggest in the history of the republic, is only the tip of the iceberg, as some seem to have suggested, then the national security of Turkey is very much at risk of being compromised. The political fallout from dirty deals apparently run by a band of graft brothers in the Turkish Cabinet will not only damage the ruling Justice and Development Party, but it will also leave a weak spot in Turkey's defenses when it comes to penetration by clandestine Iranian activities in Turkey. The mere fact that these ministers, these three musketeers of government, may have joined forces to help an Iranian national named Reza Zarrab do his own dirty bidding, both in Turkey and abroad (China, Ghana, the United Arab Emirates, and Italy were mentioned in the files), and using government powers and privileges, exposes how Turkey has become vulnerable to Iranian plots.

In a futile attempt, Prime Minister Recep Tayyip Erdoğan is mounting an offense to defend his government by highlighting so-called foreign enemies of Turkey, an implicit reference to the US, the EU, Israel, and the Jewish lobby abroad and domestic conspirators at home, which includes diverse groups, from Alevis and faith-inspired conservative groups like the Hizmet (Gülen) Movement to business interest groups and unions. These usual suspects and imaginary enemies of Turkey serve as scapegoats in Erdoğan's strategy to ride out the stormy revelations

---

[9] First appeared in *Today's Zaman* daily on Dec. 20, 2013

of the corruption scandal. He did so during the May-June Gezi Park protests as well.

The problem with this fallacy, however, is that there is no evidence to back these preposterous claims, while there is a body of overwhelming evidence, all gathered through a court-sanctioned judicial investigation and corruption dragnet run by the Istanbul Prosecutors' Office, indicating that Erdoğan's men are in it up to their necks. It is clear that Erdoğan has pushed the panic button to cover up the shady deals his government people have been involved in. The summary dismissal of police chiefs—not only in Ista+nbul, where the prosecutors discovered this major corruption scheme—but also in other parts of the country, tells a tale of great worry on the part of Erdoğan that similar scandalous details may emerge elsewhere in the country as well. It seems he does not even trust police chiefs he personally appointed a few years back.

What will the ramifications of this damaging exposé be? Well, for one, the AKP has lost the source of its primary appeal, representing corruption-free government. The ministers involved in the scheme have done a great disservice to their fellow Cabinet members and the ruling party by inflicting irreparable damage on the reputation of their fight against corruption. This will cast a long shadow on the party for some time to come and will continue to haunt each and every member of the party in political debates. Erdoğan's defensive posture only further reinforces this image. Instead of demanding disclosure and that the heads of those responsible must roll, he has tightened his grip on the ongoing investigation, shooting himself in the foot.

The impact of this scandal will surely result in a loss of votes for the AKP in the upcoming elections, more so in the presidential and parliamentary elections than in the local ones, where the candidates matter more than the party. It will likely not reach the point that the AKP will be thrown out of power, however, as long as the opposition parties remain as fractured and frayed as ever. The main opposition Republican People's Party (CHP) has surprisingly revamped its strategy based on a fresh appeal to center-right voters and has discarded some ideological trappings. It still has a credibility and trust issue with voters who suspect that all this may just be election tactics rather than a fundamental shift. The real challenge for the AKP in the short run will come from within the conservative base that has not been happy with Erdoğan's performance for some time. The corruption scandal may be a tipping point for them to organize a challenge to Erdoğan's rule. Let's not forget that President Abdullah Gül's ambitions to remain engaged in Turkish politics are as strong as ever.

Another likely result is snap national elections, currently scheduled for the summer of 2015. The AKP government will find it very difficult to run the country amid damaging corruption scandals and high levels of polarization; Erdoğan may be compelled to seek a new mandate to silence critics and lower tension in the country. It makes sense to do it sooner rather than later, because the government will lose more points with the public as the probe widens, leading to further embarrassing revelations for the government. A drop in popularity for the AKP right after the local elections of March 2014 will add more fuel to the debate of the legitimacy of AKP rule in Turkey.

Can Erdoğan contain the damage by derailing the investigation? Perhaps, but only to a limited extent. It is true that he controls the police and Interior Ministry (as opposed to a common misperception abroad that Muslim scholar Fethullah Gülen has a huge influence on Turkish security services). He can sack chiefs and appoint new ones, as he has done recently. After the story of the corruption scandal broke, he even brought in a former governor, who has no background in police work, to lead the Istanbul office, just to make sure nothing escapes his scrutiny as the probe escalates further.

As for the judiciary, he can't roam freely, thanks to the 2010 reforms that brought a more or less pluralistic and democratic structure to Turkey's judicial council that sits at the heart of the Turkish justice system. Erdoğan has some leverage, using the position of the justice minister on the council, but not to the extent that he enjoys in the police department. Therefore, the Turkish judiciary, by and large, remains independent and impartial.

The main problem is the lack of judicial police in Turkey. Since prosecutors and judges do not have a separate and independent police force to run investigations, search for evidence and round up suspects, they have to rely on the Turkish security services. Although prosecutors can instruct the police to maintain secrecy while conducting the probe and prohibit them from sharing their findings with their superiors (which was the case in the initial stages of the investigation involving the interior minister, who oversees the Turkish police), there is no guarantee that government officials and politicians from the ruling party will not be tipped off on ongoing probes by prosecutors. In fact, according to local media, Interior Minister Muammer Güler, who allegedly took bribes from Zarrab, removed a police chief who reported the Iranian national's money laundering scheme to the watchdog agency, the Financial Crimes Investigation Board (MASAK). The minister also apparently told Zarrab that he was under surveillance, prompting the Iranian national to plan an unsuccessful flight from the country.

I think the Erdoğan government is contemplating another strategy to weather this corruption crisis. He has full control of Turkey's National Intelligence Organization (MİT) through his confidant, Hakan Fidan, who leads the spy agency. Since Law No. 2937 on State Intelligence Services and the National Intelligence Organization gives MİT the right to run investigations related to spy charges rather than the police or the gendarmerie, we may very well see a series of fictitious cases launched by government to go after people who, in fact, exposed government dirty laundry. The criminal complaint filed by the Office of the Prime Minister against the liberal *Taraf* newspaper and investigative reporter Mehmet Baransu for publishing confidential documents that unveiled massive profiling of unsuspecting, innocent citizens in violation of their constitutional right to privacy is an example of just such a strategy.

Erdoğan's remarks on Wednesday pointing to a gang within the state and that his government is keen to expose this gang were part of the campaign to build a case on that logical fallacy as well. Faced with an embarrassing corruption scheme, he will likely try to invoke secret intelligence prerogatives based on treachery in a bid to establish a defense line while trying to sway the Turkish public to his side against imaginary impending threats to national security. Erdoğan hopes this strategy will confuse the Turkish people, allow him to consolidate his ranks and mobilize his own troops in a nation ready to buy into conspiracy theories. Pro-government media will support and promote this campaign, as well. Will it work? Not really. The powerful generals who abused state security courts to instill that kind of fear in Turks failed in the '80s and '90s, and the Erdoğan government's use of the same strategy will backfire as well.

What is more, Turkey is no longer the old Turkey. The affluent middle class, the young population, and stronger civil society organizations, strengthened by the digital revolution with such tools as social media, will resist any attempts to turn the clock backwards on the development of Turkish democracy. People will simply ask why Prime Minister Erdoğan is not going after his people who have been sleeping with the enemy next door if he is really sincere in addressing external threats to this great nation.

Consolidating Democracy after Scandal[10]

Right off the bat, I would like to say this: Don't let your heart be troubled much by what has been happening in Turkey recently. When all the dust settles in the aftermath of corruption, money laundering, and racketeering involving higher-ups in the ruling Justice and Development Party (AKP), we will have the chance to lay the foundation for a democracy by consensus, which is the only way to rule a large country like Turkey with a relatively young population and rising middle class. Any other scenario would create more polarization and tension, making the country very difficult to govern, no matter what party is in power.

I suppose Turks may have to learn to live with governments that are not led by such charismatic leaders who dominate the agenda, but rather by a coalition of professional politicians who take into account different constituencies and interests before reaching a compromise solution on national issues. There is always an opportunity in every crisis, and that is what Turks will discover at the end of the current government scandal over corruption. This will teach us the urgent need for more transparency in public decision-making as well as greater account-

---

[10] First appeared in *Today's Zaman* daily on Dec. 23, 2013

ability in government and will prompt Turkey to adopt a series of reforms to make sure past problems will not be repeated.

One thing is for sure: representative democracy based on a ballot box mandate every four years is no longer enough for Turks who aspire to have a truly representative government. Naturally, citizens of this country want to be fully informed and engaged in what their government is doing. They want to feel that their opinions matter, not just when they go to polling stations on election day, but between elections throughout the decision-making processes of political players. That is the lesson the nation will extract from the most recent crisis, ultimately making Turkey stronger than ever before.

As for Prime Minister Recep Tayyip Erdoğan, he blew his chance when he made a series of fatal mistakes beginning in 2011. The last one, the vast corruption dragnet sweeping up many at the highest levels that has become the largest scandal in the Turkish Republic's history, is perhaps the deadliest one for him. Since Erdoğan helped to establish his ruling AKP on the centerpiece of a corruption-free government, he will likely not recover from this outrageous scandal. The hard evidence and bitter truth will prevail over any efforts by Erdoğan in his bid to try and stay ahead of the waves with a damage control campaign. Even if Erdoğan succeeds in derailing the investigation with a flagrant abuse of government powers, the allegations of corruption will always continue to hang over his head and anybody associated with the ruling party. As a result, he has turned himself and his band of brothers in graft into a liability rather than a winning ticket for the party.

Of course, the main worry is how much damage Erdoğan might inflict on the nation as he goes down in history as the man under whose watch the country witnessed the largest-ever corruption case. Erdoğan threatened to expel the US envoy on Saturday after his close aides cooked up completely fabricated stories that the US had been involved in the corruption probe; he had this tale run on the front pages of pro-government dailies, plastering pictures of US Ambassador Francis Ricciardone there. That, in itself, shows that he is willing to burn bridges, even with Turkey's key ally and strategic partner. This spells danger for Turkish national security, given that Erdoğan had already head-butted half a dozen state leaders within Turkey's neighborhood, jamming Turkish foreign policy into tight box.

On the domestic front, the collateral damage will be felt in further polarization in society and rising risk premiums in the economy. Erdoğan has given all the indications that he wants to run a war campaign to quash opposition groups, be they liberals, social democrats, nationalists or even conservative groups like the Hizmet (Gülen) Movement that endorsed him in the past. He has already started to exploit state powers to implement his battle plan by arranging for the summary removal of hundreds of public officials, most in the police force, with no reasonable justification. He has been bending laws or even circumventing and violating legislative and constitutional articles to get what he wants.

In the economy, the mismanagement of the graft probe has already cost the nation, shaking foreign investors' confidence in the very foundations of the country's justice system with meddlesome tactics. Even well-respected economy czar, Deputy Prime Minister Ali Babacan was heard uttering the words "chaos lobby," suggesting that this mysterious group was behind the probe, when speaking from the podium in Parliament late Friday night during the budget debate. That was more troubling news than when Babacan said that state-lender Halkbank has lost a share value amounting to some $1.6 billion. Babacan knew the international risks involved when he allowed the state lender to continue payment processing for Iran on behalf of other clients such as India, and he was also aware of the dangers when the bank engaged in gold for trade deals that annoyed the Americans. I suppose Babacan should take comfort from the testimony of Halkbank General Manager Süleyman Aslan, who revealed in his court testimony during his arraignment that he had earned the country $3.6 billion from the gold trade.

The war of attrition Erdoğan has unleashed against people who disagree with him about how the corruption investigation is being handled will deal still more blows to Erdoğan himself and to the party. This war is simply not sustainable, given that the AKP government will surely face a series of legal challenges in the coming days and weeks. Despite its shortcomings, we still have a relatively independent and impartial judiciary, thanks to the 2010 public referendum that overhauled the justice system and created a more democratic and pluralistic structure. That is why Erdoğan threatened the judiciary on Sunday by saying that he will use his parliamentary majority to make the legislative changes necessary to save his government from legal troubles. That is not easy to do, however, given that the Constitutional Court may strike down any piece of legislation deemed in clear violation of constitutional articles.

Erdoğan's hatred and anger may leave scars on groups that are targeted on the domestic front, especially the Hizmet Movement, which did not pick the fight but which was compelled to defend itself against escalating attacks from the Erdoğan government on institutions affiliated with the group. Since Hizmet is not a political force but rather represents perhaps the country's strongest civic movement and is powerful at the grassroots level, it can easily bounce back and collect itself in the face of the government assault. The day of reckoning was probably inevitable, given that Erdoğan's creeping political Islam ideology recognizes no compromise whatsoever. The moderate and compromise-seeking values and ideals promoted by Hizmet are not compatible with what a politically charged Islamist ideology represents: a more confrontational and discriminatory approach.

There is no need to be pessimistic, however. Things will eventually get back to normal in Turkey. This will happen when Erdoğan is compelled to realize that he can no longer sustain beating the war drums through elections, and as the opposition picks up speed on what seems to be genuine outreach activities. As more damaging revelations will likely emerge of AKP cronies siphoning off money from contracts and tenders, Erdoğan will have no choice but to back down to save what is left for him. On a positive note, these scandals will help cleanse the state and contribute to consolidating Turkish democracy further, with strong checks and balances to be introduced to the Turkish state system. From the terrible ordeal of an authoritarian system of government under Erdoğan, Turks will draw important lessons that will be translated into reform steps to shore up democracy in Turkey. Better governance, pluralism, and a more effective use of consultation mechanisms will inevitably prevail at the end of the day.

In the meantime, the opposition will continue to pound the AKP on the largest corruption case in Turkish history in the lead-up to elections. This will not only weaken the AKP but will knock it out of the game, for sure. The only defense the AKP can mount is to amputate the diseased limbs from the party so that the main body can be saved. That seems very unlikely, however, given that the AKP is a leader-dominated party and not institutionalized with strong democratic traditions of succession and compromise. Erdoğan will fight to the end with lots of foot soldiers behind him as deciding delegates. Then, the likely scenario is that the AKP will split under heavy public pressure and criticism from the opposition. Erdoğan's blistering speeches and demonization of others will only precipitate his fall.

House of Cards Collapses[11]

Embattled Prime Minister Recep Tayyip Erdoğan's last play before his house of cards, built around imaginary enemies at home and abroad, comes tumbling down on his government, is the lawsuits of harassment he will likely unleash, using and perhaps abusing state powers entrusted to him by the electorate. Faced with a series of legal challenges stemming from corruption, money laundering, influence-peddling, tender-rigging, organized crime, and intimidation—some of which seem to be supported by formidable evidence collected by prosecutors for over a year—Erdoğan will look for a way out by launching frivolous cases loaded with petty charges.

He has already been working at building up a prime suspect with the brush strokes made in his public speeches and rallies: an unidentified "gang" nested in the police and judiciary, acting in collaboration with foreign enemies of Turkey to topple his government and harm Turkish national interests. His not-so-subtle descriptions clearly indicate that he'd like to portray well-respected Islamic scholar Fethullah Gülen as the man behind the curtain who allegedly pulls all kinds of strings to weaken Erdoğan's rule in Turkey. In other words, he picked Gülen to create a scapegoat for his own troubles as well as to create a major

---

[11] First appeared in *Today's Zaman* daily on Jan. 06, 2014

distraction in public opinion. A relentless negative campaign in the pro-Erdoğan media against Gülen and the Gülen-inspired Hizmet Movement was just a precursor to Erdoğan's next move, i.e., slapping a group of government employees, whose only "crime" is following the laws and rules to battle against corruption, with unfounded lawsuits.

Certainly, this is not an unexpected move, given its precedents in the notorious past of the Turkish Republic. When the coup-loving generals were caught red-handed with their sinister plots hatched to wreak havoc in Turkey so that a military junta could take over the civilian government, they tried to derail the investigations and trials with an attempt to launch their own legal complaints against police officers and prosecutors who had been involved in gathering a massive amount of evidence against them. Col. Dursun Çiçek, whose signature was on the secret action plan to topple the government and clamp down on the Hizmet Movement, was planning to file a complaint against prosecutors and police on charges of "military espionage" and was hoping the military justice system would take over the case.

Retired lieutenant and now-lawyer Serdar Öztürk, one of the key suspects in the Ergenekon case, who has been sentenced to 25 years in prison, also revealed similar plans when being cross-examined in court, as he said he was planning to file espionage charges against lead prosecutor Zekeriya Öz and the police chiefs involved in the investigation. His plans were foiled, however, when police discovered a 109-page confidential memo sent to then-Chief of General Staff Gen. İlker Başbuğ, asking him to prepare new action plans, including a move to ensure that military prosecutors would launch cases against the Ergenekon judges and prosecutors.

Therefore, a similar template can be used by Erdoğan, as well. Just as the junta wanted to circumvent the system through parallel and obscure military justice, Erdoğan is likely to use the National Intelligence Organization (MİT), headed by his close confidante, Hakan Fidan, to build up this baseless lawsuit related to espionage and claims of treachery. This plan was bolstered, in an unprecedented move, when Erdoğan reassigned hundreds of police officers – many of whom are senior chiefs—without any justification whatsoever to intimidate the police force and make sure his plans to go after the Hizmet Movement would not be sabotaged by fresh evidence unearthed by the police. He even ordered the Finance Ministry to reshuffle almost all senior officials, not only to silence the financial crime investigators at key watchdog agency the Financial Crimes Investigation Board (MASAK), but also to bring new foot soldiers into the revenue administration in order to go after companies that are not loyal to his absolute rule.

Well, can Erdoğan's last stand help save him from legal troubles? Unlikely. The charges we will probably see, if and when Erdoğan decides to file a case against the Hizmet Movement, will be petty charges which should not constitute a crime in a democratic country anyway. People can subscribe to different ideologies, values, and belief systems, and the government has no role in that whatsoever. Public employees can only be judged based on laws and rules, not because of their beliefs, race, or ethnicity. In a long statement, the Journalists and Writers Foundation (GYV), whose honorary chair is Gülen, has called on the government to submit whatever evidence it has on conspiracies, such as those involving a "deep state" and "parallel structures" as well as accusations of "treason," "espionage," and "collaboration with international powers" against the interests of Turkey. In other words, Gülen is standing firm and not blinking in the face of Erdoğan's preposterous threats.

What is more, Gülen has the benefit of double jeopardy, as he was acquitted of similar charges before, even under the military-dominated, not very democratic or transparent justice system. Erdoğan probably knows he cannot get a conviction in the court based on shallow evidence. But hauling a few people into court may buy him enough time to survive through the elections and help bolster the image of an enemy conducting subversive activities in Turkey. That is why his campaign people have been throwing everything they have at the problem by bringing the other usual suspects, such as the US, the European Union, Israel, the Gulf countries, minorities, wealthy families, business groups, and the media into the controversial debate. As bizarre as it sounds, Erdoğan's aides think that by lumping all these disparate groups and people together, their case will somehow grow stronger. In fact, Erdoğan is inadvertently extending the front-line and triggering further pressure from abroad while inviting more resentment from additional groups in Turkey.

The prime minister's constant bashing of the press with slanderous accusations that national media professionals are working on behalf of global imperialist powers, when in fact they have just been trying to do their best under the circumstances to provide coverage on important issues such as the corruption investigation, has now become a major concern for us. A demonization campaign in the pro-government media and social media by Erdoğan's trolls amounts to intimidation and open harassment. Even writing in an English-language daily or tweeting in English is enough for these people to conclude that you are working for foreign powers. If you chat with a foreign diplomat in Ankara over lunch, this could be enough for some of these people to label you a "traitor" who is selling the country's deepest secrets. Unfortunately, Erdoğan's harsh rhetoric has fuelled such paranoia in Turkish society that each and every critic of the government must be part of a clandestine campaign to undermine the Turkish state. Based on extremely dubious evidence, it would not be any surprise to see a case involving media professionals who have only exercised their right to freedom of speech.

Nonetheless, all these attempts are doomed to fail. Against the expected baseless lawsuits from Erdoğan's government, there are two formidable investigations going on in Turkey involving major corruption and money laundering schemes. Judging from the evidence leaked so far, there seems to be overwhelming proof implicating very senior people in the ruling Justice and Development Party (AKP) and close relatives of Erdoğan. Considering the comments from the recently resigned minister of Environment and Urban Planning, Erdoğan is personally involved in authorizing what prosecutors have described as a crime. The government has slowed down the first investigation and stalled the second one, but it will not be able to dismiss either of these cases, given that there is compelling evidence in the files.

What's more, there is now an international link to these two cases, because they involve Iranian nationals and third countries, as money had to be moved from one place to another. Perhaps more evidence will emerge soon, leading to new cases that will land the Erdoğan government in even hotter water. Then, having overplayed his hand, Erdoğan will run out of options, and he will have no choice but to watch the collapse of his house of cards.

Derailing the Corruption Probe[12]

Perhaps Turkey's embattled Prime Minister Recep Tayyip Erdoğan has discovered the ultimate battle plan to fight those seeking to expose corruption in government. He has reverse-engineered practices on how best to cope with corruption and started to attack each and every one of the fundamental pillars making up that comprehensive template to curb corruption.

First, he dealt a blow to the independence and effectiveness of the judiciary by abusing the appointment and promotion mechanism controlled by his loyal man at the helm of the Justice Ministry, Bekir Bozdağ, who is also the chairman of the key judicial council, the Supreme Board of Judges and Prosecutors (HSYK). The political interference and undue influence on the judiciary through the HSYK has resulted in the reshuffling of well over 100 prosecutors and judges who were looking into important investigations of corruption, tender-rigging, influence-peddling, money-laundering, and the al-Qaeda terror network. More are expected to be dismissed from their current posts soon.

The circulars ordering the transfers, usually issued over the summer when school is out, were pushed through the HSYK by the justice minister overnight in the middle of the winter season when it is harder for families to move and offered no explanation for the reassignments, in contrast to the established practice of providing a well-reasoned opinion for such dismissals and reassignments. Therefore, by muddying what ought to be transparent appointment, promotion, dismissal and disciplinary procedures, the Erdoğan government tried to hide the political objectives behind the unusual reshuffle that thwarted key investigations implicating people close to Erdoğan.

Second, Erdoğan has deliberately shaken public confidence in public institutions by blatantly disregarding the rule of law in violation of

---

[12] First appeared in *Today's Zaman* daily on Jan. 24, 2014

constitutional articles and contrary to the principle of safeguarding the separation of powers. The government's specific orders that law enforcement officials not enforce court judgments or prosecutors' summons brought forward arbitrariness at the expense of legal certainty. When Erdoğan intervened by not sending his son Bilal to give a deposition in compliance with a prosecutor's summons, this further bolstered a feeling of discrimination and inequality before the law in the public. The core principle of a judicial review of administrative acts was also violated in a number of draft bills that are likely to be approved in the ruling party-dominated Parliament.

Third, he is now pressuring critical media, even more so than in the past, to cease coverage of corruption and other wrongdoings in government by means of the abuse of state powers such as audits, tax fines, administrative penalties, defamation lawsuits, and criminal complaints. Erdoğan's aides are also directing pro-government media to sustain relentless smear campaigns of critics and all opponents with attacks mostly based on fabricated stories and distorted facts. Since an independent media is essential for the fight against corruption, Erdoğan is going after critical media to muzzle them in the face of damaging leaks about his government.

The fourth leg in Erdoğan's battle plan to defeat the corruption investigations is to discredit the role of civil society, important in mobilizing masses as well as generating interest for the national and international media to continue to track and condemn corruption. He chose the most powerful civic movement in Turkey, the Hizmet Movement, inspired by Islamic scholar Fethullah Gülen, despite the fact that Erdoğan had previously been supportive of the movement for years. Denouncing his own public record of praise for Hizmet from just a few years back, he has started to attack it using conspiracy theories of an obscure Matrix-style "ubiquitous parallel state," with no evidence offered to substantiate them. He thinks that if he can create a villain out of a well-respected Muslim cleric, he can easily scare all other civic groups in Turkey off and over to his side.

The fifth element in Erdoğan's sinister campaign to overcome the corruption scandal is to dismantle the independent judiciary's investigative powers and therefore, its ability to tackle corruption in government. If judicial bodies are not free from improper influence, lack effective means of gathering evidence, and cannot preserve the confidentiality of investigations, it becomes almost impossible to investigate those in political leadership. That was why Erdoğan changed the rules overnight to compel the police and the judiciary to notify the government of all ongoing investigations at once. The government decree was later struck down by the Council of State, but the government has not enforced that ruling.

The sixth point in Erdoğan's plan to reduce massive corruption claims carrying lesser charges aims to disprove the economic reasoning behind the fight against the corruption that clearly distorts competition and hinders economic development. Erdoğan often says how much Turkey has developed in the last decade under his rule. To the astonishment of his interlocutors, he even repeated the same fallacy when he was asked about corruption claims by European Parliamentarians in Brussels this week. By citing past economic successes, he purports that Turkey could not have achieved these accomplishments if corruption was rampant in government. That self-defeating logic does not, however, explain how much Turkey could have progressed further if these massive corruption scandals did not waste precious resources or cost the country taxable income on bribe money. It also defies common wisdom, since when the economy grows at an unprecedented pace there is more fertile ground for corruption, especially in a country where a full-fledged democracy with strong checks and balances does not yet exist.

The seventh element in Erdoğan's plan is to undermine the culture of integrity in the state so that corruption will thrive without a strong reaction from the public. With the consolidation of power in his hands, Erdoğan might have deliberately created a culture of corruption where everything was directed and ordered by the prime minister himself, according to the admission made by the resigned environment and urban planning minister on a live TV broadcast. By downplaying the significance of millions of dollars stashed in the home of the general manager of state lender Halkbank and vouching for two main suspects in corruption cases, Erdoğan dealt a blow to the culture of integrity in government. He described the detained Iranian Reza Zarrab, the alleged ringleader in a money laundering and graft scheme, as a man who loves charity work and called Yasin al-Qadi, designated as a terror financier by the US Treasury, a close family friend who loves Turkey. He defended his son's activities that prosecutors claim were unlawful.

The eighth point in this plan is to limit the flow of information to the public, making the government less transparent. As more information is made publicly available, civic groups and the media can more effectively apply pressure on the government to limit its interference in investigations and the judiciary will be more encouraged to take on the political leadership. The so called "name and shame" function of media can only work if they have access to judicial investigations of law enforcement officials and prosecutors as well as during the trial phases of corruption cases. Erdoğan's people seem to have encouraged suspects to obtain gag orders from friendly judges for the ongoing investigations of corruption scandals at the expense of the public's right to know while simultaneously trying to intimidate critical media with a series of lawsuits accusing them of violating secrecy rules. The justice minister's unlawful stalling tactics related to delays in forwarding the criminal complaints on resigned Cabinet ministers to Parliament also aimed to hide damaging revelations from the public.

The last component in this comprehensive plan is that Erdoğan will avoid listing his total income and assets, as well as those of his spouse and children, despite pleas from the opposition parties to lay bare of all his family wealth. His declaration from 2011 was not considered robust and does not reveal possible conflicts of interest in his dealings. There is speculation that Erdoğan hides wealth using "straw men" who are only the owners of businesses and properties on paper. The opposition parties question Erdoğan's official declaration both in terms of quality and comprehensiveness. Erdoğan will never respond to these calls, hoping that the issue will eventually fade from the public discussion.

Well, the critical question is whether Erdoğan's battle plan to beat the corruption scandal will work. He may be convinced that there is actually a way out of this using such a wide-ranging plan to bury the investigations. But I think he is making it worse; as the crisis in Turkey gets deeper and heavier, it is becoming very difficult for the ruling party to sustain its governance of the country. Despite the obstacles he has orchestrated for those pursuing the investigations, Erdoğan has never been able to gain enough traction to shift the debate away from corruption since Dec. 17. He must now be running on fumes.

Money Trail[13]

In a January meeting of European Parliament leaders in Brussels with visiting Turkish Prime Minister Recep Tayyip Erdoğan, the vice chairman of the Liberal Group in the European Parliament, Alexander Graf Lambsdorff, said it would be very surprising for a country like Turkey, coming from a modest economic background, not to have corruption considering its rapid economic growth and that in such cases, instances of corruption are more prevalent rather than less. Lambsdorff's remarks were a direct response to Erdoğan's claims that his country has developed significantly with major investments in infrastructure, urban renewal, and housing projects in the past decade of his rule. He was challenging Erdoğan's main argument that if there was rampant corruption, Turkey could not have developed as it did.

I think the German politician hit the nail on the head when he exposed a self-defeating argument raised by the Turkish prime minister to explain the corruption cases that erupted on Dec. 17, 2013, and were blamed by the government on a global conspiracy and its so-called domestic collaborators. It is true that Turkey, as an emerging economy with an export-oriented industrial base and burgeoning consumer market that is hungry for imports, has generated more opportunities for corrupt politicians and their close business associates to exploit lucrative deals and tap into government contracts and tenders. Perhaps that is what Lambsdorff was implying when he countered Erdoğan's arguments in a closed session of the European Parliament.

However, the massive corruption investigations have revealed something else that is not a typical occurrence in any developing economy.

---

[13] First appeared in *Today's Zaman* daily on Feb. 24, 2014

Judging from the prosecutors' evidence that has been leaked to the press so far, it appears there have been two main sources of cash infused into the Turkish economy illegally and under the radar of financial scrutiny and banking monitoring. One came from Iran, which desperately wanted to circumvent financial, banking, industrial, and energy sanctions. The other source was from the Gulf, mainly from the Saudis, who wanted to divert their investments from Western markets into the growing Turkish economy. While the Gulf patrons have earmarked funds for legitimate investments in Turkey, some of them started funneling cash and arms to the opposition groups in Syria in the meantime. These huge sums of money, totaling billions of dollars, obtained from Iran and the Gulf needed to be whitewashed before being legally presented as investments so that the money could circulate in the Turkish economy without raising many eyebrows. This is where the money laundering scheme came into the picture.

Suspects who stand accused of corruption have used real estate development in prime land, mining, retail business, and other industries to launder the cash. Since this has involved moving big sums of money through couriers and later via financial institutions after being laundered, they needed the cover and help of politicians who would be able to cut the red tape, bypass rigorous screenings, facilitate cross-border transit, and even secure legislative changes in Parliament to create loopholes to their benefit. Both active and retired politicians in this crime network were happy with the fat commissions they charged and lavish presents they received for any help provided for businessmen who had dealt with the dirty scheme. The dragnet generated more than enough cash for the people in government to even create slush funds to finance election campaigns, purchase media groups to establish a friendly press and set up foundations to educate and train foot soldiers for the political Islamist ideology.

In the first instance, a treasure trove of cash was provided by Iran, which had been increasingly feeling the pinch of UN sanctions as well as those imposed by the US and the EU. It was alleged that the Revolutionary Guards contracted Iranian Reza Zarrab, the key suspect in the Dec. 17 corruption probe and a naturalized Turkish citizen, and his cronies back in Iran and the United Arab Emirates to run a variety of front companies in Turkey, ranging from a company trading in precious minerals (read gold) to a private airline, from a maritime transport company to hospitality and tourism, all aimed at skirting the sanctions on the Iranian regime while laundering money from illegal oil proceeds sold on the black market. According to Turkey's main opposition party, the government was involved in irregular money transactions, mostly from Iran, that total 87 billion euros. Prosecutors identified three ministers who took bribes of millions of dollars from Zarrab on different occasions in exchange for political favors. The criminal complaint against these three, who later had to resign, is still pending due to their parliamentary immunity.

The second money supplier was alleged to be the Gulf, primarily Yasin al-Qadi, a Saudi businessman and al-Qaeda financier according to the US Treasury. He was on the UN terror list until he was delisted in the fall of 2013. He is reportedly a secret partner in some of the companies in Turkey and has stakes in some investments managed by his son, Muaz. As part of the investigation into al-Qadi's activities, prosecutors were following his every move while he had been secretly meeting with the top leadership in Turkey including Erdoğan, his son, and his intelligence chief Hakan Fidan. The abundance of cash supplied from the Gulf was injected into major contracts and tenders as Turkish business tycoons took the money to finance projects in real estate, mining, media, travel, hospitality, health care, and other areas.

For example, a report which appeared on the *T24* news website in January claimed that Forestry and Water Affairs Minister Veysel Eroğlu helped some businessmen obtain a permit for a mining facility in an Istanbul forest. According to the voice recording obtained by a court-authorized wiretap, a businessman, identified as Adem Peker, was able to secure the license after contacting businessmen Cengiz Aktürk and Osama Qutb, who are both suspects in the corruption probe and close associates of al-Qadi and Prime Minister Erdoğan. Erdoğan reportedly directed Investment Support and Promotion Agency of Turkey (ISPAT) President İlker Aycı to facilitate licensing. In exchange, Peker promised to give the businessmen 50 percent of the mining facility's shares.

In a wiretapped conversation, Aktürk and Qutb are heard discussing plans for money laundering by means of Aktürk's companies. Aktürk, who owns cosmetics companies, tells Qutb that it was not possible to "launder so much money with perfume" and that they had to find another method. Hence mining was just a front to launder money for these suspects.

There are other trails that prosecutors had identified in a months-long investigation into business moguls' dealings with Iranian and Saudi businessmen in money-laundering schemes. In exchange for favors, politicians were allegedly provided with commissions on the money laundered. In further phone conversations, this time between Qutb and several other people—including the prime minister's son, Bilal Erdoğan, and the prime minister's executive assistant, Hasan Doğan, as well as Energy Minister Taner Yıldız—Qutb informs them about the individuals who might attend a meeting planned for Nov. 9, 2013. No details were available about the content of the meeting, but it appears to have been related to energy.

In a nutshell, prosecutors were able to establish a money trail that was detected in bank wires and the trade of precious metals such as gold as well as cash in foreign exchange (using physical and wiretap surveillance) and that implicates senior people in the government. Now Erdoğan's government is trying to stifle the independent judiciary to hush up these allegations. The prime minister has created a long list of enemies, from the media to the Hizmet Movement inspired by Islamic scholar Fethullah Gülen, from business groups to foreign powers such as the US, the EU, and Israel, in order to shift the blame. Erdoğan forgets, however, that not only did prosecutors in Turkey map out this money trail, but also other countries that are interested in this money are aware of these long-running schemes that may put Turkey in trouble with its partners and allies.

The fact that the government practically stalled the investigation with a major reshuffle of the judiciary, police, watchdog agencies that track money, and finance and banking activities, while also pushing emergency laws through Parliament to prevent further investigations and leaks, casts a shadow on how far the Erdoğan government went in these dirty deals. It gives rise to rumors that circulate very fast in Ankara, which is already known as a very gossipy town. An opposition party leader, Masum Türker, even claimed that trucks that were stopped in the border province of Adana in January were not carrying arms and munitions, but rather shrink-wrapped bundles of cash and that is why the government was panicked. Another rumor is that Erdoğan allegedly took some of the cash to his plane when he recently embarked on foreign trips to unload the money in foreign banks.

It is difficult to substantiate these rumors, and we may never know what truly happened, for when legal investigations are stopped, evidence somehow disappears. One thing we can conclude, however, is that Erdoğan is in more trouble than it seems. Maybe he thought he had become invincible with the popular mandate his party received in the past three elections, bolstering feelings of impunity, arrogance, and greed. With so much cash floating around, it is bound to trigger red flags. Well, it did when the massive corruption scandal broke on Dec. 17. Perhaps that is why Erdoğan has been so angry since then. He takes out his fury on practically everybody when he constantly lashes out at the opposition, media, civic organizations, and business groups. He even threatened to expel the US ambassador in Ankara in a public speech addressed to thousands of his supporters.

Iran's Role in Corruption Case[14]

Lurking in the shadow of the massive corruption and money-laundering web that has apparently entangled senior Turkish government officials, including Cabinet ministers, Iran's pervasive influence has created a perfect storm in Turkey, its main regional rival. With billions of dollars poured into Turkey by Iran through proxies of Revolutionary Guards in an effort to circumvent sanctions, the mullah regime has triggered a domestic political crisis in Turkey while putting an important NATO member into trouble with allies and partners over shady deals Turkish authorities have brokered with Iranian counterparts.

---

[14]   First appeared in *Today's Zaman* daily on Feb. 14, 2014

The key suspect in a money-laundering and gold-smuggling ring established to dodge sanctions against Iran is naturalized Iranian national, Reza Zarrab, who was detained by the court. This 29-year-old man made a splash in Turkey when he married a Turkish celebrity and quickly built a relationship with political elites in Turkey, growing close with Turkish ministers, including Prime Minister Recep Tayyip Erdoğan and his wife. According to leaked evidence, he has bribed the ministers of economy, interior, and EU affairs and their relatives with a total of TL 137 million ($66 million) to allow his business to run unimpeded in Turkey. He has loaned his private jet to other ministers who took personal trips abroad.

How could a young man gain access to key decision makers in Turkey and what was the Turkish intelligence doing all this time as he was committing crimes involving political figures? It seems the National Intelligence Organization (MİT) warned the prime minister about his illegal and illicit activities eight months before the corruption investigation was made public, saying that if they were exposed, it would embarrass the government and would pose a grave national security risk. Erdoğan inadvertently acknowledged the existence of this report, but instead criticized those who leaked the secret document to the press.

On top of that, MİT also identified that money was wired from companies connected to Zarrab in 2011 to finance Iran's botched assassination plot to kill the Saudi ambassador in Washington. All this information indicates that the government has been very much aware of his activities all this time, yet it turned a blind eye to his criminal enterprises—perhaps even extending protection and cover. In fact, when he was asked about Zarrab, Erdoğan said he knew the guy was involved in charitable work in Turkey. The main opposition leader, Kemal Kılıçdaroğlu, said last week that the government is frantically trying to save Zarrab and would likely let him go lest he spill the dirt on government officials.

According to Turkish media reports, Zarrab appears to have been connected to Iranian billionaire Babak Zanjani, who was blacklisted in 2012 by the European Union and United States for playing a key role in helping the Iranian central bank evade financial sanctions over its controversial nuclear program. He had moved Iranian oil illegally in the black market and made billions in the process with the blessing of Iranian authorities. In return, he laundered money with some 65 companies he set up to operate in Iran, Turkey, the United Arab Emirates, Malaysia, and Tajikistan. When prosecutors ordered the arrest of Zarrab on Dec. 17, 2013, in Turkey, they were also looking to nab Zanjani, who was abroad at the time of sweeping arrests and decided to not return to Turkey.

In an interview with the Iranian Student News Agency (ISNA), Zanjani admitted that he used his companies in Dubai, Turkey, and Malaysia to sell millions of barrels of oil, making $17.5 billion, which he said he channeled to Iran's Petroleum Ministry, Revolutionary Guards, and central bank, all of which were badly in need of foreign exchange. He said this money was in the accounts of the First Islamic Bank and that he transferred it to domestic accounts via more than 9,000 transactions. The fact that he was involved in strategic industries like transportation (his name is mentioned in the sale of Onur Airlines in Turkey), finance, banking, and energy indicates that he had been working for his masters in Iran to dodge sanctions.

The valuable services of both Zarrab and Zanjani are no longer needed now that they have been exposed and have become liabilities for the Iranian regime. As Iran has been trying its best with a newly launched charm offensive due to a change of political leadership that paved the way for clinching an interim nuclear deal with major powers, it needs to dump disposable assets to appear as if it had nothing to do with the Revolutionary Guards' contractors. That is why the Iranian authorities moved swiftly on Zanjani, who fled Turkey, where he had been living most of the time. After Iranian President Hassan Rouhani ordered an immediate investigation by government agencies to identify and punish sanctions profiteers, Zanjani was sent to jail to prevent fallout from the crises in Turkey; he was hushed up.

Considering that Zanjani, the son of a railway worker, was a driver for the head of the central bank before moving to Turkey where he amassed a huge fortune, he could not move around easily in the country without Turkish authorities noticing his unusual itinerary. That raises suspicions that he must have had influential friends in the government watching his back, helping him to cut through the red tape. Now that all hell has broken loose, Turkey is left to deal with quite an embarrassing scandal at home while its credibility as a reliable partner and ally has started to be questioned. This is a huge disservice to this country that does not deserve what it has got, thanks but no thanks to the greedy and ideologically biased political leadership in Turkey.

The scope of the money laundering and corruption network apparently involves former members of the Turkish Parliament and bureaucrats as well. According to a report from the liberal daily *Taraf,* dated Jan. 28 and based on prosecutors' findings, not only ministers and security officials have been used to transfer money, but former deputies and bureaucrats who hold diplomatic passports were also employed as couriers to transfer $20 billion from sanctions-hit Iran into Turkey.

Tehran has best made use of pro-Iranian sympathy in some of the ruling Justice and Development Party (AKP) cadres, cashing in on a return derived from decades-long investments in political Islamists. The bias towards Iran by these circles has blinded them to the extent that sinister Iranian overtures were seen in the context of good neighborly relations when in fact they were simply conduits for Iranian expansionism and penetration into critical areas of the Turkish government and social structures.

No government in Turkey has signed so many agreements with Iran in such a short period of time than the Erdoğan government, paving the way for clandestine Iranian activities in Turkey to gain speed and strength. During his last visit to Iran in late January, Erdoğan reportedly called Iran his second home; he signed a series of bilateral agreements, including ones on a preferential trade deal and a high-level cooperation council. In return, Turkey has not benefited much from these deals— either in trade and investment, or in political capital, despite the access to the political leadership in Iran. The mullah regime got what it wanted from Turkey while undercutting Ankara's influence in Iraq, Syria, Afghanistan, and other places.

Now the fair question is why has the Erdoğan government been pursuing an unreciprocated love affair with Iran when Turkey is not benefiting greatly from the closer and deeper engagement—and in fact is being exposed to many threats with the mullah regime's clandestine activities? There are serious question marks in Ankara as some have speculated there might even be secret deals between the two governments that have not been made public.

The main opposition Republican People's Party (CHP) deputy chairman, Sezgin Tanrıkulu, filed a motion in Parliament on Jan. 30, asking Erdoğan whether his government signed any secret protocol, agreement, or memorandum of understanding with Iran. He also asked whether Erdoğan was pledged financial assistance by Iran and if he met with any third country representatives while in Iran. Tanrıkulu also queried whether the full transcript of the conversations Eroğan had with Iranian officials was recorded by Turkish diplomats and later filed in the state archives.

For example, the full details of an agreement to construct a pipeline to export Iranian natural gas across Turkey and Europe to Germany has not yet been disclosed. We only know that the Turkish Petroleum Corporation (TPAO), in 2010, awarded the license to Turang Transit, a subsidiary of Turkey's Som Petrol, to build an $11.5 billion pipeline and operate it for 30 years. There are too many questions around the deal, including who is providing the financing for this small and unknown company, where the gas will come from (Iran or Turkmenistan), who the buyers will be, and whether countries along the pipeline route will agree to give a right to transit under the existing sanctions.

If Iran plans to resell Turkmen gas to Turkey, this would make Ankara more dependent on Iran for its natural gas needs. In an interview with *Today's Zaman* in June of last year, Iranian Ambassador to Turkey, Alireza Bikdeli, opposed the idea of delivering Turkmen gas to Turkey through the Caspian Sea, adding that if Turkey wants to do serious business, it should do it with Iran. "There are some problems in the Caspian Sea region, and these problems prevent the occurrence of business there. Turkey is also discussing the issue with us," Bikdeli said. Iran has been advocating this idea for some time already. The Iranian Ministry of Oil and the Turkish Energy and Natural Resources Ministry signed an Agreement Protocol on Nov. 17, 2008, for transit passage of natural gas sourced in Iran through Turkey.

Not so transparent agreements with Iran like this, and possibly others, may create further troubles for Turkey down the road. Perhaps that was the message given by US Department of the Treasury Under-secretary for Terrorism and Financial Intelligence David Cohen, who came to Ankara only one day before Prime Minister Erdoğan's departure for Tehran. He warned that there are still significant sanctions in place against Iran and that business deals with Iran should be postponed. "Iran is not open for business. Sanctions [against Iran] remain in place and are still quite significant, and businesses that are interested in engaging with Iran really should hold off," said Cohen. That message, directed not only to Turkey but also other countries that may want follow the Turkish lead, should not be taken lightly.

Parallel State Lie Fails to Convince[15]

Nobody believes that the mass culling and reassignment of up to 10,000 public officials (most from the police department and the judiciary, and many of whom are mid-level and senior personnel) so far by embattled Prime Minister Recep Tayyip Erdoğan has anything to do with what the government purports is a fight against a "parallel structure," a veiled reference to members of the Hizmet Movement inspired by Islamic scholar Fethullah Gülen. The personnel movements are simply an effort by Erdoğan to contain fallout from the massive corruption investigation that was exposed on Dec. 17, 2013, and to prevent new allegations from emerging.

I think that was the prevailing perception of the members of the Committee on Foreign Affairs (AFET) in the European Parliament (EP) who debated a resolution on the annual progress report on Turkey earlier this week. When rapporteur Ria Oomen-Ruijten, the Dutch politician who wrote the report, said the counterparty for the EP is the Erdoğan government as the political authority in Turkey and not a faith-inspired civic movement such as Hizmet, it was clear that the government's ridic-

[15] First appeared in *Today's Zaman* daily on Mar. 07, 2014

ulous defense of creating a villain out of Hizmet amid corruption woes had totally collapsed.

Even an amendment that called on the Hizmet Movement for more transparency, a motion that was publicly supported by Hizmet, was dropped by the members of AFET, perhaps to send a crystal clear message to Mr. Erdoğan that European politicians are not buying into a distraction deliberately created by the ruling Justice and Development Party (AKP) to fend off embarrassment caused by the corruption scandal. The arguments raised in a private statement by Turkey's EU Minister, Mevlüt Çavuşoğlu, explaining his objections to rapporteur Oomen-Ruijten's conclusions are insulting to the intelligence of European politicians.

Çavuşoğlu said: "The recent investigations have demonstrated that there is an organization within the state, in fact, a 'parallel structure.' The adherents of this organization hold positions in different public institutions, including the judiciary and the police. A plot is set against the government by this organization at a time when Turkey is entering into an election period. ...The existence of a parallel structure as such is the greatest threat to the rule of law and democracy. Turkey has been taking some legislative measures with a view to removing this threat that alleviates trust towards judiciary and law enforcement bodies, without prejudice to the principle of the rule of law."

The Europeans, like most Turks, also understood that Erdoğan kept publicizing the unprecedented reshuffling of public officials as a fight against a parallel structure in order to mask his ongoing loyalist cadre-building in the executive and judicial branches. There has been overwhelming evidence leaked to the media in the last couple of months that reveal the systematic seeding of Erdoğan's political Islamists into government agencies and the judiciary. Not just people who sympathize with Gülen, but liberals, Alevis, Kurds, social democrats, and people who are affiliated with the opposition parties have also been profiled and targeted by the national intelligence agency. Based on this unconstitutional profiling and illegal screening, those already working in the public sector were either demoted or reassigned to low-profile positions and new applicants were barred from entering public service even at entry-level jobs.

Erdoğan's continuing paranoia about Hizmet, the media, business advocacy groups, and opposition parties (not to mention foreign powers) that, in his view, have all have joined forces to take him out of the picture, has somewhat shifted the center of the election campaign away from substantive issues. Yet he has failed to gain traction in the fight against his imaginary enemies in the face of the massive amount of incriminating evidence that has been coming out, bit by bit, every day implicating him and his family members. It is clear that Erdoğan has been micromanaging the country in practically every field. In fact, it appears that Erdoğan himself has created a "parallel structure" with his loyalists implanted not only in key positions in state institutions, but also in major corporations in the private sector.

For example, a leaked audio recording indicates that Erdoğan ordered Justice Minister Bekir Bozdağ to help reshuffle the prosecutors in the Istanbul courthouse who were assigned to investigate the corruption claims after the scandal erupted. Another recording reveals that Erdoğan tried to secure a controlling influence within the popular Fenerbahçe sports club. Erdoğan's blatant interference in the media was also exposed when he allegedly ordered media owners to fire critical editors and reporters. In yet another recording, he ordered his former Justice Minister Sadullah Ergin to get a conviction on tax evasion charges for media mogul Aydın Doğan, who had been cleared of similar charges in the lower courts. When his son's phone was wiretapped by prosecutors in the course of the corruption probe, Erdoğan was also caught directing his son to get rid of some $1 billion stashed in his residences in Istanbul on Dec.17, the day of initial police raids.

Following this leak, rushed legislation has granted the government broad powers over the judiciary by restructuring of the Supreme Board of Judges and Prosecutors (HSYK), the top legal body responsible for the regulation of judicial affairs, including the appointment and inspection of judges and prosecutors. This was part of Erdoğan's strategy to hush-up the corruption investigations.

The Internet censorship bill that has caused outrage both in Turkey and abroad was also part of this same strategy to contain the fallout from the graft scandal. Apparently, even that was not enough. On Thursday night during a live TV interview, Erdoğan said he could even ban social media such as Facebook and sites like YouTube where critical messages about the government and damning leaks can be posted.

Therefore, the picture of Turkey is rather clear for many abroad, including European parliamentarians, to whom both the EU and Justice Ministers gave rather fuzzy and muddied assessments filled with slander and lies based on parallel structures during their meetings in in Brussels. Despite Erdoğan and his loyalists' relentless demonizing rhetoric blaming Hizmet and others for all the wrongdoings in Turkey, Rapporteur Oomen-Ruijten's EP report gave a rather different and very comprehensive analysis of what is actually going on in Turkey. The EP is troubled by the allegations of major corruption and concerned about the removal of the prosecutors and police officers in charge of the original investigations, saying in the report, "This goes against the fundamental principle of an independent judiciary and deeply affects the prospects of credible investigations." The report also openly called on Erdoğan "to show full commitment to the democratic principles and refrain from any further interference in the investigation and prosecution of corruption."

On the day the report on Turkey was debated by the committee, the Turkish justice minister made a trip to Brussels to convince EU officials that what Erdoğan is doing is best for the country; he also met with a number of EU officials, including Oomen-Ruijten. During a TV interview after he returned to Ankara, Bozdağ was asked about the perception of Turkey in Brussels. He sounded frustrated and disappointed with how he was received by his interlocutors in the EU and he accused them of a lack of comprehensive knowledge about the recent legislation. He even accused them of being influenced by what he called a misinformation campaign about Turkey. It is obvious that the EU is not satisfied with the explanations provided by Turkish government officials and dismissed them as not credible.

That is why the EP report expressed deep concern regarding the HSYK law that gives the minister of justice a central role in governing the election, composition, and functioning of the judicial council. The report specifically asked Turkey to consult closely with the European Commission and the Venice Commission and called for the revision of the HSYK law. Oomen-Ruijten's report also criticized the Erdoğan government for the new Internet law, which it said "introduces excessive controls and monitoring on internet access and has the potential to significantly impact free expression, investigative journalism, democratic scrutiny, and access to politically diverse information over the internet." The government campaign to muzzle critical media through pressure on media owners, the dismissal of journalists, self-censorship, undue legal restrictions, and accreditation barriers were also criticized in the EP report.

I believe the most important conclusion in the report, and one that is very relevant to today's debate in Turkey, is the overriding theme of "inclusiveness and dialogue" that Ms. Oomen-Ruijten was able to successfully inject into the heart of the comprehensive report. The alienation and marginalization of so many diverse groups in Turkey for so many years and the lack of dialogue the Erdoğan government has with opposition parties, media, business advocacy groups, and civil society organizations including Hizmet, have all continued to generate a host of problems that weaken fundamental rights, democracy, and the rule of law in an EU-candidate country. The latest corruption scandal and the Gezi Park events prior to that simply made that bitter truth clearer. Oomen-Ruijten deserves huge credit for spelling out that key problem in Turkey in unequivocal terms.

Her report said that the European Parliament "underlines the importance and urgent need of further reforms for greater accountability and transparency in the Administration and the promotion of dialogue across the political spectrum and in society more broadly, in particular through proper involvement and a process of empowerment of civil society." Then she talked about the importance of the rule of law, full respect for fundamental rights, the principle of the separation of powers, and the importance of an impartial and independent judiciary for a truly democratic state.

Did the government get the message? I don't think so. The Erdoğan government is even keen to export the same problems to Europe, where some five million members of the Turkish diaspora live. When the justice minister was in Brussels on Monday, he only talked to the government mouthpiece *Anatolian* news agency, declining to speak with the bureau chiefs of other private media based in Brussels. When he met with civil society groups, Bozdağ only invited those who are close to the government, rejecting meetings with representatives of many other groups, including the largest and oldest community groups in Belgium.

Chapter 3

Judiciary Woes

Interference into the Judiciary[16]

Perhaps Turkey's embattled Prime Minister Recep Tayyip Erdoğan has already lost the battle against the judiciary over massive corruption investigations involving senior members of his ruling Justice and Development Party (AKP), businessmen close to him, and even his relatives. He just does not know it yet, as it will probably take some time for the bitter facts to sink in.

The nation's prosecutors are not stupid enough to go after the country's most powerful people without having solid evidence that can hold up to scrutiny in a court of law. It seems that even the few pieces of evidence that have leaked to the press amid the government's relentless efforts to suppress them have easily convinced the Turkish public of the massive wrongdoings in the upper echelons of the government. In people's minds, the Erdoğan government is already guilty and there is no appeal, which will in turn lead to the collapse of his "comeback kid" strategy and his efforts to survive through elections.

The prosecutors are also not incompetent people who disregard judicial procedures to the extent that their case might be thrown out of court. All the talking points whispered by Erdoğan's men into the public's ears have failed. For example, the government argued that he should have been informed of the investigation in advance. It turns out the laws prohibit prosecutors from notifying the government, which is in line with the rule of separation of powers between the two branches. Erdoğan

---

16   First appeared in *Today's Zaman* daily on Dec. 27, 2013

rushed overnight to change the rules of engagement through an executive order, which triggered a series of legal challenges on the grounds of legality and constitutionality.

The deadliest blow to the government came from Turkey's top judicial body, the Supreme Board of Judges and Prosecutors (HSYK), which came out very strongly against the government interference with an ultimatum-like statement condemning this executive order and the pressures imposed on the judiciary. The fact that the judicial council stood behind prosecutor Muammer Akkaş, who was removed from an investigation involving a corruption scheme worth $100 billion, is testament to the fact that there is no violation of rules and procedures, unlike chief prosecutor Turan Çolakkadı, whom the opposition accuses of being a spokesperson for the government. I suppose the Council of Europe's (CoE) Venice Commission, which endorsed changes to the HSYK in 2010 and has a big stake in Turkey's judicial woes, must be very happy to see that the judicial council is actually taking a very principled stand against the government's interference in the judiciary.

For the first time, we are seeing the executive branch in this country blatantly disregarding the letter and spirit of the law and meddling in judicial investigations openly and flagrantly. Erdoğan's mishandling of the corruption cases by unnecessarily dragging his feet for a week about the resignations of four ministers who were implicated in the graft has turned what was a judicial case into a government crisis. Now Erdoğan, by inventing imaginary enemies at home and abroad to shift the blame and justify his meddlesome tactics in the judiciary, has escalated the government crisis into a state crisis where the executive is trying to usurp the powers of the judiciary as well.

On the sidelines, President Abdullah Gül, acting as if he is the head of state of Mars, has simply been watching to see how this crisis will unfold before making any decisive moves. He even waited for a week after Dec. 17, when the country's biggest corruption probe was made public, to comment on the investigation. Even then, he did not say much, seeking refuge in the principles of the rule of the law, the separation of powers, and democratic ideals. Gül, who has always avoided taking risks in his long political career, is holding his fingers up in the air to try to feel where the wind is blowing before taking a clear stand on Turkey's major state crisis. In the meantime, however, he is not stopping Erdoğan from dismissing senior officials to replace with loyalists by putting his signature of approval on decrees. If he resisted, for example, appointing a former spy as the head of the Telecommunications Directorate (TİB), which is Turkey's listening post charged with complying with court orders on wiretapping suspects' phones, Erdoğan would have not succeeded in turning the state into a major intelligence machine.

It is simply unacceptable for Gül not to come out and put a stop to the government interference in the judiciary when even Turkey's allies and friends, worried over the government's attempts to cover up corruption, have been suggesting that Turkey not derail the investigations and act in line with legal and democratic principles. Well, I guess these are testing times for everyone. İdris Naim Şahin, who has been with Erdoğan for almost 30 years and served as secretary-general of the AKP and interior minister for the government, taught everyone a lesson by resigning from the party and issuing a manifesto-like statement accusing Erdoğan of running the country with a small gang of people whose intentions are questionable. He is now being targeted with character assassination by the same gang he was blaming for steering the country in the wrong direction.

The stakes in Turkey are quite high. Three fundamental principles are at great risk right now with the way Erdoğan is handing government affairs: democracy, fundamental rights, and the rule of law. All are key determinants of whether Turkey has a role to play in global affairs as a responsible actor. For one, Erdoğan sees democracy as merely a short trip to the ballot box where people cast their votes every four years. He sees the ballot box as the ultimate arbitrator in deciding everything, even settling the claims in the massive corruption investigations, which have to be sorted out in a court of law. He has repeatedly made all these arguments publicly in rallies and even dared business communities, the media, and civic groups critical of his government on some issues to challenge him in the elections by forming political parties.

In terms of fundamental rights, Erdoğan does not tolerate any dissent or critical media at all. He publicly bashes reporters, labeling them traitors or foreign agents just because these members of the press corps are exercising their right to freedom of expression. When business advocacy groups expressed their concerns over problems that might affect their investments or trade, he started name-calling, labeling them domestic collaborators for international conspiracy groups that want to harm Turkish national interests. Civic groups like Hizmet are unable to avoid his wrath as well and are easily accused of running "parallel structures" or "gangs" within the state apparatus with no shred of evidence to back these claims.

The last, but not least, blow to the rule of the law in this country came under Erdoğan's watch. An independent and impartial judiciary is critical in Turkey to deliver justice and ensure transparency and accountability in governance. Unfortunately, Erdoğan is trying to turn the judiciary into a submissive state agency that does his bidding, just like he has done with Parliament with his domination of the AKP. For all intents and purposes, he is seeking an ultimate consolidation of power and does not care much about separation of power. The judicial council's outcry on Thursday over the government's interference is testament to that bitter fact. In a veiled criticism of the government, even the military came out strongly on Friday, saying it respects the rule of law in Turkey and abides by the rules even when military personnel are involved in judicial investigations.

If Erdoğan has his way, Turkey, to be cast in his own image, will no longer be interested in membership in the European Union, and it will dump the CoE, of which it was one of the founding members. It will likely withdraw its signature from the European Convention on Human Rights (ECHR) and will no longer accept judgments by the European Court of Human Rights (ECtHR), which are currently binding on Turkey. Turkey's transatlantic strategic partnership is also at risk, with Erdoğan making new overtures to solidify ties with newfound partners in the East and alienating decades-long alliance members for no justifiable reason whatsoever.

The question boils down to whether Erdoğan can actually turn the clock back on Turkey's democratic journey. Hardly, given the transformation that has taken place in Turkish society over the past several decades. He may perhaps postpone the day of reckoning by exerting pressure on the judiciary and skewing the checks and balances in the state system in his favor, but he cannot avoid being eventually dragged under public scrutiny to give his account on the massive corruption in the government. Ultimately, the buck stops with him. His government will eventually be caught with what seems to be serious claims based on overwhelming evidence, and Erdoğan will have to respond to the charges.

I think Erdoğan did a great disservice to his fellow comrades in the ruling AKP by resisting and trying to thwart the judicial probe, which was perhaps the only avenue to put this scandal behind him. He blocked the only way to clear himself and the party in the eyes of the people. As details of these massive corruption scandals will reverberate across coffeehouses, town hall meetings and family gatherings in each and every corner of Turkey, all AKP politicians conducting campaign tours for the elections will be looked at suspiciously or even as potential culprits involved in corruption. The AKP cannot simply carry that burden as we have already seen a flurry of defections and resignations from the party in protest of Erdoğan's mismanagement of the corruption probe.

Erdoğan has accused pretty much everyone in this country of treachery, from the media and businesses to intellectuals and civic groups. But in fact, it seems that it was he who betrayed his friends, party, government, and country.

Abusing the Criminal Justice System[17]

If beleaguered Prime Minister Recep Tayyip Erdoğan gets his way and convinces his old pal President Abdullah Gül to sign recent bills into law, written ostensibly in the name of democratic reforms and judicial overhaul, then Turks will experience one of the most blatant abuses of the criminal justice system by political authorities in Turkey's history.

The opposition's challenge to Erdoğan's tightening grip on the judiciary in the Constitutional Court can limit the damage to a certain degree, but will not be able to completely thwart the encroachment of the executive branch on the judiciary. In other words, Erdoğan will be able to

---

[17] First appeared in *Today's Zaman* daily on Feb. 17, 2014

consolidate absolute power in his hands when he effectively ends the independence of the judicial branch in a grand scheme of reordering the balance of power among state institutions.

The most important indicator for the presence of politically motivated abuse of the criminal justice system is discrimination, which is clearly visible in the latest corruption investigation. Erdoğan's son, businessmen close to the Prime Minister and even Cabinet ministers have been afforded special protection by the government, while legal proceedings against opposition figures were put on a fast-track.

For example, the summary of proceedings' documents filed against four ministers who were forced to resign due to corruption allegations were stalled by the justice minister for one-and-a-half months before he then returned them to the prosecutor's office in violation of the established practice and legal rules that require the justice minister to simply forward them to Parliament immediately for possible trial proceedings in a high court.

In contrast, the summary of proceedings filed against main opposition Republican People's Party (CHP) leader Kemal Kılıçdaroğlu and junior opposition Nationalist Movement Party (MHP) leader Devlet Bahçeli for public remarks, a minor offense, were sent to Parliament by the justice minister in a very short period of time. The fact that most of the detainees in the corruption investigation were released after an abrupt change of the lead prosecutor in the case is also evidence that the government has manipulated the procedure itself, allowing suspects to avoid pre-trial detention and likely soon defeat the charges.

It is clear that the Erdoğan government has been abusing the criminal justice system in a prejudiced way. With new legislative changes that subordinated the judiciary to the rule of the executive, Erdoğan will not hesitate to target his political and non-political opponents in an even more crude and vicious way than ever before.

The harsh public statements made by Erdoğan and his ministers alleging that people and groups critical of the ruling Justice and Development Party (AKP) government have committed a crime is another indicator that Turkey is moving quickly to a stage where politically motivated criminal justice works overwhelmingly in the favor of the government. It has almost become a daily routine on the campaign trail for Erdoğan to accuse the media, business groups, civic organizations, and opposition parties of "treachery" and "betrayal of the nation" without offering a single shred of evidence.

With relentless, systematic public smears, Erdoğan tries to intimidate any opposition that might dare stand in his way. He will likely try to engineer an even larger politically motivated lawsuit against journalists, civil society organizations, and business groups using the government's undue influence on the criminal justice system.

He constantly attacks the Hizmet Movement inspired by Islamic scholar Fethullah Gülen and calls it a "parallel state," an invented term to divert public attention from the government corruption scandal. His constant diatribes denouncing business groups like the Turkish Confederation of Businessmen and Industrialists (TUSKON), the country's largest business advocacy group, and the Turkish Industrialists and Businessmen's Association (TÜSİAD), the business group representing the nation's wealthiest and most powerful, for conspiring with the "interest lobby"—another term made up by Erdoğan—is another reflection of this dangerous trend. The national media, including the largest dailies *Zaman* and *Hürriyet*, feel the wrath of Erdoğan practically every day. The international media get their share of being the subject of tirades from the prime minister, as well. These public remarks raise the specter of a dangerous environment where politically motivated criminal justice can easily use guilt by association to thwart businesses, media, political parties, and civic groups.

The third indicator of the scary prospect of Turkey being dragged into a politicized judiciary are the vague charges floated by Erdoğan and his people in government. In authoritarian regimes, the easiest way to attack opponents is to cast doubt on their patriotism and raise questions of espionage and violations of state secrecy. It sounds absurd and totally ridiculous, but if you send a message written in English on Twitter or Facebook, you can be accused of espionage by senior people in this government. If you participated in the Gezi Park protests in May and June of last year out of concern for the environment, you could be accused of being a member of an organized criminal gang working in tandem with global conspiracy groups. Unclear legal charges may complicate the defendant's case in a court of law, and if and when the original charges prove to be too weak to sustain the court challenge, the government can always blindside opponents with completely unrelated investigations like tax audits.

The most troublesome sign that Turkey is moving toward a politically motivated criminal justice system is the recent judicial bills—some of which have already been approved in Parliament—that will deal one blow after another to the independent and impartial judiciary. The prosecutors and judges in Turkey were already open to some degree of political influence before these changes were introduced. The government-orchestrated reshuffle of the judicial council paved the way for the reassignment of hundreds of judges and prosecutors, most of whom were looking into critical cases such as corruption, money laundering, and the al-Qaeda terrorist network. If the controversial bill on the Supreme Board of Judges and Prosecutors (HSYK), Turkey's judicial council, is approved by the president, it will be almost impossible for judges and prosecutors to ward off political interference in investigations and trials.

In defending the HSYK bill, Erdoğan and his ministers, including Justice Minister Bekir Bozdağ and Foreign Minister Ahmet Davutoğlu, repeatedly point out that Germany does not even have a judicial council for appointments, promotions, and disciplinary measures for members of the judiciary. This logic has a couple of fallacies. First, Germany has been criticized heavily for not having an independent judicial council as exists in most European states, not only by European organizations such as the EU and the Council of Europe, but also the Deutscher Richterbund, the German Association of Judges, the most representative professional organization of judges and prosecutors in Germany. Secondly, the German judicial system is a federal one, in contrast to Turkey's highly centralized system. While the federal government is in charge of federal courts, 14 German states (*länders*) have their own courts and rules for the promotion and appointment of judges. Some German states have their own judicial council and others are planning to introduce one. Since political authorities at the state level may represent different political parties from those at the federal level, it is difficult to subordinate the judiciary to one specific political group.

The fact that the German justice minister has the power to give specific instructions concerning individual cases, although rarely used in practice, is greatly criticized in Germany today. The Deutscher Richterbund believes that this mandate gives a public perception that politicians manipulate the judicial process for their own purposes and that it undermines public trust in the objectivity and independence of the criminal justice system. Hence, Germany will likely reform its judiciary as the UK did in 2006 by creating the Judicial Appointments Commission (JAC) to strengthen the principle of independence of the judiciary from political influence. Therefore, presenting Germany as an example for Turkey is not the best way to defend the Turkish government's attempts to rein in the judiciary.

If Turkey has to look for guidance, it should seek the counsel of the Venice Commission, the top authority in Europe on judicial and constitutional reforms. Erdoğan rushed to this body when his party faced a closure threat in the Constitutional Court in 2008. Faced with fierce opposition from the military and others, he again enlisted the Venice Commission's help for the 2010 referendum on judicial reforms. Now he does not even utter the words Venice Commission and, in fact, he has criticized the Venice Commission's comments on the failed constitutional drafting process and the HSYK changes. The commission made it very clear that new democracies such as in Central and Eastern European states should have an independent judicial council to guarantee the independence of the judiciary as well as recommending that old democracies also establish independent judicial councils. "In all cases the council should have a pluralistic composition with a substantial part, if not the majority, of members being judges elected by their peers," the commission underlined. In Turkey, the Venice Commission welcomed the new constitutional amendment related to the HSYK in 2010 and urged some changes to the HSYK bill in 2011 to further improve the council. Since the current corruption scandal, the Erdoğan government has rolled back these gains, neutered the council, and effectively put it under the justice minister's control.

Turkey will pay a price for a politically motivated criminal justice system in several ways. For one, this will open the floodgates to serious flaws in investigations and court proceedings. Second, it will increase the political risk premiums for Turkey, making foreign investors jittery when it comes to committing millions, if not billions, of dollars to the country. Third, the democracy indices monitored by intergovernmental and nongovernmental organizations on issues ranging from transparency to corruption and from the investment climate to accountability will get worse. Fourth, it will be difficult for Turkey to successfully extradite suspects from abroad because trust in the delivery of fair justice in Turkey will be tainted. The European Convention on Extradition clearly indicates that extradition can be refused when prosecution is politically motivated.

The only courts that can withstand the crude treatment of Erdoğan will be the Constitutional Court in Turkey and the European Court of Human Rights (ECtHR) in Strasbourg, two courts over which Erdoğan does not have political leverage. It would not be surprising, however, to even see the Erdoğan government ignore injunctions from the top Turkish court and the Strasbourg-based rights court.

Hate Crimes Get Worse[18]

Despite the fact that Turkey has recently adopted legislation against hate crimes, Turkey's divisive Prime Minister Recep Tayyip Erdoğan has not stopped his attacks with verbal expressions of intolerance and hatred directed at the judiciary, opposition parties, the media, business groups, and members of the Hizmet Movement. In fact, his hateful speech has increased in gravity, indicating that he is not interested in effective implementation of the law at all.

The prime minister's hateful rhetoric and his government's discriminatory policies using the vast profiling of Hizmet members, Alevis, Kurds, and supporters of opposition parties have led to many groups being victimized and created divisions in Turkish society. It has also dealt a big blow to cohesion in the Turkish social fabric, violated fundamental

---

[18]   First appeared in *Today's Zaman* daily on Apr. 21, 2014

human rights and liberties, and threatened the rule of law, ultimately endangering Turkish democracy.

It appears that Erdoğan's government will easily disregard its own revisions to the penal code that defined hate crimes in Turkish law for the first time and provides for additional penalties for offenders. The amendment was made to Article 122 of the Turkish Penal Code (TCK) (also known as Law No. 5237, adopted in 2004). The bill was approved in Parliament on Feb. 2 as part of the democratization package announced by the government last September and signed into law by President Abdullah Gül on March 12. Instead of toning down his hateful discourse, Erdoğan has, in fact, ratcheted up his belligerent tone targeting and stigmatizing his opponents. For example, at election rallies, he attacked members of Hizmet by calling them deplorable names such as "assassins," "traitors," "viruses," "evil," and "mafia." Others, too, received their fair share of bashing from Erdoğan, including Gezi Park protesters and critical media.

This clearly shows that Erdoğan is not interested in the rule of law or implementation of his own government's recent legislative action. Otherwise, he would have been careful to respect the amended article, which says, "A person who bars the selling, turning over, or rental of movable goods or real property to a person; who prevents a person from using certain services offered to the public; who bars employment; and who prevents a person from running a regular economic activity because of hatred stemming from a difference in language, race, nationality, color, gender, disability, political views, philosophical belief, religion or sect will be sentenced to prison for a period of one to three years."

Now, let's see how Erdoğan measures up against the four benchmarks cited in this hate crime law he helped push through Parliament. Thanks to the liberal *Taraf* daily, it was revealed that the Erdoğan government has been profiling unsuspecting citizens in Turkey on a massive scale according to their race, sect, political affiliations, or philosophical leanings. Documents published by the paper indicated that the government prevented businesspeople affiliated with the opposition parties from being awarded major contracts, tenders, and direct purchases. The same discriminatory practices were also applied in valuable land leases or sales for lucrative residential and commercial property developments. There was an alleged direct phone link between the National Intelligence Organization (MİT) and the Prime Ministry to run illegal background checks on people to see whether they are close to the government or not. This is a clear violation of the first part of the sentence in the hate crimes amendment.

The two major corruption investigations that were made public in December also revealed how public lands and properties were allegedly handed over to businesspeople close to Erdoğan. It exposed how the prime minister personally directed some sales and leases of valuable state properties. For example, an audio leak in March, purportedly between Erdoğan and Housing Development Administration of Turkey (TOKİ) Chairman Ahmet Haluk Karabel, revealed the prime minister chiding the official for selling a valuable plot of land in the Ataşehir district of Istanbul to a company called Biat İnşaat without informing him beforehand. "From now on, you will get my approval before selling any valuable land," Erdoğan allegedly instructs Karabel according to a transcript accompanying the voice recording. Karabel was fired from his position last week.

Leaks also exposed how the prime minister apparently instructed a well-known shipping magnate, Metin Kalkavan, to engineer the reopening of a public bid on the national warship project (MİLGEM), valued at $2.5 billion. The contract, won by Koç Holding subsidiary RMK Marine in January 2013, was canceled after Erdoğan asked Kalkavan to file a complaint with his office saying that the necessary conditions for competition had not been met in the initial bidding for MİLGEM. In September 2013, the contract was canceled by the government. In another exposé, Erdoğan instructed his former justice minister to "closely monitor" judicial proceedings in a tax case against Aydın Doğan, whom the prime minister has criticized on a number of occasions over the years, so that the media mogul would not get off scot-free. Both the Koç and Doğan groups have been repeatedly attacked by Erdoğan in recent years for not endorsing his government.

When it comes to preventing a person from using certain services offered to the public, as is described in the second part of the law, the discriminatory practices are, unfortunately, abundant. For example,

Erdoğan slammed the popular Turkish Olympiad, held annually for years by Hizmet with the participation of some 160 countries around the world, at his election rallies and threatened to refuse to grant a location to the event's organizers. Now, municipalities that are run by Erdoğan's Justice and Development Party (AKP) have started to deny applications or revoke those that were already granted for these activities. The government has also refused to open up Taksim Square to unions to gather and celebrate Labor Day on May 1, a national holiday.

When it comes to employment, the Erdoğan government infringes on the rights of law-abiding and tax-paying citizens of this country on a massive scale. Not only are entry-level jobs in government generally offered to partisan candidates, barring others from attaining a position in the government using a merit-based selection process, but Erdoğan also purges employees who have served the government for years with distinction, citing their affiliation with a so-called "parallel structure," a reference to members of Hizmet. Opponents are all lumped together under the same banner and subjected to firings, reassignments, and demotions without transparent procedures and reasonable legal justification. Again, the government fails in the third part of the protection offered in this new hate crimes law.

The last protection in the law is granted to those who are prevented from running their regular economic activities due to hate crimes. Erdoğan fails utterly on this benchmark as well because he openly attacks business groups not loyal to his rule. For example, he called a powerful business group, the Turkish Industrialists and Businessmen's Association (TÜSİAD), "traitors" for its chairman's remarks in January that warned that foreign direct investment (FDI) would not be made in a country with no respect for the rule of law, where legal codes conflict with European Union rules, where public procurement laws have been amended dozens of times and where companies are pressured through tax fines.

Erdoğan's list of enemies in the business world also includes the Turkish Confederation of Businessmen and Industrialists (TUSKON), the country's largest trade advocacy group, whose chairman disclosed to The Wall Street Journal back in January that the group was threatened with being "wiped out of the market" by the government after TUSKON issued statements critical of government policies. Hizmet-affiliated business firms have come under intense pressure from the Erdoğan government abusing auditing and licensing procedures to bully major companies. Even US companies like Twitter, Facebook, and YouTube have been openly attacked by Erdoğan in public rallies and the complete severance of access to these sites from Turkey has been threatened. Employing anti-Western and anti-Semitic rhetoric in his discourse, Erdoğan is violating provisions of the law that criminalized bias-motivated actions.

The Erdoğan government's public record of hate crime and hate speech violations since the relevant amendment became law in March has worsened even further, signaling that the rule of law in Turkey has effectively been suspended and that laws are valid only on paper.

Law of the Jungle[19]

Failure to execute court judgments when it does not serve the interests of the political authorities, a lackluster performance in the effective implementation of judges' orders and foot-dragging in their enforcement have now become hallmarks of the ruling Justice and Development Party (AKP) government under the authoritarian Prime Minister Recep Tayyip Erdoğan. Although the situation has certainly taken a sharp turn for the worse against the backdrop of a huge corruption scandal implicating Erdoğan and some of his family members, the arbitrariness in the observance of the rule of law during the AKP era is definitely not a new phenomenon. There have been several road markers indicating the government's flagrant disregard of court judgments when it was not pleased with the decision.

The case law of both the European Court of Human Rights (ECtHR) and the Turkish Constitutional Court provide an ample window into decoding the policy of the Erdoğan government with regard to respecting the rule of law. For example, the privatization tender for the state-owned Cellulose and Paper Factory (SEKA) in Balıkesir on March 25, 2003, only a couple months after the AKP came to power, represents the

---

[19] First appeared in *Today's Zaman* daily on Apr. 25, 2014

classic mindset of the Erdoğan government on how to sell state assets to pro-government businesspeople for far under their prevailing market value. The state enterprise—situated on 1,800 decares of land (approximately 538 acres) with 185 housing units, social facilities and other buildings and assets—was sold to Albayrak Turizm Seyahat İnşaat Ticaret A.Ş. for $1.1 million through direct negotiations, during which the company was the sole bidder.

The sale of the paper mill gave Albayraklar Holding—the owner of daily *Yeni Şafak*, a staunch supporter of Erdoğan—a great advantage over its competitors, which were forced to import paper. The Cellulose Workers Union sued the Supreme Privatization Board (ÖYK), a government agency controlled by Erdoğan, to cancel the sale. On July 28, 2003, the Bursa 2nd Administrative Court ruled that the sale of the mill—which had been valued at $51 million—for just $1.1 million violated the public interest as well as the privatization law. In an interim decision, the court granted an injunction against turning SEKA over to its prospective owners and later decided to cancel the sale on Oct.15, 2003, notifying the Privatization Administration (ÖİB) in Ankara of its ruling.

The ÖİB was supposed to initiate procedures to repossess SEKA, yet it challenged the interim ruling by the Bursa 2nd Administrative Court in a higher court, the Bursa Regional Administrative Court. It lost the appeal on Sept. 18, 2003. The ÖİB later filed a challenge in the top administrative court, the Council of State, to reverse the lower court's rulings but again lost the legal suit when the Council of State refused to cancel the injunction decision on May 7, 2004, and upheld the lower court's rulings on June 6, 2005. On Feb. 2, 2004, the ÖİB was finally compelled to notify Albayraklar Holding to return the properties it had acquired in the tender and filed two lawsuits against the company when it failed to do so. The company lost the first lawsuit in the court, and the decision was upheld in the appellate court as well. The decision on the second lawsuit is still pending.

When the Erdoğan government realized that it would not be able to bypass strict rules and regulations governing privatization deals by invoking administrative privileges, it decided to circumvent checks in the system using Parliament, where the ruling party has a majority and can push through any law it likes. The first attempt was made in December 2010 when the government buried a substantial revision in an omnibus bill to render legal challenges against completed privatization tenders futile. The provision in the draft cited the impracticability of implementing court decisions to reverse privatization deals and as such justified the failure to enforce court rulings. Faced with the opposition's stand against the provision and the ensuing critical coverage in the media, the government had to drop the provision during deliberations on Law No. 6111 in the Planning and Budget Commission.

When the AKP's maneuver in routine legislative work backfired in the commission, the Erdoğan government resorted to a new and more subtle approach. It parachuted a similar provision overnight into Parliament and had it tied to another omnibus law, No. 6300, in April 2012, during a debate on the assembly floor. The opposition did not have a chance to mount a significant challenge to this last-minute motion, and the issue escaped public and media scrutiny. Erdoğan immediately made the best use of this new law and had the Cabinet issue a decision in June 2012 that made challenging the SEKA privatization deal—among others—in a court of law impossible, citing "impracticability" issues.

Not only did Erdoğan bypass constitutional protections of judicial review on administrative decisions, he also tried to escape from the legal consequences of his government's actions. For example, in another privatization deal that awarded Eti Alüminyum A.Ş. to Ce-Ka A.Ş. for $305 million in June 2005, an Ankara court issued a judgment against Erdoğan, five Cabinet ministers, and two government officials for disregarding various court decisions that canceled the sale and ordered the restitution of the properties that had been handed over to the company. Erdoğan had to pay a fine for proceeding as if there had been no court decision and pressing ahead with the privatization deal nonetheless. Hence, the last-minute change in the omnibus bill allowed Erdoğan to escape the consequences of his contempt of the judges' orders and to act with impunity in lucrative contract and tenders.

However, Erdoğan's jubilation turned out to be short lived because the Constitutional Court—acting on a petition for annulment from the main opposition Republican People's Party (CHP)—decided to cancel this provision of the law. On Oct. 3, 2013, the Constitutional Court ruled that the provision which gave the Cabinet the power to bypass judicial review on administrative decisions based on a "physical impracticability" proviso violated the Constitution. It said the provision contravened several articles of the Turkish Constitution that emphasize the rule of law, the independence of the courts, and judicial review of government actions. It also warned that the Cabinet cannot assume the role of the judiciary in adjudicating legal disputes over privatization tenders.

What is more, most of the Constitutional Court judges did not find the government's defense of the amendment "credible." For example, in defense of the new provision in the law, the government cited lengthy judicial proceedings that last for years and that make it difficult to reverse privatization deals because the company would have invested already and it would therefore be costly to return properties to the government. That is not true, however; the court granted an injunction against the SEKA deal after four months, but the ÖİB intervened very late and tried to return the properties handed over to Albayraklar Holding. Hence the damage due to delay cannot be attributed to the court, but rather to the government agency that was initially reluctant to comply with court judgments. The court also said that it is always possible to calculate the amount of compensation to be awarded to a company for capital investments and other costs incurred in the meantime.

According to the Constitutional Court, the provision violated the right of access to the courts and the right to fair trial because the administrative body—the Cabinet—is empowered to prevent implementation of court judgments. The Turkish Constitution mandates that only the courts can adjudicate legal disputes and not the executive branch. It also said that the law in its current form violated the rule of law enshrined and protected in the Constitution. Though the top court announced its interim decision on Oct. 3, 2013, the government did not enforce the Constitutional Court's decision, claiming that the reasoned decision had not yet been published in the Official Gazette, according to Finance Minister Mehmet Şimşek, responding to a parliamentary question on March 11, 2014. The court's decision was published in the Official Gazette on March 27, 2014, and we still do not know when and how the government will enforce this judgment. SEKA is unfortunately just one example, and there are many other cases like it.

As with the Constitutional Court's decision ordering the lifting of the Twitter ban in Turkey, a decision which Erdoğan said he did not respect, he probably loathes the court for the decision that canceled the law to bypass the judicial system in privatization tenders. The SEKA case clearly reveals how the Erdoğan government wanted to circumvent the rule of law in Turkey ever since the first days of his rule. Erdoğan just feels more comfortable now in blatantly disregarding the court rulings as he has consolidated so much power in his hands over the 12 years of his rule. That is why he defied a court decision reiterating the illegal nature of the destruction of an Ankara forest where the government is currently finishing the construction of a huge new complex for the Prime Ministry in a first-degree environmentally protected zone. Despite the Ankara 11th Administrative Court's decision to halt the construction on Feb. 17, the government has continued with the construction and Erdoğan has vowed, "I will open it and sit inside it."

Fearing that investors will be scared away from investing in Turkey with the suspension of the rule of law, Turkey's economy czar and Deputy Prime Minister Ali Babacan warned this week that the country cannot be governed by what he called "the law of the jungle." Perhaps it is "the law of Erdoğan" that keeps undermining the rule of law and prevents the full and expeditious compliance of the government with the courts' judgments.

Rushed Bills Weaken Turkey[20]

Millions of dollars spent by the European Union and the Council of Europe (CoE) on programs to help Turkey overhaul its criminal justice system and train members of the judiciary and police have all been wasted, thanks but no thanks to the embattled Turkish Prime Minister Recep Tayyip Erdoğan, who effectively suspended the rule of law, turned the whole criminal justice system upside down with a series of rushed bills from Parliament, decimated the police force with an unprecedented num-

---

[20]   First appeared in *Today's Zaman* daily on Jun. 09, 2014

ber of reshuffles and purges, and reined in the independence and impartiality of the judiciary.

Erdoğan has done all this just to save himself, his family members, and his close associates in politics and the business community from incriminating corruption investigations. Now another package of ostensibly judicial reforms has been brought to Parliament's agenda by the government in order to pave the way for Erdoğan and his associates to overcome legal troubles.

Unfortunately, these revisions will not help Turkey get out of the post-monitoring process, a type of probationary measure imposed by the Parliamentary Assembly of the Council of Europe (PACE) back in 2004 against serious violations it observed in a member state. One of the conditions for Turkey, a founding member of the CoE, to graduate from the post-monitoring process is the completion of the revision of the criminal code in line with judgments of the European Court of Human Rights (ECtHR), reviewing the legislation dating from the Emergency Rule Region (OHAL) period, and the training of judges and prosecutors as well as the police and gendarmerie to fully comply with CoE rules and values.

Yet it seems Turkey is far from meeting the conditions laid out by the CoE. Erdoğan's discourse as well as his government's policy actions since 2011 have all dealt a big blow to the right to freedom of expression, the right to freedom of assembly, and the right to enjoy practicing one's religion of choice without interference. The police brutality against peaceful protestors with explicit orders from the government, censuring a critical press including social media with undemocratic laws, putting pressure on corporate owners of media through tax auditing and license revocations, as well as raining down defamation lawsuits on journalists, have been the hallmark of the Erdoğan government in its frantic search for ways to restrict the free flow of information to the electorate.

Therefore, PACE's invitation to Turkey to undertake the reforms in order to protect all fundamental and individual freedoms have been not only disregarded, but some of the accomplishments made so far have now been reversed. The most worrisome development is the attempt by the Erdoğan government to set the stage for politically motivated abuses of the criminal justice system through bills that curtail judicial independence. The government not only destroys the legal and administrative structures in order to usurp powers of the judiciary, but also makes attacks on the personalities of individual judges and prosecutors, at all levels, in order to break the courage and determination of members of the judiciary to ward off any politically motivated interference.

For example, the amendment submitted by the government to Parliament in May and currently being debated in the General Assembly would allow the prime minister, ministers, and high-ranking officials in the Ministry of Justice to influence prosecutors' investigations. The bill aims to change Article 277 of the Turkish Penal Code (TCK), which concerns "attempting to alter the course of an investigation through pressure on members of the judiciary who are carrying out their duty." According to the bill, if interference in the judiciary occurs during the investigative stage conducted by the police or prosecutors, it will not be a crime.

The current law says that suspects or defendants who try to influence an ongoing investigation and members of the judiciary in order to obscure the truth will be sentenced to from two to four years in prison. The government plans to remove the phrases "an ongoing investigation" and "suspects or defendants" from the article. With this, the Erdoğan government wants to let off the hook those implicated in a corruption scandal that became public on Dec. 17, 2013. Recalling that a summary of proceedings was filed against Justice Minister Bekir Bozdağ, who was in hot water after an exposé that he in fact called the chief public prosecutors of İzmir and Adana regarding ongoing investigations into allegations of tender-rigging and corruption in order to derail the investigations, the revisions of the criminal code are needed to save him and his boss, Erdoğan.

Another provision in the package of amendments also reduces the punishment for the crime of forgery of documents to a month-long prison sentence from an offense that is punishable by from one to three years' imprisonment. That means all suspects who are currently being tried or face similar charges would be set free. Some of the charges filed during the corruption investigation that forced four ministers to resign in the Erdoğan government involve "document forgery."

For example, former Economy Minister Zafer Çağlayan, who is accused of accepting 28 bribes amounting to $52 million from Iranian national Reza Zarrab, stands accused of "conducting imports with fake documents" among other charges. The Turkish minister allegedly helped Zarrab to move Iranian state funds, which were deposited in foreign banks as part of payments for oil and gas but were prevented from being transferred back to Tehran because of financial sanctions, to Iran using trade in gold, staples, and medicine.

In one of his phone conversations with the Iranian businessman, which were legally wiretapped by the police and prosecutors involved in the corruption investigation, the ex-minister is claimed to have said: "The current account deficit is falling. Let's move to export gold for three months." Çağlayan was involved with Zarrab in efforts to bring 1.5 tons of gold from Ghana to Turkey by plane on Jan. 1, 2013, declared at customs as a "mineral sample." Çağlayan also allegedly gave Zarrab fake documents permitting the export of 150,000 tons of cargo on a ship with a capacity of only 5,000 tons.

The rushed amendments on the criminal code reflect the general pattern we see during the reign of the ruling Justice and Development Party (AKP): whenever Erdoğan feels the heat from the judiciary, he resorts to the parliamentary majority to save himself and his associates from legal troubles. With the current revisions, 157 amendments on 89 articles of the TCK have been made since 2004. The criminal justice system has been revamped to let Erdoğan and his partners in crime act with impunity while bringing harsh sentences for those who report, write, or talk about these serious allegations.

The hasty changes have damaged the fundamental pillars of the law, such as foreseeability and predictability, which is not good for the business environment and political stability. Worse, the citizens' trust in the justice system and the judiciary has been seriously damaged. This will open a Pandora's box of all sorts of ensuing problems within Turkish politics, economy and civil structure.

Chapter 4

Political Islamists Polarize

Failure of Political Islamists[21]

The undercurrent of growing discontent with the structure of the Turkish political system, currently dominated by the almost Baathist political Islamists of the ruling Justice and Development Party (AKP) under the polarizing figure of Prime Minister Recep Tayyip Erdoğan, is a harbinger of a new era in Turkey. The Islamists' moves have resulted in the ambivalence of Turks, who believe that Erdoğan's vision has faltered a great deal amid corruption, social tension, economic woes, and foreign policy failures. It means the time is ripe for a realignment of Turkish politics.

An opening in the political spectrum is definitely there to exploit for potential contenders who have a broad agenda, the proper organizational structure, and the necessary leadership skills. Neither nationalism nor social democratic values alone can offer a credible alternative ideology to rally the nation and pose a strong challenge to Erdoğan's political machine. As was the case in the '80s and '90s, the new political party must be able to incorporate all four major ideological strands to appeal to liberals, conservatives, social democrats, and nationalists in order to gain enough traction to pull Turkey's disparate political interests together.

The general sense among many Turks is that there is a growing void at the center/center-right of Turkish politics that can only be filled by a new progressive party that will appeal to Turks from all walks of life.

---

[21] First appeared in *Today's Zaman* daily on May 26, 2014

This will happen with a new start-up political party or one that will branch out from an existing party with heavyweights who have some political capital to spend. Turkish politics have always been resilient, innovative, and have proved time and again that they can produce viable alternatives to protect the republic's institutions. The military, judiciary, critical media, and vibrant civil society groups stand as a bulwark against Erdoğan's intrusive ideological tilt in government while offering corrective measures against the encroachments of political zealots who may harm the interests of Turkey.

I think we have reached a critical juncture in Turkish politics. The fractured state institutions, deepening of divisions, and a society that has fragmented under Erdoğan's political Islamist stewardship all prevent Turkey from making vital progress on many issues that need urgent attention for the security and viability of the Turkish state. Erdoğan's political discourse—intolerant of dissent and highly incoherent because of corruption scandals that have pushed his government into a defensive posture—has dealt a significant blow to Turkey's national interests, both at home and abroad.

Erdoğan and his band of brothers try to manipulate the masses in Turkey into helping them maintain their power. Corrupted at the core, they do this by using government assets. This is the main problem thwarting Turkey from adopting true political, economic, and social reforms. Erdoğan's announcement of new reform packages has proven to be merely window-dressing, as it lacks substance and credibility. Even good pieces of legislation were apparently undermined during the implementation phase because they expose the dirty laundry the Erdoğan government has accumulated when these laws are put into motion. This inevitably pushes Islamists in the ruling party to be further disconnected from people and disillusioned with the reformist agenda.

Faced with significant political and non-political countervailing forces to his Islamist agenda, Erdoğan is obviously struggling to make his way ahead. The cumbersome Turkish bureaucracy, already notorious for its lackluster performance, has been rendered more inefficient by a McCarthyist witch-hunt and an unprecedented reshuffle among government employees. Various government agencies have been bloated by incompetent political Islamist cronies who are not qualified to undertake the tasks such government positions require. This leads to further mistakes in government as many political appointees continue to make errors of judgment. In the end, the government has to foot the bill, as in the case of the recent mining accident in Soma, which killed 301 miners.

This means that Erdoğan, Turkey's divisive figure, will have to further amplify political Islamist ideology in order to downplay problems in governance. In the past, this ideology helped him ride out domestic challenges, albeit temporarily. He has no fallback position left and has run out of reasonable choices. The only exit strategy is to play on divisions that will sideline debate on the substantive matters that the nation is struggling with. This Islamism is part of Erdoğan's overall organizational strategy and provides him with an ideologically motivated party cadre. He needs these loyal foot soldiers to do the canvassing in election times or to demonstrate en masse in rallies in order to prove to his challengers that he still has populist backing.

Moreover, Erdoğan often abuses religious values when he talks about the economy in order to give an impression that domestic troubles in the national economy are not due to failure on his government's part but rather have everything to do with the global economy, one that is ruled by interest-seeking and profit-maximizing Jewish money, according to many insiders in Erdoğan's close circle. His "interest lobby" remarks during the Gezi Park protests of May-June 2013, and in the aftermath of the corruption investigation that shook his government, are good illustrations of his reliance on an Islamist agenda.

There is a strong association with ultra-leftist ideological leanings in the mindset of the people surrounding Erdoğan, which reveals itself as anti-American, anti-Israeli, and anti-Western discourse. The fact that some of Erdoğan's close aides feel strong sympathy toward Iran also fuels the enthusiasm for West-bashing discourse in government. Hence, when credit rating agencies shave off a couple notches in the sovereign rating of the Turkish economy based on structural deficiencies in the economy or rising political uncertainty, Erdoğan and his aides attack these organizations as if they were driven by other interests. Erdoğan is quick to claim that credit agencies simply do not want to see Turkey growing economically. This helps Islamists shift the blame from their own doing to outsiders.

While in opposition, political Islamists complain about corruption, lack of transparency, and accountability, as well as unfair and unjust use of state coffers by ruling parties during elections. Yet when they come to power, similar complaints are downplayed and are in fact justified because Islamists pursue the lofty goal of a worldwide campaign to assert the supremacy of their religion. For that, they need financing, economic leverage, and political capital at any expense. In other words, for political Islamists, the end justifies the means and it does not concern them whether the tools they employ are in conflict with mainstream Islamic values and ethics.

Since Islamists do not believe richness lies in diversity and plurality in society with their narrowly focused ideology of "one size fits all," they try to impose their own views on others. On face value, they pretend to take on liberals and social democrats, yet in fact Islamists pose the gravest danger to conservative and faith-based groups, first and foremost. This is because they need to consolidate their support base in order to maintain power; conservatives are the main challenger to Islamists, as they have more in common with these voters than leftists and liberals.

This is the main reason why Erdoğan attacks the Hizmet Movement inspired by Islamic scholar Fethullah Gülen and tries to vilify this moderate cleric who has been highly critical of Erdoğan's abuse of Islam for political purposes. Gülen's unwavering stand against Erdoğan's cycle of corrupt power—despite pressure, threats, and intimidation—has already exposed how much damage political Islamists have dealt to the religion of Islam as well as the Turkish nation. The appeal of politically exploited Islamist ideology has lost its shine and its strength has been diluted or broken during Erdoğan's version 2.0 regime. The pendulum will eventually swing back to the political center, where the majority of Turks cluster.

Now, Turkey can finally move forward, even if it takes some time to realign the broken pieces of its social harmony and political cohesion. That is definitely good news.

Engagement vs. Exploitation[22]

The exploitation of politically sensitive issues—such as the plight of Muslims abroad—for domestic political gain rather than displaying a genuine effort and sound diplomatic outreach to help contribute to resolving their problems with the cooperation of the relevant authorities has been a leading characteristic of political Islamists in Turkey. Since there is no strong support for this among a Turkish public that overwhelmingly subscribes to a centuries-long Sufi-oriented tradition, political Islamists cleverly seize upon human rights abuses that target mainly Muslims in other countries and play back their sufferings to the Turkish audience with the hope that Islamists will pick up more political support on the home front.

Speaking at a parliamentary group meeting on April 22, 2013, Turkish Prime Minister Recep Tayyip Erdoğan suddenly uttered the name of Pattani, a southern province of Thailand where the long-standing animosity of the province's majority Malay-Muslim population towards the central government has been a lingering issue fueling violence amid reported abuse by law enforcement forces and a weak justice system. The Thai government has been trying to address the problems in this deep southern province with reforms in local governance and judiciary, albeit with limited success. The Thai government was also compelled to deal with violence generated by some factions that use extremist religious ideology to channel Malay Muslims' frustration into recruitment to their ranks.

I may be wrong, but as far as I remember, this was the first time that Turkey's Erdoğan raised the Pattani issue publicly in Parliament. He later repeated the line in a meeting organized by an advocacy group called ÖNDER, which represents members and alumni of religious high schools. It was also interesting because the issue was brought up only a couple of days after the visit of Malaysian Prime Minister Najib Razak to Turkey. In his fiery parliamentary address, Erdoğan said: "This morning I saw a picture of Pattani, where Muslims are under pressure from Buddhists and hundreds and thousands of Muslims have been killed in

---

[22] First appeared in *Today's Zaman* daily on Apr. 28, 2014

recent days. I saw an elderly Muslim man who prays for Turkey. ... He said 'Be patient, Erdoğan,' and then cried."

Portraying this picture in vivid terms, Erdoğan told his deputies that Turkey, heir to the vast Ottoman Empire, has a responsibility to reach out to these people and slammed Turks whom he said do not understand this historic responsibility. In his address to young students in Istanbul later, he said that Pattani is their brother, just like Bangladesh, Palestine, Egypt, Somalia, Iraq, Afghanistan, and Myanmar. Erdoğan's picking up on the Pattani issue follows an emotionally charged broadcast story run just two days ago by the pro-government and Islamist *Kanal 7* station featuring human rights abuses suffered by Muslims in that province.

Nobody bothered to check the facts regarding the little-known Pattani issue and whether hundreds and thousands had been killed in recent days, as claimed by Erdoğan. There was no awareness of this issue among the Turkish public and Pattani had never been heard in public discussion before. Therefore it was easy for Erdoğan's speech writers to add a couple of provocative lines to his addresses as it served to mobilize Islamists around the political cause ushered in by the beleaguered Turkish prime minister who has been fighting the biggest challenge of his political career amid massive corruption scandals implicating him and some of his family members.

Pattani was just the latest example of how Islamists in Turkey manipulate sensitive issues involving Muslims in foreign countries and how far they are disconnected from reality. It almost appears that the main priority for them is not to improve conditions for Muslims in the first place but rather to dwell on their sufferings in order to expand the political-Islamist agenda in Turkey. Small religious parties in Turkey have played on these issues for so long but failed to make inroads in Turkish society. Unfortunately, the current government in Turkey, dominated by a few powerful and overzealous political Islamists, is able to thrust Islamist issues onto the national agenda. During town hall meetings and public rallies, the senior leadership in the ruling Justice and Development Party (AKP) has started to parrot the same talking points devised by Islamists in order to mobilize supporters.

Using the pro-government media financed by businesspeople, and fattened up by commissions and contracts disbursed by Erdoğan, Islamists are able to project these issues to a larger audience and are now slowly gaining ground in raising awareness on foreign policy matters that are ripe for political exploitation back home. The downside of this, however, is that these ill-advised initiatives risk creating tension in Turkey's relations with other countries and can be easily construed as blatant interferences into the domestic affairs of sovereign nations.

What is more, by injecting enthusiastic Islamist philosophy into foreign policy choices, political Islamists in the government do not seem to mind squandering hard-earned political capital and goodwill credit that Turkey has accumulated over decades. This is a highly dangerous, counterproductive strategy, and one that is set to backfire because it lacks constructive engagement with authorities who are entrusted with managing the problems in their own territories. Instead of producing positive results through different instruments, including silent diplomacy and engagement through regional and international partners and organizations, Ankara's unilateral approach combined with harsh public rhetoric risks irking Turkey's friends, partners, and allies.

The same mistake was repeated in Egypt, where Erdoğan, who feels strong sympathy for the Muslim Brotherhood, has relentlessly slammed the interim government backed by the military. During the campaign period before the March 30 local elections, Erdoğan publicly and on many occasions slammed army chief Gen. Abdel Fattah el-Sisi, who deposed the Islamist President Mohamed Morsi last year and is likely to be the next president of the world's most populous Arab nation. The result is that Turkey lost its political dialogue with Egypt and its ambassador in Cairo was declared persona non grata.

One can be highly critical of a military coup and strongly oppose capital punishment; this is quite understandable. In my opinion, Turkey should raise objections to both, but turning these into major domestic policy debate and escalating the harsh rhetoric against Egyptian leaders beyond an acceptable level of criticism only burns the bridges of dialogue which jeopardizes Turkey's valuable access to the leadership in Egypt. Unfortunately, that is what happened in our ties with Egypt, as Ankara lost credibility when it adopted a clear partisan attitude. If

Erdoğan had some political capital with Egyptian rulers, he could have made the lives of Brotherhood members much easier.

Erdoğan appears to have made the same mistake with Bangladesh when he announced publicly that he had pleaded with Bangladeshi Prime Minister Sheikh Hasina in a phone conversation in December last year to suspend the execution of Abdul Quader Mollah, a convicted war criminal. Erdoğan's public rhetoric was seen as flagrant interference by a Bangladeshi government that had come to power on the promise of bringing to justice those who it claimed to have been war criminals during the war of independence. Mollah, who belonged to an Islamist party, Jamaat-e-Islami, was one of the leaders who were tried and convicted, and his sentence was upheld by the Supreme Court. Again, Bangladeshi officials say that they understood Turkish concerns over the trials but were left bewildered at why the Turkish prime minister publicly mentioned the issue time and again, and that it may risk destroying the almost picture-perfect relationship between the two countries.

Unfortunately, this is what happens when foreign policy preferences are based on ideological choices motivated by a political Islamist philosophy aimed at influencing a domestic audience rather than producing a result. The Erdoğan government made similar mistakes in its relations with Serbia, Palestine, the Gulf countries, and even with some of the European countries that are home to sizable Turkish and Muslim communities. It is rather a naïve approach adopted by Islamist politicians who have a big appetite for destructive drama and fiery rhetoric. They think that they can reach out to Muslim populations in other countries over the heads of state and governments, and get away with it. Not only did this approach lead to failures on many foreign policy fronts, but it also left Turks with a sense of disillusionment due to populist rhetoric and empty promises.

Undermining the Fight with Islamophobia[23]

Over the past couple of years, increasingly hurtful and pointedly hateful discourse adopted by Turkey's chief political Islamist, Prime Minister Recep Tayyip Erdoğan, has done a huge disservice in the effort to com-

---

[23] First appeared in *Today's Zaman* daily on May 05, 2014

bat Islamophobia in the world today, dealing a blow to decades-long efforts done by organizations such as the Organization of Islamic Cooperation (OIC) in international forums. The rabble-rousing speeches he has delivered on the campaign trail and defamation articles published by Erdoğan-controlled media stigmatize Jews, Christians, and even Muslims who do not subscribe to Erdoğan's firebrand political Islamist ideology that has a close affinity with its brethren in other countries, albeit marginal ones.

Erdoğan's parochial political Islamist ideology defies the richness in multiplicity and diversity of viewpoints among Muslims, setting a bad example for opponents of Islam to capitalize on. Instead of resisting marginalizing different religious groups with the same commitment and engagement that he tackles signs of Islamophobia, Erdoğan rather implements discriminatory practices to dominate his authoritarian Islamist version among Muslims, imposing an exclusionary vision of non-Muslims altogether.

The latest example of Erdoğan's destructive discourse was seen last week when Erdoğan, responding to well-placed criticism by visiting German President Joachim Gauck on press freedom woes and tightening control over the judiciary in the EU candidate country, accused Germany's head of state of not acting like a statesman probably because Gauck still thinks of himself as a pastor and that he should keep his advice to himself. Instead of addressing legitimate concerns raised by the German president, who merely repeated similar criticism uttered by Turkey's top judge, Haşim Kılıç, a week ago, Erdoğan chose to attack Gauck based on his past record of being a Lutheran pastor.

What is the point here for Erdoğan in recalling Gauck's religious background, which is perfectly all right with German citizens? Perhaps he was trying to score politically among his core political Islamist constituency and keep their spirits up by humiliating a visiting dignitary. This is conduct totally unbecoming for a Turkish head of government, let alone for a Muslim. By attacking someone for his Christian roots as a pastor, Erdoğan plants seeds of religious hatred in Turkish society, which is very dangerous for dialogue and outreach activities long-endorsed by the United Nations' Alliance of Civilizations, an effort initiated by former Spanish Prime Minister Don José Luis Rodríguez Zapatero and Prime Minister Erdoğan.

Toeing the line with Erdoğan, one of the government-controlled newspapers, the *Star* daily, ran a headline story on Sunday in which it accused US-based watchdog Freedom House, which downgraded Turkey from "Partly Free" to "Not Free" in its annual report last week after citing a significant decline in press freedom, of being a mouthpiece of pro-Israel lobbies and of being financed by Israel. It also singled out the president of Freedom House, David Kramer, as being Jewish and to have alleged close ties to neocons in the US. The story, followed by a full-page analysis inside, was mostly based on distorted facts and run without a byline and signature, hinting that it was serviced by the government, probably by intelligence directly controlled by Erdoğan's close confidant, a common pattern that has been seen in the Turkish media landscape recently.

Raising Jewishness in order to discredit a report or any opponent of the government for that matter has now become a hallmark of Erdoğan's government. He frequently claimed a Jewish conspiracy as being behind last year's Gezi Park protests when he said the "interest lobby"—a murky and veiled reference to Jewish investors and bankers—was driving the anti-government rallies. When a vast corruption scandal broke on Dec. 17, 2013, incriminating Erdoğan and his close associates, the prime minister again accused Israel and the West of orchestrating investigations to topple his government. On the campaign trail before the March 30 local elections, Erdoğan had also scapegoated what he called domestic collaborators for that conspiracy such as opposition parties, business groups, media, and the Hizmet Movement.

He has done so in order to shift the debate away from corruption scandals, but in the meantime has hurt decades-long investments many others worked hard to build—efforts that were made to strengthen dialogue and engage in outreach activities across the divide among cultures, civilizations, and religions. The corruption scandal revealed that Erdoğan's hate speech is not limited to non-Muslims. He has singled out Fethullah Gülen, an interfaith dialogue advocate who inspired a powerful, non-political social movement that places emphasis on the empowerment of Muslims through science education, as his number-one enemy for the past six months. He has done so by going against his own record of having praised Gülen publicly and having been supportive of Gülen's work at home and abroad for years.

Gülen's critical stand against corruption in the ruling Justice and Development Party (AKP) government and refusal to be cowed into silence disturbed Erdoğan, prompting his government to take a position openly hostile against the Hizmet Movement. In public rallies, Erdoğan slammed this elderly Muslim cleric for having met with Pope John Paul II in 1998 and called him all kinds of slanders such as "traitor," "hollow preacher," "virus," "false prophet," "hashashin"—a member of a medieval order that spread political influence through assassinations—and others. This unprecedented attack on a Muslim cleric was so appalling that Danish Prime Minister Helle Thorning-Schmidt was clearly startled during a press conference in Copenhagen in March when a journalist asked the visiting Turkish premiere whether Erdoğan's hate speech against the Hizmet Movement conflicts with the Turkish authorities' fight against Islamophobia in Europe.

It is clear that with this kind of rhetoric, Turkey's embattled Erdoğan is hampering efforts to bridge the great divide among religions on the basis of fundamental human rights, such as freedom to practice a religion. This hateful discourse also makes it difficult to combat growing Islamophobia in the West because it gives ammunition to Muslim haters who pick up on the views of the increasingly authoritarian Erdoğan, who blatantly disregards the rule of law, fundamental rights, and democratic principles. Erdoğan acts like a political entrepreneur benefiting from hateful speech that stigmatizes Jews and Christians as well as Muslims who defy political Islamism. It appears as if the prime minister raises Islamophobic issues deliberately, but has no interest in actually solving them. It seems as long as there is more conflict, the better for him to seize upon the conflict for electoral purposes.

The Erdoğan government's smear campaign against Ekmeleddin İhsanoğlu, the former OIC secretary-general and Turkish diplomat, is the ultimate display of how a few Islamists in Turkey have dominated the current government and can damage Muslims' fight against Islamophobia. İhsanoğlu, the man who changed the face of the world's second largest intergovernmental organization, is perhaps the most accomplished international personality in raising awareness about Islamophobia. He has successfully worked with the US administration and the European Union on advancing measures to tackle discriminatory practices against Muslims. He helped produce powerful resolutions in the UN tackling Islamophobia.

Since he is not a political Islamist within the strict definition of Erdoğan's thought process and he refused to take a position on the Egyptian coup that ousted former Muslim Brotherhood member Mohammed Morsi, İhsanoğlu was subjected to a character assassination in Turkey. İhsanoğlu, who was born in Cairo to a Turkish family and is a graduate of Cairo's Ain Shams University, is perhaps one of the most knowledgeable diplomats on Egyptian affairs in Turkey. He knew it would not be wise to go against the interim government backed by the military and the overwhelming majority of the Egyptian people. It was also improper for him, as secretary-general, to try to impose Turkish views on the 57-member nation bloc with regard to Egypt.

The OIC secretary-general also said that if the Turkish government really wanted to raise this issue, it could certainly call an emergency session of the OIC on the Egyptian situation, something Ankara declined to do after realizing that it was in the minority. Yet Erdoğan publicly slammed the OIC for not doing anything in Egypt while his ministers attacked İhsanoğlu when he was still OIC secretary-general. Just as pro-government dailies attacked Gülen for meeting with Pope John Paul II, İhsanoğlu was also targeted for meeting with Pope Francis in December of last year. Speaking to reporters following the meeting in Rome, İhsanoğlu said his visit is the first of its kind and aims to deepen cooperation between the Catholic Church and the OIC to contribute to reducing tension in international politics. This is the difference between a respected diplomat who wanted to go the extra mile to make a difference towards world peace and a politician who simply wanted to leave conflicts unresolved so that he can continue to profit from a political windfall.

The harsh narrative and extremist language employed by Erdoğan publicly is certainly taking a toll on combating discriminatory practices targeting Muslims. It builds new walls, destroys bridges of trust, and puts more distance between communities. It affects the ability to counter extremist narratives and impairs an objective assessment of the situation for Muslims in Turkey and abroad. What is more, instead of dispelling common misperceptions that feed prejudices against other religions, Erdoğan is in fact reinforcing biases towards non-Muslims.

As the head of government, Erdoğan must in fact encourage active participation of people who belong to vulnerable or underrepresented groups in positions of responsibility based on professional competence and merits. Yet he appears to have been doing completely the opposite. The widespread reporting on massive profiling of Turkish citizens based on ethnic, religious, or ideological affiliations in the workplace is alarming. Erdoğan is promoting the worst practices and his way is definitely eroding the struggle of Muslims to combat Islamophobia in the world today. This is totally uncalled for.

New Army of Political Islamists[24]

The recently passed intelligence legislation that Turkish spymaster Hakan Fidan lobbied hard for with Islamist politicians, including the Turkish president and prime minister, contains such head-spinning initiatives in the national education policies that the Erdoğan government increasingly reflects Iranian influence on this country. In fact, the bill was introduced because the intel chief considered it a crucial tool to allow to him to restructure his agency to be on par with Iranian intelligence, according to insider accounts from the Turkish capital.

The dramatic shift in the main parameters of educational policies and youth engagement programs, also covered in the bill, reflect the strong desire of Prime Minister Recep Tayyip Erdoğan, the top political Islamist in Turkey, to raise a new generation of young political Islamists to support his ideologically motivated political party as well as to sustain his legacy when he exits from politics one day. For that to happen,

---

[24] First appeared in *Today's Zaman* daily on Jun. 02, 2014

the level and intensity of the indoctrination of young students must be ratcheted up at the expense of teaching science, math, and other essential academic subjects. In this politicized campaign, Islam is not a religion, per se, but rather, it is used and abused for self-serving ideological inclinations, a practice that will damage the spirit of tolerance and respect for others in the next generation.

That is how the mullahs in Iran, the architects of politically driven Shiite ideology, have been able to cling to power since the revolution of 1979. They replicated what the former Soviet Union, the predecessor of today's Russia, did when the highly oppressive regime praised and venerated the ideology of communism above everything else in schools and universities, defying reason, logic, and critical thinking. Perhaps Erdoğan and his band of brothers in political Islam have discovered that education is the main conduit to implant political Islamist ideology in Turks, a predominantly Sufi-oriented society. Erdoğan knows that the orthodox and rigid definition of religion in the political Islamists' ideology does not resonate well with most inside Turkey and, in fact, has been met with the stern disapproval of Turks for centuries—yet he pushes for the survival of this ideology.

The main casualty of this newly revamped education policy of the Erdoğan government will be the decades-long efforts to overcome fear and ignorance among Turks and to promote respect, diversity, pluralism, and mutual appreciation. If political Islamists somehow succeed in this endeavor, it will perpetuate strong anti-Western discourse for generations in Turkey, hampering efforts at dialogue to bridge the divide between the Muslim world and the rest of the world. The takeover of Islamists in Turkey's ruling Justice and Development Party (AKP) originally represented a progressive umbrella platform, but in 2011, the government moved into activism for a political Islamist ideology and away from rhetorical and substantive moderation.

Legislation approved in Parliament on March 1 gave the government sweeping powers to overhaul the Ministry of Education from the top down, representing a drastic restructuring in education, the likes of which have not been seen even in extraordinary periods such as during military coups. Law No. 6528 terminated the employment of thousands of senior officials in the ministry, including the president of the Ministry of Education's Board of Education and Discipline, the board's other members, the ministry's deputy undersecretaries, the general directors, the chiefs of education branches, and the provincial education directors of all 81 provinces. Some 100,000 school principals and vice principals were also sacked after the bill was adopted.

The hasty changes in the education system, made without consulting education specialists, unions, or the opposition parties, are aimed at creating a political recruitment program, one that will cater to political Islamists in Turkey. Now, the newcomers to those vacated positions will play a significant role in the development of the public school curriculum, most notably the religious education components. What is more, Erdoğan also turned the powerful Directorate of Religious Affairs (DİB), with some 100,000 employees, over 80,000 mosques, and a huge budget, into a political tool to communicate the ruling party's messages via press statements and Friday sermons. The DİB was also used as a steppingstone by the government: a vast number of political appointees were transferred from the DİB to other state institutions. The publicly funded DİB, which only represents Sunnis, has now become a mouthpiece of the Erdoğan government, justifying whatever policy decisions the ruling party's cronies decide to implement.

It is a hair-raising development that this political Islamist cabal has been able to lay siege to the Sufi-oriented and moderate Muslim thinking that has the allegiance of the overwhelming majority in Turkish society. Erdoğan has not fully succeeded in his endeavor yet because of the secular tradition in the education system and the existence of restraining measures in the state—such as the judiciary and the military, as well as the vibrant media, civic society, and diversified leadership in Muslim communities across Turkey. But he will not give up easily in his efforts to consolidate more power in government by weakening state institutions and eroding checks and balances while simultaneously monopolizing his undeclared leadership in religion by co-opting conservative and faith groups with lavish offers or cowing them into submission with threats and intimidation.

Unfortunately, the Erdoğan government's Islamist policies will hinder the education system from performing the role of fighting against intolerance, hate speech, racism, and xenophobia in society with an emphasis on rights starting at an early age. Moreover, the sham education reform under Erdoğan's rule will be permitted to clear all hurdles in its path so that political Islamist ideology may develop deeper roots in Turkey. A series of highly controversial education initiatives, such as banning privately run schools which assist students in preparation for college and university entrance exams and Erdoğan's continuous pleas for his supporters to withdraw their children from the schools associated with the Islamic scholar Fethullah Gülen and the Hizmet Movement have all been aimed at advancing Erdoğan's agenda of raising "a vengeful religious youth."

However, Erdoğan obviously misjudged Gülen. The prime minister expected the well-respected, 73-year-old Muslim scholar—who has expressly stayed away from politics throughout his life in order to preserve Islamic principles and values rather than enter an environment of political bickering, factionalism, and the "end justifies the means" approach of political Islamists—to take a back seat and remain passive in the face of the encroachments of political Islamists who merely want to drill slogans into the minds of Turkish youth using the name of religion. Perhaps Gülen had to take a stand, not seeking power for himself at his advanced age, but to protect the fundamental teachings of Islam that emphasize humility, moderation, justice, accountability, and transparency in governance.

Erdoğan's attempt to put a stranglehold on religion with Iranian-style indoctrination and imposing political Islam's values on Turkish society has not been able to shake the bedrock of power in Sufi-dominated Turkish society. That is why he has grown impatient and frustrated, prompting him to replace education ministers frequently and to appoint an undersecretary to directly do his bidding. Erdoğan hopes to sustain his rule by dividing society further into sectarian and ideological camps with the hateful rhetoric he employs against Gülen, the media, business and civic groups at home, and his constant bashing of Turkey's Western allies, especially the US, as well those in the Middle East and the Gulf.

The inflammatory xenophobic hostility and anti-Western sentiment leads to the potential radicalization of Turkish youth. Erdoğan needs a restless generation to channel voters' growing dissatisfaction and disillusionment with his government, as we saw in his desperation to find scapegoats for allegations of corruption, in order to shift the blame. The youths who show up at Erdoğan's rallies wearing shrouds and chanting slogans like, "Tell us to die for you, we will die; tell us to hit, we will hit," is something never before seen in Turkey, and it unfortunately raises just such a specter of radicalization.

The well-organized and hard-working members of Hizmet, savvy in modern education that promotes interfaith and intercultural dialogue in the early years of schooling, stand in the way of Erdoğan's political Islamist ideology. That is, perhaps, one of the main reasons why Mr. Gülen has topped Erdoğan's enemy list recently. However, there is no need to be pessimistic about Turkey's prospects. Erdoğan's new emphasis on political Islamist indoctrination in religious education in public schools—a divisive issue during the best of times—will surely fail, given the vibrancy and dynamism of Turkish society, but it will inflict some damage in the meantime.

Chapter 5

Education and Prep Schools

Frontal Assault on Free Enterprise[25]

T he way Turkey's power-hungry Prime Minister Recep Tayyip Erdoğan and his small cadre of yes-men advisors, most of whom are subscribers to politically charged Islamist ideology, are running the country as a shadow government has taken the nation to a breaking point, where the pressure on the Cabinet members and deputies of the ruling Justice and Development Party (AKP) has intensified beyond a healthy limit. The opposition voices in the AKP parliamentary group, with several deputies openly questioning Erdoğan's decisions on several issues, and cracks in the government shown by government spokesperson Deputy Prime Minister Bülent Arınç chastising Erdoğan over differences of opinion on co-ed housing, are recent evidence of the wounds Erdoğan and his advisors are inflicting on their own government.

The public outrage over a controversial government plan to ban all privately run college prep schools, which have been in operation for decades as educational institutions that supplement the failing public schools to help students enroll in top-notch colleges and universities, is just the latest example of how Erdoğan and his yes-men misread the mandate given them by the voters to run the country until the next election. By attacking prep schools and threatening them with forced closure by law, Erdoğan hopes to hide the miserable public education record that saw the reshuffle of five education ministers and six major overhauls during the AKP's three terms. The colossal mistakes the AKP govern-

---

25   First appeared in *Today's Zaman* daily on Nov. 18, 2013

ment made in education, with fast-tracked reforms that did not take into account the concerns expressed by education specialists, parent-teacher associations, unions and other stakeholders, have frustrated millions of parents.

Underage drinking, smoking, and drug use and abuse are rampant problems in the Turkish education system and the government's track record is not so good when it comes to addressing these problems. According to a survey of 32,000 students in Istanbul released in Nov. 2013, 45 percent of ninth graders smoke cigarettes, 32 percent drink alcohol, and 9 percent use drugs. The survey was conducted between 2010 and 2012 in ninth grade classes at 154 high schools in all of Istanbul's 39 districts. It was led by Professor Andres Pumariega, chair of the department of psychiatry at the Cooper Medical School of Rowan University in Camden, New Jersey, on the request of the Istanbul Police Department and Provincial Education Directorate. A government-backed education project, the Movement to Increase Opportunities and Technology (FATİH), launched at pilot schools in February 2012 to fulfill an election promise from the 2011 elections, has not yet been completed and is now being investigated for corruption claims.

The shortage of teachers and lack of sufficient school facilities has not been resolved, either. Creating a villain out of privately funded prep schools that have proven to be successful sanctuaries for parents to get extra tutoring for their kids in order to boost the children's chances of getting into better schools has served as a useful tool in shifting the blame away from the government. Erdoğan is abusing this issue as a distraction from his own failures.

What is more, Erdoğan fired a warning shot across the bow of the Hizmet Movement, which operates some one-third of the more than 3,500 prep schools, hoping that the movement would fold under the pressure and shy away from criticizing the government on lingering corruption charges, the lack of bold reforms, the stalled EU membership process, the failed constitutional work, its intrusion in people's ways of life and privacy, blunders in foreign policy, and the weakened transparency and accountability in governance. Judging from the remarks of Mr. Fethullah Gülen, who has vowed to remain steadfast against these threats, urging his millions of followers to never be shaken, not to give in to despair, and to be patient, I believe the movement is keen on maintaining its principled stand on these issues and committed to upholding the very values that make this nation great. Erdoğan is gambling away his good fortune on the eve of the elections because his attempt to ban these educational institutions will certainly backfire on him, possibly costing him his presidential ambitions.

Erdoğan's government is also undertaking a huge risk with this manifestly ill-advised move. It may very well scare away foreign investors whom Turkey needs desperately because of its chronic current account deficit (CAD) and low saving rates. This will add a big chunk to the pile of concerns already being expressed by international investors who deal with Turkey. It will ring alarm bells among investors who already feel uneasiness about Erdoğan's government, which exploits the law against legitimate businesses for political purposes. Several ambassadors in Ankara have told me that some of these concerns have made it to the agenda in bilateral ties because of complaints from foreign companies to their respective governments. For example, a Western ambassador told me in confidence that a major investment scheme has been waiting for approval on the prime minister's desk for far too long despite an appeal made by the Investment Support and Promotion Agency of Turkey (ISPAT) to lure that company to Turkey. He was complaining about red tape and the lack of transparency and predictability in the government bureaucracy. This downward turn in the investment climate and undermining of basic principles and values like transparency and accountability may spell bigger risks for the Turkish government when the Federal Reserve begins tapering off its funds and money becomes scarce and expensive to attract.

The government's move to shut down private prep schools once again highlights the danger of the few checks and balances we have in Turkey against the abuse of the executive branch, which uses the majority it has in Parliament to push through unpopular bills with impunity. The government uses this legislative power to intimidate or coerce its political opponents wherever and whenever it feels like it, undermining the rule of law in the sense of universally acceptable standards. This gives rise to claims of the authoritarian tendencies Erdoğan has not been shy to show off.

It was also widely reported in the media that the witch hunt apparently targeting Turkish citizens who do not subscribe to the Islamist ideology of Erdoğan has been going on for some time, and many moderates, including people who sympathize with Gülen's teachings, were terminated, suspended or moved to low-key positions. The specter of political Islam now looms large and dominates the government bureaucracy as the AKP sacrifices its democratic credentials with the rapid erosion of pluralism at the expense of diversity in government agencies.

Another worrying result that could stem from the possible ban would be the burgeoning of the unregistered economy in Turkey. The prep schools have emerged as a necessary and corrective measure in the liberal market, where supply and demand shape the economy. Some 100,000 people are employed in the prep school system, valued at some TL 2 billion to TL 3 billion. Banning them will not wipe out this major economic activity as long as strong demand is there—and it is quite likely there will be demand, as students will naturally compete for good schools. But the ban will push the system into the gray area of the unregistered economy, which is already a big problem for the government.

According to data released by the government in November, nearly 40 percent of the 26 million workers currently employed in Turkey are not registered in the social security system. Companies usually opt for unregistered workers to avoid high payroll taxes, social security premiums, and severance benefits. Banning prep schools will move more people to the informal economy, resulting in a loss of revenue. This issue is also a major handicap for Turkey in attracting foreign investment because foreign investors who choose to follow the rules and register their workers in the system face unfair competition from Turkish companies that do not.

Erdoğan's government, which attacks the right to private ownership, the right of establishment and freedom to provide services, the right to free enterprise, and the right to education, will deal a blow to business confidence and the climate of investment in Turkey. The business community values predictability and frequent changes to the legal and regulatory environment scare it off. If this draft bill becomes law, how will the Turkish government argue that private entities may freely establish, acquire, and dispose of their interests in business enterprises in Turkey anymore? If Erdoğan is stubborn enough to go after the largest civil organization, which partially owns and operates the prep schools, the daunting message is that he can do anything and everything to whomever he pleases, whenever he likes. The cascading impact from this pattern will be a rising risk assessment for Turkey, which will in turn make insurance premiums on lending expensive as investors are forced to re-evaluate their plans for Turkey. Private Turkish companies that have been benefiting from low-interest foreign loans and credit will feel the pinch. Eventually, the government will have to make a choice whether it can sustain structural changes and reforms.

Arbitrary Rule[26]

On Nov. 18, in a Cabinet meeting that lasted more than seven hours, Prime Minister Recep Tayyip Erdoğan discussed the ban on private prep schools with his ministers for almost four hours. The meeting came only four days after the draft bill on the ban was leaked to Turkey's largest circulated paper, *Zaman*. In what seemed to be a divided house in the Cabinet on the issue, Justice Minister Sadullah Ergin was one of those who voiced his opposition to the blanket ban, arguing that the legislative change to that effect is destined to fail a possible legal challenge in the Constitutional Court. Even if it passes the test in Turkey's top court, Ergin said, the bill would in all likelihood not withstand a challenge in the Strasbourg-based European Court of Human Rights (ECtHR), a leading rights court in Europe whose decisions are binding on Turkey.

Not impressed by his justice minister's reasonable concerns, Erdoğan brushed aside other opposing voices in Cabinet as well, vowing to go ahead with the ban despite legal challenges, economic ramifications, and political consequences. An insider's recollection of this Cabinet meeting tells the tale of the prep school ban in plain truth: It is a politically motivated move on the part of Erdoğan, who took it upon himself to stig-

---

[26] First appeared in *Today's Zaman* daily on Dec. 02, 2013

matize Turkey's largest civic movement, Hizmet, which has differences with his own line of thinking on a number of issues. Hence, it was useless to discuss the ban on merit at all, be it in legal challenges, economic consequences, or basic rights and liberties. Erdoğan had no interest in hearing all these arguments that ran contrary to what he personally set out to accomplish. That is why the bill lacks a comprehensive impact analysis statement, legally required for draft bills so that the public, including members of Parliament, has an idea of the bill's ramifications, economically and socially.

It is clear that Erdoğan does not trust Ergin and the Justice Ministry in formulating such laws that will have drastic implications for the justice system, let alone in other areas. The fact that some crucial legislative changes were drafted in the past by a small cadre of Erdoğan's trusted men at the Prime Ministry, bypassing the Justice Ministry, which is the traditional venue for draft bills according to established practice, worries many in Turkey over the state of affairs in the Turkish government. The Justice Ministry had learned about some of the draft bills only after they were submitted to Parliament for debate. Erdoğan believes if he involves the Justice Ministry, the process will be stalled or at least slowed down, and possibly amended to reflect better alignment with the existing laws and constitution.

If it was up to the justice minister, we would have seen the merging of both the third and fourth judicial reform packages into one when it was submitted to Parliament. Erdoğan even had the drafts that were prepared at the Justice Ministry watered down in his office. The same can also be said about Ergin's relations with the Foreign Ministry. Ergin, who is well respected by his Western counterparts for his rights-based and reform-minded approach, has been thwarted by Foreign Minister Ahmet Davutoğlu and his diplomats on more than one occasion when he wanted to work on judicial cooperation with regional organizations like the Council of Europe and the European Union, as well as with Turkey's allies and friends. His personal appeals to Davutoğlu to cut the red tape at the Foreign Ministry to allow the Justice Ministry to better interact with interlocutors in Brussels and Strasbourg were left unaddressed most of the time. He had to appoint his own representatives to these two important cities to do business, bypassing Davutoğlu and the Turkish embassies.

Ergin, who deserves credit for successfully reducing the backlog of cases from Turkey with a series of agreements with the ECtHR, including friendly settlements and compensation commissions, helped Turkey drop two notches, down to fourth place, in terms of the total number of cases pending against the country at the Strasbourg court. He is now worried that if Erdoğan gets his way, that success will become only a temporary blip on the radar. Although Erdoğan does not seem to care much about the legal consequences of ECtHR decisions and can order his government to overlook the court's decision by not enforcing judgments, for the sake of legal entertainment, let's look at how a class-action legal challenge from some 3,000 private prep school owners would fare at the Strasbourg human rights court.

Based on case law at the ECtHR, one can predict fairly easily which way the court will lean on the prep school ban in Turkey. For one, the closure of perfectly legal and legitimate businesses amounts to an interference with the right to the peaceful enjoyment of possessions guaranteed by Article 1 of Protocol No. 1 of the European Convention on Human Rights (ECHR). The convention says that "every natural or legal person is entitled to the peaceful enjoyment of his possessions. No one shall be deprived of his possessions except in the public interest and subject to the conditions provided for by law and by the general principles of international law."

Second, in the court's assessment, any interference with the peaceful enjoyment of possessions should be lawful. Simply legislating the ban by Parliament does not meet the criteria of lawfulness for such interference. Since the prep schools' owners will be deprived of their businesses and properties, I do not think that claiming the existence of the law will satisfy the court. ECtHR precedents state that the legal basis must have a certain quality—namely, it must be compatible with the rule of law and must provide guarantees against arbitrariness. Closing down perfectly legitimate businesses and halting their operations abruptly qualifies as an arbitrary step by the Turkish government. Case law also underlines that the legal norms used by the government should be sufficiently "accessible, precise and foreseeable" in their application. In the prep school controversy, there was no guarantee for owners who would have not signed long-term leases or bought properties otherwise. The principle of foreseeability affords a measure of protection against arbitrary interference by public authorities.

Third, the ban must be justified in terms of "general interest," which is lacking in the prep school controversy, too. The European court can accept the public benefit argument if the prep school issue involves public funds and is related to social justice. These are privately funded schools, and students enroll in these institutions voluntarily. Actually, the ban will make the education problems worse in Turkey. Millions of parents in Turkey are worried that they will have no outlet to educate and train their kids for highly competitive and state-administered exams once the prep schools are banned. They have to hire private tutors, which cost more, or they have to rely on the failing public education system. Education specialists say the ban will have a more drastic effect on lower and middle income families, dealing a blow to the general interest principle in case law of the ECtHR.

The Strasbourg court will also look at the ban from the point of view of whether the government measure is proportionate to the aim pursued. Even though the court recognizes that states enjoy wide latitude with regard both to choosing the means of enforcement and to ascertaining whether the consequences of enforcement are justified in the general interest, there is a clear arbitrariness that infringes upon the principle of proportionality in the current case of the prep schools. The broad and blanket ban will have a negative impact on the acquired rights of legitimate businesses. If the aim is to establish equal opportunities for students, then banning private prep schools is not the way to accomplish that goal. Perhaps subsidizing students who can't afford prep schools makes more sense, rather than punishing privately funded prep schools for the troubles in public education.

The ban will also give rise to compensation claims by the prep schools for loss of revenue, severance payments for staff, loss of income on immovable properties, and interest accrued over years until the case is settled in court. Because Article 41 of the ECHR stipulates that when there is a judgment in which the court finds a violation, the defendant state has a legal obligation to put an end to the violation and make reparations for its consequences to restore, as far as possible, the situation existing before the violation. Considering that the prep schools represent some TL 3 billion (roughly $1.5 billion) worth of economic activity annually, this means the Turkish government may be compelled to pay some $15 billion plus interest in pecuniary damages if the case settles 10 years from now.

There may be other articles in the convention, such as the right to education (Article 2 of Protocol 1), the right to respect for private and family life (Article 8), non-discrimination (Article 14), and the right to freedom of expression (Article 10) inter alia that prep school owners can invoke when contesting the government ban. But, as I said, Erdoğan has no interest in sorting out this matter from a legal point of view, let alone economic and social perspectives. What a pity.

Erdoğan Is His Own Worst Enemy[27]

The real challenge to the legacy of Prime Minister Recep Tayyip Erdoğan in the Turkish political landscape now comes from Erdoğan himself, as he has been rapidly moving from a progressive stand through which he was able to appeal to a broad-based electorate to an authoritarian conservative platform which is dominated by political Islam. A growing disillusionment among Turks, something the weak opposition parties have failed to capitalize on, is now being fed by the leader of ruling Justice and Development Party (AKP) himself, albeit unconsciously and inadvertently. As Erdoğan tries to unload what he considers excess baggage en route to an ultimate consolidation of his power, he has started making a series of mistakes that may prove to be difficult to recover from.

For one, he lost his reformist and progressive appeal when he introduced an Islamist agenda on both domestic and foreign policy choices. At home, he has strengthened the anti-Erdoğan opposition camp by alienating more groups, including liberals and moderate conservatives. Turks are no longer buying into sugarcoated legislative reforms embed-

---

[27] First appeared in *Today's Zaman* daily on Dec. 09, 2013

ded in an actually regressive and hidden policy agenda. Rigging the fourth judicial reform package, which was supposed to align Turkish legislation with the judgments of the European Court of Human Rights (ECtHR), with a last-minute amendment before summer that actually reduced sentences for those who squandered taxpayers' money in public contracts, was a recent example, passed in order to save political cronies. Now Erdoğan offers harsher penalties for those who exercise the right to freedom of assembly, in what was ostensibly a democratization package the government forwarded to Parliament last week. I suppose the proverbial saying of "Fool me once, shame on you; fool me twice, shame on me" is in order in the eyes of voters.

Abroad, foreign policy choices along ideological lines have contributed to the near-isolation of Turkey, both in the Middle East and North Africa region and beyond. Although Foreign Minister Ahmet Davutoğlu dismisses criticism flat out by highlighting the frequent flyer miles he has clocked, the meetings he has held and the number of Turkish embassies around the globe, the bitter fact is that Turkey has been sidelined on many issues in its own region, to say nothing of in world affairs. Erdoğan vows that the world will eventually agree with the Turkish view on Syria and Egypt, two countries with which Ankara cut off ties. The efforts to pick up the broken pieces on the foreign policy front by trying to repair relations with Iraq and finally agreeing to the EU's position on the readmission agreement after dragging its feet are testament to a failed foreign policy. That is why Erdoğan scrambled Davutoğlu and his diplomats to fix the picture on the eve of the election period in Turkey.

Erdoğan's democratic credentials at home were dealt severe blows in just four weeks alone when he attempted to shut down privately funded popular prep schools that train and educate schoolchildren by offering supplementary courses for highly competitive state-administered exams. The move—which was seen by many as an assault on the right to free enterprise and the right to education—to forcefully close some 4,000 prep schools sparked outrage among millions of parents. It turned out the government did not even calculate the economic costs, let alone the legal and social challenges emanating from such a closure. It was Erdoğan himself who pushed the agenda with a small cadre of his advisors and now the plan has blown up in his face, as even Cabinet members and AKP deputies have started to question the wisdom of such a drastic ban. Erdoğan had to take a step back and has shelved the idea for the time being. He ended up with his reputation greatly damaged.

Then came the massive profiling revelations when the liberal daily *Taraf* published confidential National Security Council (MGK) documents, dated 2004, where Erdoğan and his minister signed on to a plan to crack down on faith-based groups in the country, including the powerful Hizmet Movement inspired by Islamic scholar Fethullah Gülen. The daily continued publishing more documents indicating that the profiling and blacklisting of people and diverse groups, from Alevis to Christian missionaries, went on even in 2013. The government admitted the authenticity of the documents but denied it ever acted upon them. That turned out be false when the daily published articles detailing how people profiled by the government were denied public service or shifted to low-key positions. As a last resort, Erdoğan turned to intimidation tactics, just as meddlesome generals in this country once used to do, by launching criminal and civil lawsuits against the paper and its investigative reporters who uncovered the government's dirty laundry. That followed with financial threats as auditors from the revenue administration started to show up at businesses.

This was the second big mistake Erdoğan committed in a month. He could have easily come clean by offering a simple apology to the public for the profiling programs that victimized people and violated their constitutional right to privacy. Instead of cutting his losses and allowing an independent judiciary to investigate the culprits behind the profiling, Erdoğan decided to fight back using, and perhaps abusing, state powers. Perhaps his administration was up to its neck in profiling dirt. As Erdoğan got angrier in his public speeches, he crossed the fine line of separation of powers between the executive and judiciary. He called on the judiciary to intervene and punish those who publish scandalous government documents. He even said if the judiciary remains idle and does nothing, it would violate the constitution. *Taraf* fired back at Erdoğan, accusing him of violating constitutionally protected rights such as the right to privacy and the right to free speech.

Where do we go from here? I think Erdoğan is fighting a losing public battle. Turks historically and traditionally feel great sympathy towards victimized groups and very much despise condescending, uncompromising, and overbearing leadership. That was the key point once-powerful generals overlooked for years before realizing that it was too late to make changes. Second, this is not a fight for sharing power between Erdoğan and Gülen, as government people tried to portray it. It is much more than that. Erdoğan, the strongman of Turkey, wants to railroad any and every opposition that comes in his way so that he can create a new Turkey in his own image. These opponents may be generals yesterday, liberals, and conservative groups, including Gülen, today, and President Abdullah Gül loyalists tomorrow. As Erdoğan tries to impose values of his own orthodox version of political Islam on Turkish society, he will keep clashing with many diverse groups that may disagree with his vision of Turkey.

Is this sustainable, though? Hardly. In a very vibrant and dynamic society like Turkey, which boasts a young population, Erdoğan's push will trigger stronger push-backs, eventually trapping him in his own corner. The polarization of Turkish society may become unbearable, and Erdoğan is risking a big backlash from the public by forcing his own agenda. The business community is not comfortable with the foreign policy choices of the Erdoğan government because they are losing market share and opportunities. Considering that the economic outlook has not looked so gloomy during election periods, the AKP may not be able to ride out the stormy impact of global economic changes as easily as it once thought. That is why Erdoğan kept slamming what he describes as the interest lobby, because roll-over debts on credit cards have snowballed to the point that people feel squeezed as they are trying to make ends meet under the burden of consumer debts, including car loans and mortgages.

What card is left for Erdoğan to play? As he has proven himself to no longer be so keen on building coalitions, I believe the Turkish prime minister decided to fight back with the way he knows best: Creating a villain dressed up with all kinds of crazy conspiracy theories. Erdoğan will attack his opponents by floating ideas, such as the one that the world

Jewish lobby and imperialist powers are after him and his government. He did so during the May-June Gezi Park incidents by claiming that an interest lobby was behind the anti-government protests, perhaps an implicit reference to the Jewish lobby. When he was pressured on Egypt, where his government has burned all bridges with the interim government backed by the military after Mohammed Morsi's ouster by a coup, Erdoğan said Israel was behind it and had evidence to back that claim up. It turned out he was referring to a YouTube video where French intellectual Bernard-Henri Lévy, who is Jewish, made some comments two years ago in a panel discussion at Tel Aviv University. Similar attacks against the Hizmet Movement and Mr. Gülen by hired guns in pro-government media lately are also part of the same pattern.

I suppose we will see an aggressive campaign period in Turkey where conspiracy theories sell easily and serve as a convenient tool for politicians to distract the public from real and substantive issues. As the elections get nearer, Erdoğan will turn up the volume on his Chavez-style rhetoric.

Girls' Education Hampered[28]

Adalet Binici, a 14-year-old Kurdish girl in eighth grade, became the champion in last year's Level Determination Examination (SBS), a high school placement test administered by the Turkish government to over a million students nationwide, thanks to the supplementary education and training provided by a prep school run by the Hizmet Movement, which is inspired by education-savvy Islamic scholar Fethullah Gülen. Coming from a poor family of seven, Ms. Binici did not even have her own room to study in, so she spent most of her after-school time at the prep school studying and preparing for this very competitive exam.

Her province, located in southeastern Turkey at the Iraqi and Syrian borders, is perhaps the most impoverished part of Turkey, yet she achieved the opportunity to enroll in any top high school of her choosing in Turkey, thanks to Hizmet volunteers' educational investment in this predominantly Kurdish province.

---

[28] First appeared in *Today's Zaman* daily on Apr. 18, 2014

Terrorized by the Marxist-Leninist armed group called the Kurdistan Workers' Party (PKK), the residents of the province had not had much cause for hope for decades and had to rely mostly on social assistance because border trade, livestock breeding and crop farming did not bring much income. Government employees, be it doctors or teachers, always saw the province as a place of exile and rushed to flee from there at the first opportunity, despite additional payroll incentives.

It was under these challenging conditions that members of Hizmet volunteered to go to the province to educate and train Kurdish children. That was the hope that became reality with many bright students like Ms. Binici getting the educational opportunity to be able to compete with students in the western part of the country.

The proven record of Hizmet-affiliated educational institutions successful performance over the years is not limited to the southeast, of course. The champion of the year 2014's Transition to Higher Education Exam (YGS), a national university entrance examination run by the government, Oğuz Türkyılmaz, who prepared for the exam with the Hizmet-affiliated FEM University Preparation School in Malatya, said he owes most of his success to his prep school teachers. There are numerous other examples of similar success stories and the Turkish media has reported extensively on their achievements over years.

Now Turkey's divisive Prime Minister, Recep Tayyip Erdoğan, who loathes Hizmet's Sufi-oriented Islamic perspective and sees it as a direct challenge to his political Islamist ideology, pushed a bill through Parliament earlier in year 2014 to have these prep schools shut down by 2015. By doing so, his government, dominated by Islamist zealots, has dealt a big blow to women's empowerment in Turkey, especially in less developed regions where public schools have been failing terribly. The only successful outlet that provided educational opportunities for this mostly conservative part of society has, for some time, been Hizmet-run educational institutions, be it the prep schools, study halls, or private colleges.

After the prep schools, Erdoğan has now begun to clamp down on private schools as well; an army of inspectors has been sent out to harass students, parents, and school administrators at Hizmet schools as part of the government-backed intimidation campaign. The relentless, hateful campaign Erdoğan has sustained for the last five months—a frontal assault on these educational institutions—will take a particularly big toll on girls' education and undercut the long effort to empower women in Turkey. Many families who send their daughters to Hizmet-run educational outlets are conservative and many maintain strong traditional values. They take great comfort in knowing that these educational institutions are trustworthy, dependable, and observe the family and social values seen in predominantly conservative Turkish society. Erdoğan is taking this option away from these families.

Given that subjects such as female illiteracy, better access to quality education and employment, and violence against women are major issues in Turkey, cracking down on Hizmet schools—which are all run privately with funds raised by volunteers and do not cost taxpayers in Turkey a dime—is certainly a counterproductive campaign to empower women. Perhaps that is what the political Islamists running the government want to see in this country and perhaps they have no interest whatsoever in seeing women empowered. Undoubtedly, education is a key to addressing important matters such as the low participation rate of women in the labor force, violence against women, underage marriage, the underrepresentation of women in politics, economic life and government, and many other challenges.

Take the problem of violence against women in Turkey, for instance. When questioned, Erdoğan's apologists list a number of legislative measures adopted by the government to curtail violence against women—training programs for officials in law enforcement conducted by the Ministry of the Interior, action plans adopted by the Ministry for Family Affairs and Social Policy, and ratifying international conventions—as evidence of the government's commitment to combatting violence against women. Yet it has been a lackluster performance, because the government did not seize upon these new legal and regulatory instruments to build substantive educational initiatives to improve the position of women. According to a Human Rights Watch study done in May 2011, 42 percent of women over 15 years of age and 47 percent of female rural residents have undergone physical or sexual violence at the hands of their spouse or partner at least once in their lives.

Turkey cannot resolve these issues without addressing the root of the problem, which is limited access to quality education for women. Focusing too much on punitive measures will not produce the intended results, as the European Court of Human Rights (ECtHR) concluded in its judgment in the Opuz v. Turkey case in September 2009. The court criticized Turkey for a lack of diligence on the part of the authorities to take action against the perpetrator of domestic violence in the case as well as an overall insufficient commitment to taking appropriate action to address the problem of domestic violence.

Another dire picture can be seen in politics. The Erdoğan government also failed to narrow gender inequality in governance. His party has only 45 female deputies among 313, corresponding to merely 14.4 percent of the ruling Justice and Development Party (AKP) parliamentary group. In local government, less than 1 percent of mayors have been women and that did not change in the last election on March 30. In the Cabinet, there is only one female minister. What is more, Erdoğan's close advisors are all men, with the exception of his daughter.

The economic picture is not so different. Women's participation in the labor market was 30.5 percent in 2011 as opposed to 63 percent in the European Union. The main reason for this low rate is a lack of education. Female illiteracy continues to be major obstacle to women's participation in public life and the business world. According to government estimates, the number of illiterate women in the country is approximately 3 million; most are in the less developed regions of the southeast, where the literacy rate increased by only 10 percent between 2000 and 2010, reaching 70 percent.

The restricted access to education for girls also has social implications. For example, child marriage is a big problem confronting girls in Turkey, where one in three marriages is a child marriage and half of these are between illiterate boys and girls, according to a UN Population Fund (UNFPA) survey in 2012. This research highlights the link between poverty, illiteracy, child brides, and the greater risk of girls being exposed to physical, psychological, and sexual violence. When all these factors are combined, it is not surprising to see that Turkey ranked 120th of 136 countries in the Global Gender Equality Gap Report 2013, which measures economic participation and opportunities, educational outcomes, health and survival, and political capabilities.

Gülen has always advocated for the education of women and advocated for their empowerment, a progressive view that stands in contrast to the views of other Islamic leaders. His ideals were not only given life in Turkey, his homeland, but they also led to the establishment of girls' schools in Afghanistan and other countries where the education of girls has traditionally never been a priority. Now Turkey's number one political Islamist, Prime Minister Erdoğan, threatens to shut down these institutions not only in Turkey but also in other countries where his government has leverage. Erdoğan is lobbying his counterparts to crack down on these schools, the first Turkish leader to do so in republican history.

Erdoğan does not seem to realize it, but the downside of this shameful policy is that he is also sabotaging his own vision of making Turkey one of the top economies in the world. Without an increased contribution to economic life from women as a vehicle for growth, Turkey cannot tap into its full potential and can never be a major economic powerhouse in the world. For that, girls' education must be a priority for his government—and for any government, for that matter.

Chapter 6

Smear Campaign against Gülen

Why Mr. Gülen Was Targeted[29]

The main difference between Islamic scholar Fethullah Gülen and the politician who became Prime Minister, Recep Tayyip Erdoğan, is that the former is vehemently opposed to the use and abuse of Islam as a political ideology and party philosophy, while the latter sees the religion as an instrument to channel votes and to consolidate his ranks among supporters. Whereas Gülen talks first and foremost about building bridges established on basic humanistic values and democratic principles as part of interfaith and intercultural dialogue efforts, Erdoğan has only been interested in building his leadership around a political Islamist ideology with which he thinks he can appeal to conservative Muslims, not only in the Turkish streets but in the former territories of the Ottoman state.

Gülen talks about education as the most important institution needed to establish a society through which most of the world's problems and malaise can be resolved, ranging from low schooling for girls to insufficient transparency and accountability in governance, and from substance abuse among young people to soaring crime rates and fanaticism/terrorism. He believes that if family values centered on a strong character in individuals can be promoted through education, then this will have a trickle-down impact on neighborhoods, towns, cities, nations, and even the world. That is how he aspires to help contribute to world

---

29   First appeared in *Today's Zaman* daily on Dec. 30, 2013

peace, albeit in his humble ways from self-imposed exile in a small retreat in the Pocono Mountains of Pennsylvania.

On the other hand, Erdoğan's way represents a top-down imposition of Islamist values that are distinctly separate from the mainstream Sufi orientation in the predominantly Sunni population of Turkey. He wants people to show off their religiosity and to help state powers make it more visible, as opposed to Sufism's mystic and inner-oriented, soul-searching character. Erdoğan's authoritarian tendency is only equaled by the now-defunct, repressive, military-backed Kemalist attitude that had an oppressive, stigmatizing impact on much of the history of the republic. Just as the hard-core secularists failed to achieve what they sought for years, i.e., establishing a society in their straightjacket image, Erdoğan's Islamist agenda is doomed as well, given the strong, vibrant civil society, affluent middle class, and very dynamic young population in Turkey. That, though, does not mean that Erdoğan's style of governance will wither away without leaving scars on Turkish democracy, just as the meddlesome generals did in the past.

The recent corruption scandals that have rattled and perhaps even threatened Erdoğan's rule were wrongly perceived as a fight for power between Erdoğan and Gülen. For one thing, Gülen, a 75-year-old cleric, has never been interested in politics in his life and has publicly refused to engage in it. He is not seeking to govern the country and never will. Based on issues, he has supported candidates and parties that he believed might benefit the nation. On the eve of the public referendum in 2010 that brought further freedoms and rights with the constitutional overhaul, he said that he would have applauded the main opposition or junior opposition parties as well, if it had been they who brought such reforms that benefited the people of Turkey.

The fact that he has never committed himself blindly to a single party platform put Gülen in an independent position to criticize Erdoğan's ruling Justice and Development Party (AKP) government when warranted. For example, regarding the 2010 flotilla incident where a humanitarian aid convoy en route to Gaza was attacked by Israeli commandos who killed eight Turkish civilians and one Turkish-American, he said that the organizers' failure to seek accord with Israel before attempting to deliver aid "is a sign of defying authority and will not lead to fruit-ful matters." Erdoğan, whose government allowed the ship to sail with-out any protection or assurances from the Israeli side, seized on this tragedy to mobilize people around his Islamist agenda in Turkey and ratcheted up his anti-Israeli rhetoric. Gülen, on the other hand, saw this as dynamite blown up under the bridge of a religious interfaith cam-paign. His focus was more on the substance of easing the plight of the Palestinians and making their daily lives better, rather than exploiting the sensitive issue with mere symbolism.

The difference between Gülen and Erdoğan emerges in other for-eign policy areas as well. The EU membership process seems to be a tac-tical rather than a strategic choice for Erdoğan, who used the accession talks as leverage against the once-powerful military and later dropped the agenda after he had pushed them to their barracks. The fact that Erdoğan is now trying to roll back some of the accomplishments Tur-key has achieved in areas like the judiciary and fundamental rights and freedoms is a strong indication that he does not really have his heart set on advancing Turkish democracy with strong checks and balances. Gülen, on the other hand, has been supportive of the EU process, even during the 1990s when Erdoğan was publicly bashing the EU and call-ing it a "community of Christian Catholic countries." (As strange as it sounds, that is what he said in a YouTube video dated March 1990.) Gülen, however, has always seen the EU process as an opportunity to give substance to his interfaith and cultural dialogue efforts and has sincerely endorsed the idea from the beginning.

There are of course various reasons why Erdoğan has now started attacking Gülen, an intellectual and scholar who is neither a political figure nor a religious leader seeking a revolution in Turkey. Faced with massive corruption investigations that implicate people in his govern-ment with criminal charges, Erdoğan is trying to make a villain out of Gülen and make him the scapegoat of government problems so that he can distract the public from the fallout of the damaging revelations. He did this during the Gezi Park protests also, when he floated the murky idea of an "interest lobby" acting with international powers and media groups. Since Gülen has always been highly sensitive about combating corruption in Turkish society and has harshly criticized people who have squandered taxpayers' money, he came out strongly against Erdoğan in the face of hard evidence exposing a major graft network. Erdoğan targets Gülen with smear campaigns in public rallies to silence him and his followers while at the same time trying to derail investigations with a purge of police officers and prosecutors.

Not surprisingly, Gülen is not the only one in a long line-up of suspects, a list that includes the main opposition Republican Peoples' Party (CHP) and the junior opposition party, the Nationalist Movement Party (MHP). Both of them are public enemies, according to Erdoğan, who has openly described them as being involved in "treachery" against the Turkish nation. Turkish media outlets who run critical stories of government corruption scandals are also traitors. Business groups like the Turkish Industrialists and Businessmen's Association (TÜSİAD), the club of the wealthiest businesspeople, and the Turkish Confederation of Businessmen and Industrialists (TUSKON), the largest trade advocacy group, are also on the same list. By the definition of his ideology, the list goes on to include unions, leftist groups, Kurds, Alevis and even football fans who chant against the government during a match. Hence, this is not a fight between Erdoğan and Gülen, but rather Erdoğan's war with every group that is critical of his government on corruption and other issues. Erdoğan wants total subordination and commands loyalty with no questions asked, as an outgoing former Cabinet minister bluntly described it.

As for the claim of infiltration of the police department and the judiciary by Gülen sympathizers, this is an old argument in Turkey that has been trotted out time and again with no evidence to back it up. The junta-dominated military pursued these allegations against Gülen in the Turkish courts with frivolous lawsuits and they all resulted in Gülen's acquittal. Erdoğan leveling similar accusations against Gülen now is just another attempt to shift the blame and turn the focus elsewhere. If Erdoğan has any evidence of wrongdoing, he should have settled it in a court of law, which seems quite unlikely. Just like the use of terms like "interest lobby" or "chaos lobby," Erdoğan plays to the gallery by raising the specter of "gangs" within the state, a veiled reference to

Gülen sympathizers. It is, of course, very natural for people who like Gülen's ideas to work in public agencies as full-fledged citizens of this country, based on their merits and not because of ideology, value, or personal preferences. As long as they act within the laws and regulations, they should not be profiled or targeted, as President Abdullah Gül said last week when he commented on the corruption investigation.

Since the Turkish state has always been authoritarian and not allowed any religious or non-religious orders to officially exist in Turkey apart from the state's Religious Affairs Directorate, faith-based groups were forced to operate in a gray area. This included Alevis, religious orders, and many other diverse groups that make up the vibrant whole of Turkish society. This was not unique to Muslims, of course. Even non-Muslims who were officially recognized in the Treaty of Lausanne of 1923 have had great difficulties in Turkey due to a major democratic deficit in governance. When most Turks, including the government, were looking at non-Muslim minorities with suspicions of subversive activity in 1990s, Gülen was reaching out to the ecumenical patriarch and Jewish rabbis in a bid to promote understanding. Hence, the claims of a lack of transparency leveled at Hizmet today are part of the larger problem in Turkey, a country with a notorious past of profiling its citizens based on their beliefs, race, and ethnicity. Even now, we have learned from recent media leaks that the Erdoğan government has maintained massive profiling schemes on citizens, including those in the Hizmet Movement.

In a nutshell, Erdoğan's creeping Islamist agenda, with a heavy focus on symbols rather than substance, has started threatening the very fabric of Turkey's variegated social structure. The richness of diverse views and perspectives is an important asset that makes Turkey perhaps one of the rising stars of its neighborhood. It offers a good and workable model in which Islam and democracy can function, despite all its current shortcomings. However, dressing down Turkish society with an Iranian mullah-type domineering agenda of political Islam will sabotage the future of Turkey and all others who have pinned their hopes on Turkey. We have never seen, for example, young people wearing shrouds in public and chanting "Jihadist Erdoğan" at government-endorsed rallies before. This is very troubling in a country with a young population that might be easily pushed to radicalization if left unchecked.

Since Erdoğan is playing with fire in Turkey and pushing the country off the cliff with symbolism and adventurism, perhaps Gülen felt compelled to take a stand to protect the very values he has been advocating his entire life.

Gülen's Defense[30]

In April 2011, I asked the main opposition leader Kemal Kılıçdaroğlu about what he thought of the slanderous remarks uttered by his deputy İsa Gök. Gök had targeted Islamic scholar Fethullah Gülen while at the speaker's podium in Parliament. Without hesitation, Kılıçdaroğlu criticized Gök's remarks, saying Parliament is a platform to criticize the actions of the government. "Targeting non-political people in Parliament is wrong and unacceptable," he said, asking his deputies to refrain from criticizing people without any solid evidence. Let's contrast that with Prime Minister Recep Tayyip Erdoğan's unrelenting attacks against Gülen since the corruption investigation of Dec. 17, 2013, which implicated the Prime Minister, his family, his ministers, and businessmen close to his government.

In an effort to find a scapegoat for the colossal wrongdoings in government—including graft, money laundering, re-zoning land, and influence peddling allegedly committed, according to the opposition, with the full knowledge and consent of Erdoğan—the Turkish prime minister has staged an unprecedented onslaught against Gülen with all kinds of name calling. He has accused Gülen of plotting a coup against his government without offering a single shred of evidence. Gülen, who inspired a worldwide, faith-inspired civic movement called Hizmet (service), is not a political figure. He has expressed time and again that he is not interested in entering politics, especially at his advanced age. Yet the politician that is Erdoğan keeps insulting a man who has tried to remain apolitical his entire life, a man who has not shied away from taking strong positions on democratic principles and respect for the rule of

---

[30] First appeared in *Today's Zaman* daily on Feb. 10, 2014

law and fundamental rights. Now, he is being forced by Erdoğan to defend himself and the Hizmet Movement he has inspired.

I think the president of the US-based Freedom House, David J. Kramer, hit the nail on the head when he described the increased harshness of Erdoğan's verbal assault on Gülen as part of a pattern long pursued by the ruling Justice and Development Party (AKP) government in discrediting opponents. "The current rhetorical attack on TÜSİAD [the Turkish Industrialists and Businessmen's Association], local and international media and the Hizmet Movement (which is also known popularly as the Gülen Movement in the West) are part of a pattern of demonization and intimidation of opponents that has been going on for years," Kramer told *Today's Zaman* in an interview on the eve of the release of a damning report about freedom of press woes in Turkey. "What is new is that the attacks have gotten harsher and that the Gülen movement is now also a target," he added. Erdoğan repeated his line of offense on Sunday at a public rally as well, lumping TÜSİAD, the opposition parties, the media, and Gülen all together in the same basket as traitors and domestic collaborators for global power circles.

Gülen does not have a political platform from which to defend himself, nor does he have a seat in Parliament. He chose to respond to Erdoğan's slanderous accusations the same way he has been fighting similar claims in the past: in the courtroom, where his lawyers launched civil slander cases and defamation proceedings to protect Gülen's reputation and honor as part of his right to a private life. In Feb. 2014, Gülen filed a defamation suit against the prime minister for remarks Erdoğan made about him in recent speeches, which Gülen's lawyer says is full of derogatory and inappropriate comments. Gülen's lawyer, Nurullah Albayrak, said Erdoğan crossed the line in terms of freedom of expression and that the prime minister excessively and harshly insulted the Islamic scholar. Gülen is demanding TL 100,000 in damages for the denigrating remarks.

Gülen's legal challenges will most likely succeed in Turkish courts as he has successfully won many cases in the past. He has never had to go to the Strasbourg-based rights court, the European Court of Human Rights (ECtHR), because even a criminal case against him launched by the military-backed judiciary failed to produce a conviction in Turkish courts. He has been cleared of all charges leveled against him, and the appeals court upheld the lower court's judgment.

However, in the likelihood he has to go the ECtHR, he has a very good chance of winning as well. In many cases, the ECtHR has opted for protection of someone's reputation against freedom of expression. For example, in a 2009 judgment that the ECtHR delivered in the case of A. v. Norway, the court voted for the right of the applicant to have his honor, reputation, and privacy protected under Article 8 of the European Convention on Human Rights (ECHR) against safeguarding the freedom of expression, which is protected under Article 10. In order for Article 8 to come into play, "the attack on personal honor and reputation must attain a certain level of gravity and be in a manner causing prejudice to personal enjoyment of the right to respect for private life." Erdoğan's slanderous remarks against Gülen, made without openly naming him, include referring to him as a "traitor," "hollow preacher," "virus," "false prophet," "hashashin"—a member of a medieval order that spread political influence through assassinations—and others. I suppose these qualify as being grave.

Gülen and Erdoğan are not on an equal footing to face off on defamation charges. According to ECtHR case law, the status of the person against whom remarks have been made is also an important factor in deciding whether criticism amounts to freedom of expression or defamation. The court upholds the general principle that the limits of acceptable criticisms are wider in regards to a politician acting as a public personality compared to a private individual because the former "inevitably and knowingly lays himself or herself open to close scrutiny of his or her every word and deed, in particular by a political adversary," according to the court's case law. The court also tends to favor claims on the right to privacy when there is no factual basis to support the other side. In this case, Erdoğan has not presented a single piece of evidence indicating any wrongdoing on the part of Gülen.

Unlike Gülen, who is a private citizen, Erdoğan enjoys broad parliamentary immunities that protect him from criminal proceedings. According to Article 83 of the Turkish Constitution, a member of Parliament who is alleged to have committed an offense before or after elections cannot be arrested, questioned, detained, or tried unless Parliament waives his or her immunity. The criminal proceedings against a deputy are suspended until he or she ceases to be a member of Parliament, but the statute of limitations does not include their time in office. Erdoğan has faced several criminal complaints already. Graft prosecutor Zekeriya Öz, who was later removed, filed a lawsuit against the prime minister for launching a defamation campaign, making slanderous remarks, and directing false accusations at him to discredit him in the eyes of the public. Last month, a number of lawyers and law associations filed a criminal complaint against the prime minister, alleging that he has made attempts to influence the judicial process in relation to the corruption scandal.

Erdoğan's frontal assault on the Hizmet Movement also violates the state's obligation to ensure that those who are part of Hizmet enjoy their right to freedom of thought, conscience, and religion. If Erdoğan's criticisms amount to hate speech, the state has an obligation to fight against these stereotypes, especially when they are spread in the media. Let alone fighting with stereotypes, Erdoğan is encouraging people to go after Hizmet members and has directed his aides to disseminate all kinds of fabricated articles in the pro-government media. Erdoğan's policy of purging public officials who sympathize with the Hizmet Movement and his hateful speeches targeting Gülen follow a familiar pattern of policies that are usually adopted by authoritarian governments that display hostility toward religious groups, fail to address intolerance, and support institutionalized bias and discrimination against religious groups.

As such, Erdoğan is violating Article 9 of the ECHR, which states, "Everyone has the right to freedom of thought, conscience and religion; this right includes freedom to change his religion or belief and freedom, either alone or in community with others and in public or private, to manifest his religion or belief, in worship, teaching, practice and observance." The court has extensive case law on the freedom of religion, as it is a pillar of a democratic society. It emphasized the individual and collective features of freedom of religion while limiting the state's interference into religious communities, underlining that the state should remain neutral and impartial when it comes to religious groups. Erdoğan is infringing on the rights and freedoms of Hizmet members.

This certainly does not mean that Gülen is immune to all kinds of criticism. He is an important figure and, as such, there has been huge interest in his works, speeches, and activities. That is why Gülen openly welcomes scrutiny, advocates transparency, pays attention to criticism, and gives interviews to national and international media. His public record is wide open for anybody to see. The Hizmet Movement has repeatedly and positively responded to calls for greater transparency and supported all democratic reforms in enhancing the rule of law, fundamental rights, transparency, and accountability in the governance of the country.

According to rumors in the Turkish capital, the last straw Erdoğan may pull is orchestrating a lawsuit based on fabricated stories of Hizmet working in collaboration with foreign intelligence agencies. He will use assets of Turkey's National Intelligence Organization (MİT), headed by his confidante Hakan Fidan, to build a frivolous case against people who sympathize with the Hizmet Movement. The spy agency has reportedly been busy producing false documents and asking for the help of foreign intelligence agencies while false witnesses are being arranged in the bureaucracy. With this move, Erdoğan plans to kill two birds with one stone in a baseless lawsuit: First he will discredit the police and prosecutors who exposed the government's dirty laundry in the massive corruption scandal. Second, he will turn Turkish public opinion to his side against an imaginary enemy that he has built overnight.

Will this strategy work? It hardly can against the background of huge and hard evidence piled up against Erdoğan's government by prosecutors in criminal investigations. As the opposition keeps ratcheting up criticism of the government in terms of corruption, with new evidence leaked to the press every day, Erdoğan will be swimming against the tide. Going after the Hizmet Movement, which is respected by millions in Turkey, will only make the situation for Erdoğan worse than it already is on the eve of elections.

Gülen's Contribution to Pluralism[31]

The Hizmet Movement, inspired by Muslim scholar Fethullah Gülen, is a formidable actor in catalyzing change for a better Turkey and will remain so for the foreseeable future as a non-political force to be reckoned with. It does not need to transform itself into a political party to express its views or to influence the political decision-making process, just like a variety of other actors that are not part of the traditional state apparatus or political organizations, such as unions, the media, business advocacy groups, interest and pressure groups, lobbies, and other networks of influence that are commonly seen in modern democracies.

In fact, Hizmet promotes a pluralist democracy in an age of declining public interest in politics and a sharp reduction in citizens' confidence in state institutions, particularly given the beleaguered Prime Minister Recep Tayyip Erdoğan government's suspension of the rule of law. Gülen has taken a strong stand against weakening state institutions and the lack of full transparency and accountability and has fully supported the investigation of the allegations of massive government corruption. It was important for Gülen, representing perhaps the strongest faith-inspired civic movement in Turkey, to speak up at a difficult time, emboldening others to be vocal as well. He has paid for that stance, however, as Erdoğan, who once praised Hizmet but suddenly turned against it in order to hush up the corruption investigation, has attacked him mercilessly with unwarranted smears and slander.

In an effort to cast a shadow over Hizmet, Erdoğan called on Gülen to establish a political party, as if only political parties have a right to voice criticism of the government. Gülen was not an exception, of course, as Erdoğan also called on critical members of the media, business groups, bar associations and others to start a political party when they expressed their frustration with the policies and rhetoric of Erdoğan. The prime minister does not seem to understand that various non-political and extra-institutional actors may exist in a democracy and may exert influence on the decision-making process in the legislature and government. It is actually desirable in advanced democracies to have diverse pres-

---

[31] First appeared in *Today's Zaman* daily on Mar. 17, 2014

sure and interest groups. They are hailed by the UN, the EU, the Council of Europe (CoE), and other international organizations as an indication of a healthy pluralistic democracy.

For three months, Gülen has not responded to the verbal assaults and threats made by Erdoğan, who made him a focus of the election campaign and is giving more airtime to Hizmet than any political opponent. Erdoğan has worn himself out with flurries of fast punches that connect with nothing but air. He got his facts completely wrong in the talking points he has raised in campaign speeches and he has made a fool of himself. He is cornered, on the ropes, and is lashing out in an attempt to regain his footing. Leaders of the opposition parties quickly tapped into the real facts and have used the visible fear, anger, and frustration Erdoğan feels, hammering Erdoğan harder than ever before. When Gülen finally decided to speak to the Turkish media recently in order to respond to Erdoğan's continuous verbal abuse, he was calm, soft, and gentle in his criticism. He kept the moral high ground as he explained what lies at the core of the issues that separate him from Erdoğan.

Addressing the old argument that Hizmet is not transparent, Gülen said that every institution established and run by members of Hizmet is open to public scrutiny and operates in full compliance with the law. "In other words, there is a completely transparent structure in place," he said, lamenting the fact that the volunteers of the Hizmet Movement are depicted as members of a clandestine organization. Gülen is right, because Hizmet-affiliated institutions operate within the law, abide by the relevant rules and regulations, and are subject to rigorous inspections by the appropriate government agencies, including the Finance Ministry, which is vigilant about accounting methods and taxes. Even Prime Minister Erdoğan, who has claimed he will launch a lawsuit against the movement for months, has not been able to produce a single piece of evidence indicating wrongdoing by members of Hizmet. The Journalists and Writers Foundation (GYV), of which Gülen is the honorary chairman, has been calling on the government to start legal procedures if it has reasonable proof, or to otherwise stop demonizing and threatening Hizmet volunteers with hate-filled speeches. The GYV, acting as an official spokesperson for the Hizmet view on issues of interest, is fully accessible to media inquiries, regularly issues press statements, and holds press briefing to inform the public. It is worth mentioning here, too, that the GYV is the first institution from Turkey to earn consultative status with the United Nations Economic and Social Council (ECOSOC) and regularly attends the relevant UN meetings.

It is only natural for some members of Hizmet to hide their affiliation out of fear of discrimination in public employment because the Turkish government has been notorious for its profiling of unsuspecting citizens, including Alevis, leftists, social democrats, nationalists, Kurds, and others. Leaked confidential documents have recently revealed that the Erdoğan government has, in fact, expanded illegal and unconstitutional profiling activity and denied public sector positions to citizens based on ethnicity, religion, or ideology. When Turkey finally becomes a full-fledged democracy where merits matter rather than personal views, color, creed, or ethnicity, then Hizmet members and other vulnerable groups will naturally become more transparent.

The contribution of Hizmet to the development of Turkish democracy by encouraging wider participation in civic and public life, especially in the realms of education, charity, and dialogue efforts, has been highly appreciated. The movement generated an important framework for individuals to come together, to better represent specific interests, and to jointly express and defend their views. For example, the Abant Platform, a signature workshop featuring free debate and organized by Hizmet, has become an important venue for others to speak up, gather support and advocate for their positions. Over the years, the platform has organized workshops to tackle tough issues ranging from the status of Alevis to the grievances of non-Muslims, and from women's empowerment to resolving the Kurdish problem, in order to encourage wider debate in society and to prod the government into adopting reforms to improve their rights.

Hizmet, a volunteer-driven movement, understands that it does not represent the whole society nor does it seek such a mandate or to make such a claim. It simply wants to lead by example. It knows the representation of the movement is limited; that is why it partners with others to address lingering problems in Turkish society with a view that this can be a good experience for others—including the government—to emulate for the advancement of society. For instance, the start of construction of a mosque and a *cemevi* (an Alevi place of worship) sharing a complex in Ankara's Mamak district in September 2103, a project that was jointly undertaken by Hizmet and Alevi groups, represents such an endeavor.

Hizmet also partnered with local businessmen in the southeast of Turkey to open hundreds of courses that provide free supplementary tutoring for Kurdish children in low-income neighborhoods in order to give them a better chance on college entrance exams. Gülen has openly suggested that the government should honor the right of Kurds to be educated in their mother tongue without making ethnic identity a condition for any kind of grand bargain in the course of the settlement process. Hizmet has also been a leading force in pressuring governments to grant rights and recognition denied to non-Muslim minority groups in Turkey, including the opening of the Halki Seminary. Gülen was the first Muslim scholar in the 1990s to reach out to Christian and Jewish minority group leaders and had a series of dialogue meetings with them, despite huge criticism from conservative groups and the government at the time.

Hizmet, just like other advocacy and pressure groups, also enjoys freedom of association and freedom of expression as guaranteed by Articles 10 and 11 of the European Convention on Human Rights (ECHR). In the case law of the Strasbourg-based European Court of Human Rights (ECtHR) that interprets Article 11 on freedom of association, the court has said that while political parties play an essential role in pluralism and democracy, associations "formed for other purposes" are also important. The court explains that "Where a civil society functions in a healthy manner, the participation of citizens in the democratic process is to a large extent achieved through belonging to associations in which they may integrate with each other and pursue common objectives collectively."

Similarly, Article 10, which guarantees the right to receive and impart information and ideas without interference from public authorities, also awards groups like Hizmet protection, to ensure their ability to exist with autonomy from undue interference from the state. It is perfectly legitimate for members of Hizmet to organize and lobby for their interests. At the same time, Hizmet welcomes regulatory legislation and restrictive measures as long as they do not target a specific group unfairly and are proportionate to secure legitimate aims such as public order, security, and preserving an effective democracy. This is the general guideline provided by the ECtHR, as well. That said, Hizmet is well aware of speculation about the internal functioning of the movement and its members' relations with public institutions and officials. This is why it welcomes scrutiny and urges inquiries into its operations. As for relations with the government, Gülen has said time and again that members of Hizmet need to comply with laws, rules, and regulations or face investigations, judicial scrutiny, and disciplinary proceedings.

All in all, Gülen has made a significant contribution to the democratic advancement of Turkey and stepped up to the plate to resolve difficult issues when so many others allowed themselves to be cowed by authoritarian regimes backed by military or civilian governments.

Debunking the Smear Campaign[32]

Acting as prosecutor, judge, and executioner, Turkey's chief political Islamist, Prime Minister Recep Tayyip Erdoğan, has already convicted a well-respected Islamic scholar, Fethullah Gülen, of what he called a civilian coup attempt, a fabricated charge devised by Erdoğan to discredit the vast graft scandal that incriminates him and his associates, including his family members. The beleaguered Prime Minister Erdoğan has publicly declared Gülen—who is critical of the corruption and the lack of transparency and accountability in Erdoğan's government—as his enemy number one without presenting a single shred of evidence to prove Gülen's involvement in clandestine activities against the Turkish government, including orchestrating the graft probe.

Having failed to demonstrate any evidence of guilt, let alone a smoking gun implicating Gülen, the Islamist politician Erdoğan launched a smear campaign to discredit the 76-year-old Islamic scholar, who has

---

[32] First appeared in *Today's Zaman* daily on May 02, 2014

preached the importance of education, science, moderation, dialogue, and outreach activities across religions and cultures throughout his life. Since the Dec. 17, 2013 exposure of the graft investigation, Erdoğan's propaganda machine has been busy disseminating lies, distortions, and insults. Angry over his shattered legacy due to the corruption scandal, Erdoğan has scapegoated Gülen and engaged in hateful rhetoric. He frantically tried to build a perception that there is a strong legal case against Gülen, when, in fact, there is none. Going to the extreme, he even floated the idea of requesting Gülen's extradition from the US, who is facing no judicial investigation, much less a trial.

Fethullah Gülen, who bears no political or criminal responsibility whatsoever in any illegal activity, is unfortunately the victim of a witch hunt conducted by Erdoğan, who drew a bull's-eye on the back of this Islamic scholar in what the opposition parties describe as part of a deliberate government campaign to shift the public debate away from the corruption scandal. By rehashing old claims about Gülen that were proven to be false in a court of law, perhaps Erdoğan hopes to orchestrate another baseless legal suit against him with fabricated stories and false reporting run in pro-government media. Since Erdoğan is the head of government, with significant powers, his remarks must also be interpreted as a means to pressure the judiciary and negatively influence Gülen's ability to receive a fair trial if such a case ever arises in the future.

Haşim Kılıç, the president of Turkey's top court, the Constitutional Court, lashed out at Erdoğan a week ago for making up claims, such as there being a parallel structure or gangs in the judiciary—veiled references to the Hizmet Movement inspired by Gülen—saying that the government should produce evidence to back up these claims and investigate thoroughly. Otherwise, he implied, Erdoğan needed to shut his mouth, because the hateful discourse and harsh rhetoric the prime minister has adopted has been taking a toll on members of the judiciary in terms of polarization, tension, and divisions. He warned that social harmony is at stake if the executive branch continues to attack the Turkish judiciary.

Erdoğan knows that he has no basis for a legal case against Gülen. A court of law will have to reach an objective, impartial and independent assessment of the facts after examining the credibility of the evidence professionally, in accordance with generally recognized principles of legal interpretation. Since professional courts that comply with the case law of the European Court of Human Rights (ECtHR), whose judgments are binding on Turkey, will not do Erdoğan's dirty work against Gülen, the prime minister needs to find a court that will blatantly disregard the articles of the Turkish Constitution as well as those of the European Convention on Human Rights (ECHR) and thereby violate the protections built into the legal code, both in terms of procedure and substance.

There are no shortages of friendly judges and prosecutors, of course, especially in the lower courts, where young and inexperienced members of the judiciary are willing to pay their dues to the Erdoğan government by initiating baseless lawsuits. One of the audio tapes leaked during the election campaign exposed a phone conversation in which then-Justice Minister Sadullah Ergin was telling Erdoğan how the government had been able to bring some 2,000 partisan hacks into the judiciary. Therefore, orchestrating a frivolous lawsuit against Gülen will not be that difficult. The judicial proceedings will merely be used as a disguise to execute Erdoğan's wishes to sideline opponents that are critical of his government, including Gülen. In other words, Erdoğan aspires to abuse criminal proceedings to penalize dissent and opinions that conflict with his way of governing in Turkey.

Acting more like a bitter politician who has found himself with his back against the wall in a massive corruption scandal rather than a statesman, Erdoğan does not seem to mind that the judiciary is politicized. With his public statements already concluding that Gülen is guilty before even beginning an investigation or a trial, Erdoğan has clearly trampled over the principle of presumption of innocence. During a recent interview, Erdoğan even dressed down a reporter for calling the Hizmet Movement the "Gülen community," insisting that the reporter describe the movement as a "gang." At other times, Erdoğan has even called the movement a terrorist organization. Some ministers have gone even further, suggesting that Gülen should prove his innocence in court. All these statements are clear signals to prosecutors and judges about the desired and expected outcome of any judicial proceedings launched against Gülen.

The Erdoğan government is looking for a court that won't bother with independence or impartiality and one staffed by young, inexperienced political lackeys. What seems to be a politically orchestrated illegal wiretapping case in Adana, in which a judge ordered the arrest of six police officers last month, may provide some hints as to how the Erdoğan government intends to pursue Gülen. The judge in that case, İbrahim Sağır, is known to be a strong supporter of Prime Minister Erdoğan. The judge's social media posts in which he expressed his close affinity to the prime minister with comments such as, "Those who don't love you [Erdoğan] don't love this nation, either. Because Zionist Israel and its collaborators don't love you," tell the tale. In another post, the judge celebrated the victory of Erdoğan's Justice and Development Party (AKP) in the local elections: "Yes, friends, the real winner is the great Turkish nation. And the loser is Israel, the neocons, and their collaborators here [in Turkey]."

Judge Sağır also expressed his dislike of Islamic scholar Gülen and the Hizmet movement in his Facebook posts. On April 1, the judge wrote: "One day, a young man came and presented a petition to me. I asked him what his petition was about. He said he wanted to change his name. I checked his name. It was Fethullah. I asked the man why he wanted to change his name. He said he doesn't want to share a name with that traitor [referring to Fethullah Gülen]. At first I felt sad. Then I admired the man's sensitivity." The higher court suspended the arrest warrants for the police officers and let them go, citing a lack of sufficient evidence. The move infuriated Erdoğan, who slammed the judge that ordered the release of the officers pending trial and called him a member of the gang in the judiciary affiliated with Gülen.

Gülen is not the only one targeted by Erdoğan. Kemal Kılıçdaroğlu, the leader of the main opposition Republican People's Party (CHP), was summoned by prosecutor Mehmet Demir to testify in a probe after receiving a complaint from Bilal Erdoğan, the son of the prime minister. The subpoena was later canceled, because the CHP leader enjoys parliamentary immunity and cannot be called to testify without the consent of

Parliament. CHP spokesman Haluk Koç described the prosecutor's move as a scheme against the main opposition party and accused the prosecutor of acting under instructions. "Under whose instructions was this plot carried out? [...] Where did this person [the prosecutor] get the courage?" Koç asked in a press conference at Parliament, implying that the prosecutor is connected to the government.

Prosecutor Demir is known for making pro-government remarks in the media. Demir had previously called the Dec. 17 and Dec. 25 graft operations a coup attempt against the ruling AKP. "A government can decide if there is a coup attempt in progress or not. All the events that began after the Dec. 17 graft operation are clear signs that the AKP government is under threat," he commented.

The government also applies a sort of psychological pressure on Gülen. It orchestrated illegal leaks of a telephone conversation purportedly between Gülen and his associates, allegedly recorded by Turkey's National Intelligence Organization (MİT). Gülen's picture gets plastered on front pages with fabricated headline stories in the pro-Erdoğan press every day. Businesspeople sympathetic to Gülen's teachings and ideals have been threatened with audits, license revocations, and permit difficulties. These are all part of well-orchestrated government intimidation campaign that was planned and managed by a small cadre of political hacks, reportedly acting on explicit orders from Erdoğan.

Erdoğan knows that his charges against Gülen are untenable in the high judiciary, the Constitutional Court and in the international arena, including the Strasbourg-based rights court, the ECtHR. He also realizes that Gülen is protected by the "ne bis in idem" rule, which bars prosecutors from initiating legal action on charges for which Gülen has already been acquitted unless there is new evidence, and certainly not as part of a politically motivated campaign. Erdoğan has also been making harassing statements since the corruption case was exposed in a futile attempt to get members of Hizmet to give in. He is just trying to buy time until the presidential and national elections while distracting the public from the corruption scandals.

Chapter 7

Abusing Foreign Policy

Hollow Rhetoric and Empty Promises[33]

S ince corruption in government of an unprecedented magnitude
was exposed on Dec. 17 of last year, Turkey has been on a slippery slope sliding toward anarchy, where the rule of law does
not apply to the political leadership that was implicated in the ongoing
investigations. In panic mode, embattled Prime Minister Recep Tayyip
Erdoğan has reshuffled thousands of public officials, mostly in the police
department and the judiciary, in order to stall the damaging investigations and thwart the emergence of new ones. The notion of the separation of powers and the balance of power, first coined by French political philosopher Charles de Montesquieu and later taken up by German
philosopher Immanuel Kant and entertained by American founding
fathers like James Madison in "The Federalist Papers," is effectively
dead in Turkey.

In Brussels last week, Erdoğan tried to paint a picture where the
judiciary is trying to dominate the executive branch in Turkey. Yet the
EU leaders did not seem to be at all convinced by the story Erdoğan told.
I think Herman Van Rompuy, president of the European Council, made
an excellent summary of what happened in a closed session and what
the EU plans to do next. In the question and answer session with the
press, Van Rompuy, standing next to Erdoğan, said: "We have to deal
with acts and legislative texts. And that is what we're monitoring and
that's what we're giving our opinion on."

---

[33]   First appeared in *Today's Zaman* daily on Jan. 27, 2014

In other words, what Van Rompuy was saying is that the EU won't pay much attention to rhetoric and made-up stories like an international conspiracy, global media campaign, judicial coup, parallel structures, an interest lobby, or war lobbies—words of distraction that Erdoğan has used constantly back at home yet never uttered publicly a single time in Brussels. It is actions and the legislative process that Brussels will look at, and they will measure them against the core principles of the EU in terms of the Copenhagen criteria, which put an emphasis on the rule of law, democracy, human rights and a market economy. Erdoğan has deliberately dealt damaging blows to the relevant institutions designed to preserve these concepts in his efforts to save himself and the government from the lethal effects of the corruption scandals.

Now, let's look at the legislative actions the Erdoğan government has undertaken so far, as Van Rompuy suggested that the EU should and would do, in order to get an understanding of how the rule of law was suspended and democracy degraded in Turkey. First, the controversial bill on the judicial council called the Supreme Board of Judges and Prosecutors (HSYK) will subordinate the whole judiciary to the government—if enacted. Though the bill was frozen temporarily after its first 21 articles were approved on the floor of Parliament, we have not seen the constitutional amendment that was offered as an alternative solution to the bill. Yet Erdoğan's suggestion of turning the HSYK into a highly politicized body with political parties appointing their own loyalists to the council is by no means less damaging to the judiciary than the draft bill itself.

Second, it is obvious that the government is keen to usurp the powers of the judiciary with other legislative moves as well. For one, the restrictions proposed for the Internet in the name of protecting privacy give a broad mandate to the government to shut down websites or remove content without requiring a judge's order. The lengthy and costly review by the judiciary would come afterwards, if anyone decides to contest the government decision. The bill cleared the key commission in Parliament and will soon be sent to the floor for a likely approval. Even before the bill has been enacted, the government has started to shut down websites arbitrarily.

The third legislative effort that gives us a hint of where Erdoğan wants to take the country is the proposed changes to award extraordinary immunity from prosecution to key staff at Turkey's listening post, the Telecommunications Directorate (TİB), which is authorized by law to intercept, monitor, and record communications. Erdoğan's move came six days after he appointed a former spy, Ahmet Cemaleddin Çelik, as president of TİB. Çelik later removed five senior officials leading different departments at TİB as part of the latest round of mass removals in state institutions by Erdoğan's government designed to disrupt investigations. On top of that, Erdoğan is now planning to introduce a review board to examine judges' rulings on wiretap orders that were requested by prosecutors in connection with an ongoing investigation. In other words, Erdoğan will be able to overrule judges' decisions through his people on the board. The government's similar attempt in 2009 failed after the Constitutional Court canceled a provision that "lawful interception activities are inspected by an individual or commission to be authorized by the prime minister."

A fourth legislative proposal that sheds light on Erdoğan's thinking is the draft law on state secrets, which is pending discussion and voting in Parliament. The bill envisions redefining the identification, preservation and disclosure of classified information and documents. It gives a higher board called the Supreme Board of State Secrets (DSÜK), chaired by the prime minister himself, the ultimate authority to define the concept of a state secret and to classify documents accordingly. Those who fail to keep classified state documents secret will be punished severely per the penal code. If state secrets are revealed through the media, the punishment will be increased by half. Hence, Erdoğan will decide what constitutes a state secret in Turkey and if the press reveals a classified document that may indicate the illegal profiling of unsuspecting citizens, for example, as the liberal *Taraf* daily did recently, the reporters who exposed the government's dirty laundry will face the wrath of the state.

A fifth effort was clear in the government's attempt to weaken Turkey's top administrative court, the Council of State, by rattling the internal balance of the court as well as limiting its powers. The ruling party-dominated Justice Commission has already signed off on the 16-article bill and it has been sent to the floor of Parliament. It is expected to pass easily. If passed, the bill will deal a major blow to the right to a fair trial in the Turkish judiciary while significantly weakening individuals' ability to defend their fundamental rights against government encroachment. The bill seeks to eliminate the option to appeal that is currently available to citizens in cases where the court renders a judgment on a request to suspend an executive decision made by the government.

It will pave the way for the government to effectively seize the top administrative court by opening a new chamber in the Council of State and appointing an unprecedented 32 new judges to the court. The bill was brought forward in the wake of a decision by the Council of State last month to cancel an executive order requiring the police and prosecutors to notify their superiors of all investigations, which would have effectively given government officials suspected of wrongdoing advance notice that they were being investigated. The decision struck at the government's efforts to derail the corruption investigations with overnight decrees and purges of police departments and lead prosecutors.

The sixth road marker that may be useful to Van Rompuy is not a legislative act, but rather an arbitrary action of the government to damage the investigative powers of the judiciary by instructing law enforcement officers not to comply with court orders or prosecutors' summons. On several occasions, the police have not complied with court judgments to round up suspects in ongoing cases for questioning, citing incomplete paperwork or procedural deficiencies. In other words, the police have started to exercise the core function of the judicial system which lies in fact-finding and determinations of law. If there are problems in procedure, which is highly unlikely and unprecedented, then the authority to review and correct these problems is the judiciary itself, not law enforcement officers. Since the promotion, investigation and appointments of law enforcement officials are directly controlled by the government, they are being illegally instructed to stand down in the face of orders to execute search, seizure, and arrest warrants.

The seventh sign of arbitrary rule in Turkey was witnessed in the Ministry of Justice, when newly appointed Justice Minister Bekir Bozdağ was slapped with two criminal complaints by prosecutors in İzmir and

Adana for attempting to derail an ongoing judicial investigation with illegal interference. According to the complaints, Bozdağ personally telephoned the chief prosecutors in both cities to halt the investigations that implicated people close to the government and is now facing serious charges for having attempted to unduly influence the judiciary.

Bozdağ, who is also the president of the HSYK, reportedly orchestrated a scheme in the HSYK through the reorganization of chambers and helped reshuffle prosecutors and judges in key investigations. There was no evidentiary basis for the reassignment of these prosecutors and judges and the decision failed to provide judges and prosecutors with basic due process guarantees. It was merely based on the fact that these prosecutors were conducting graft, money-laundering, and al-Qaeda terrorism-related investigations implicating people close to the government. This decision perpetuates and extends the government's improper influence and effective control over the judiciary in Turkey.

I believe all these signs are more than enough to convince Van Rompuy, or anybody else for that matter, of the worrying state of affairs in an EU-candidate country. In a written statement he read out loud during the briefing, Van Rompuy expressed the EU's uneasiness regarding developments in Turkey since Dec. 17. "I stressed that Turkey, as a candidate country, is committed to respect the political criteria of accession, including the application of the rule of law and the separation of powers. It is important not to backtrack on achievements and to assure that the judiciary is able to function without discrimination or preference, in a transparent and impartial manner," he said.

Erdoğan listened to Van Rompuy's remarks; however, he has shown no interest in hearing what was said. Perhaps Turkey is already on the verge of proving Madison's identification of tyranny, which he said was "the accumulation of all powers, legislative, executive and judiciary, in the same hands, whether of one, a few or many, and whether hereditary, self-appointed, or elective, may justly be pronounced the very definition of tyranny."

Saving the Iranian Suspect[34]

It is absolutely appalling to realize how far Iranian clandestine activities have penetrated into Turkish state institutions; they have practically unhindered access to the top political leadership of the country, which is dominated by political Islamists and Iran sympathizers.

Thanks to the vigilance of the Turkish police and due diligence on the part of prosecutors, the massive corruption scandal removed the lid on the extent of Iran's money laundering, sanctions-busting illegal trade, and smuggling activity within Turkey. At the epicenter of this sits a 29-year-old Iranian, Reza Zarrab, who was most likely hired by the Iranian Revolutionary Guards to do dirty bidding on behalf of the mullah regime. He seems to be considered a disposable asset by Iran, which is committed to a new charm offensive, but Turkey seems to hold a different view of Zarrab.

When Zarrab was arrested by the police and later sent to jail pending trial by the court, it was clear that Turkish Prime Minister Recep Tayyip Erdoğan was panicked. The voice recording allegedly between Erdoğan and his son, Bilal, within minutes of sweeping operations launched by prosecutors on Dec.17, 2013, shows that Erdoğan talks about Zarrab with his son as if he is a household name in the family. It made more sense later when pictures of Zarrab emerged while he was posing in the front row protocol order with Erdoğan on one occasion and with members of his family and Cabinet ministers on others. Erdoğan even acknowledged publicly that he knew Zarrab as a philanthropist.

Therefore, saving Zarrab—who knew too much and could very well expose those involved in the money laundering and smuggling network—was of paramount importance to Erdoğan. The government immediately moved to remove prosecutors from the case in order to stall the investigation.

First, the newly appointed Istanbul chief prosecutor, Hadi Salihoğlu, whom the opposition claims made a trip to Ankara just two days before his appointment, allegedly struck a secret deal with the justice minister. As soon as he took over his new post, he removed prosecutors Celal

---

[34] First appeared in *Today's Zaman* daily on Mar. 03, 2014

Kara and Mehmet Yüzgeç from the corruption case that landed Zarrab in jail. It's interesting that Salihoğlu was the prosecutor in the alleged cover-up of a fatal traffic accident in 1998 involving Erdoğan's son, Ahmet Burak Erdoğan, who fled the scene where Turkish classical musician Sevim Tanürek got killed while trying to cross the street. Perhaps his services were needed once again to save Erdoğan's family as well as Zarrab.

The plan has worked. Even though the indictment was already completed by former prosecutors who demanded 37 years of jail time for Zarrab on some 100 counts of bribery, smuggling, and money laundering charges, the new prosecutor, Ekrem Aydıner, assigned to the case by Salihoğlu, said he would disregard the original indictment.

The main opposition Republican People's Party (CHP) raised allegations in Parliament that Aydıner had a bad record. He had been reprimanded and demoted by the judicial council on charges of "influence-peddling" and "dishonorable conduct." The motion filed by the CHP asked whether there was a deal involving his record impugned in exchange for favorable treatment of suspects in the corruption case.

The CHP had been saying for a month that Zarrab would be released soon with a plot orchestrated by the government. That is exactly what happened, and Zarrab was let go last Friday after a friendly judge who turned out to be an Erdoğan fan on his Facebook profile was arranged to hear the lawyer's petition to release him. But before Zarrab was out, Justice Minister Bekir Bozdağ, acting on explicit orders from Erdoğan, reportedly visited Zarrab in prison some time ago where he spent three hours with the Iranian suspect trying to convince him not to speak, assuring him that he would be out soon. According to claims, the whole surveillance network in the prison was shut down when the justice minister paid the visit to Zarrab.

The next step is to clear charges leveled against the Iranian suspect using new amendments to the penal code rushed through Parliament by the ruling Justice and Development Party (AKP). According to the 22-article law, ostensibly the fifth judicial reform package, radical changes were introduced to make wiretapping and the technical follow-up of suspects, as well as police searches at the addresses of suspects, more difficult. "This is a package aimed at acquitting those who are involved in the graft probe," a CHP deputy told Parliament. For example, the law requires the review of all court-sanctioned wiretapping orders while removing Article 220 of the Turkish Penal Code (TCK), which mentions forming an illegal organization to commit a crime, from the list of crimes that can be documented through a wiretapping order, and preventing authorization of warrants for wiretaps on these crimes.

The changes also make it very difficult to obtain a decision to order an asset freeze, requiring a unanimous decision by a panel of judges in high courts as opposed to a single judge, as is the current practice. The prosecutor needs to prove that the assets in question were obtained through criminal activity and s/he needs to obtain a report from government agencies to that effect. In other words, judges will not be able to order an asset freeze without the consent of the government in advance. With the new legislation, anti-money laundering and financing of terror measures were unfortunately weakened significantly by the government that shamefully kept Turkey on the gray list of the Financial Action Task Force (FATF). These changes will likely pave the way for judges to dismiss charges for Zarrab and other suspects in the corruption scandal.

In fact, judge İslam Çiçek, a temporary judge covering for the main judge who is on leave, disclosed how the plan would work when he let Zarrab off the hook on Friday. In his reasoned decision, Çiçek said without supporting evidence of any other kind, the technical surveillance and wiretaps alone cannot be considered evidence by themselves. He was setting the stage to acquit Zarrab. Considering that the government already subordinated the judiciary to the executive branch with recent changes to Turkey's judicial council, the Supreme Board of Judges and Prosecutors (HSYK), it will be very difficult to find a judge to convict Zarrab now.

In the meantime, Erdoğan's government, through newly appointed prosecutors, has started to destroy evidence collected in the course of the investigation. A document revealed to the media in late February has confirmed the claim that three prosecutors from the Istanbul Public Prosecutor's Office ordered the Istanbul Police Department on Jan. 8 to destroy wiretapped recordings that had been carried out by the police. In the document, the prosecutors ordered the police to stop wiretapping and carrying out physical surveillance of suspects based on court orders and to destroy any kind of collected voice recordings and any other evidence regarding the ongoing corruption and bribery investigation that was carried out after Dec. 15. It is clear that Erdoğan is trying to get rid of the damning voice recordings with his son, which were recorded on Dec. 17-18.

Erdoğan, who expressed joy within hours of Zarrab's release by saying that justice was served, must be relieved that the plan to save the Iranian swindler is going like clockwork. It is simply mindboggling to see how the court could release Zarrab, whose Iranian accomplices all fled the country when they learned about the investigation. There was more than enough incriminating evidence to hold him in pre-trial detention. According to the summary of proceedings sent by prosecutors to the Justice Ministry, Zarrab is alleged to have bribed former Economy Minister Zafer Çağlayan with a total of $52 million on 28 different occasions, gave former Interior Minister Muammer Güler a total of $10 million on 10 occasions, and provided former EU Affairs Minister Egemen Bağış with a total of $1.5 million in bribes on three separate occasions. The sons of Çağlayan and Güler, who were released from prison on Friday along with Zarrab, are also accused of receiving bribes from the Iranian businessman.

Zarrab also provided cash to the prime minister's son, Bilal Erdoğan, and the Foundation of Youth and Education in Turkey (TÜRGEV), where he serves as the chairman of the board. The $100 million wired to TÜRGEV's account allegedly originated from Zarrab's front company in Dubai. The voice recordings confirm that Zarrab was talking to TÜRGEV director Salih Koç about his desire to make a "donation" to TÜRGEV. Investigators were able to photograph the alleged money transfer through Zarrab's courier who entered the TÜRGEV building with bags full of cash. Zarrab was also on very friendly terms with the former manager of state lender Halkbank, Süleyman Arslan, who is also a suspect in the corruption case. On a secure line, Arslan explained to Zarrab how he had facilitated financial transactions for him.

Zarrab must have taken out an insurance policy by recording every transaction he had ever made with politicians, businesspeople, and their relatives. In fact, a document that was seized during a police search exposed some of the names who received bribes from Zarrab along with the amount of cash. There may be more incriminating evidence Zarrab must have kept in case things went south.

Zarrab has created a big hole in Turkey's national security by exploiting the vulnerabilities of politicians, Islamists, and Iranian sympathizers. Now the Erdoğan government has adopted a scorched-earth policy to hush up any corruption and save Zarrab to stop him from spilling the beans. Will the patriotic people of this nation in the military, police, intelligence, and judiciary let that slide? Given the strong tradition of the Turkish state over centuries, I would not bet on that.

False Flag Operation[35]

Drawing a lesson from the confrontation over two small and uninhabited islets called Imia/Kardak in the Aegean Sea, which led to a quick escalation in tensions between Turkey and Greece in 1996 and helped to boost then-Prime Minister Tansu Çiller's popularity amid a heightened fever of nationalism, today's embattled Prime Minister Recep Tayyip Erdoğan might have planned a regional provocation to help himself recover from a sharp decline in the polls ahead of local elections that have turned into a critical referendum for his future amid an unprecedented corruption scandal.

There are worrying signs in the Turkish capital that the Erdoğan government has been working on a secret plan to create a crisis in Syria in order to distract public attention away from the corruption allegations while unleashing a nationalistic furor to pick up some points in the election. This would be a sort of false flag operation using downright lies and distortions for the purpose of saving the beleaguered Erdoğan politically. The target, according to rumors circulating in Ankara, would be Jaber Castle—a historic castle considered a territory of Turkey within Syria's borders—a highly sensitive location protected by a contingent of the Turkish army.

---

[35] First appeared in *Today's Zaman* daily on Mar. 21, 2014

According to the Treaty of Ankara, which was signed on Oct. 20, 1921, between the colonial power, France, and the Turkish Parliament, Jaber Castle, which is situated 120 kilometers from the city of Aleppo in Syria and some 25 kilometers from the Turkish border, is considered Turkish territory. Article Nine of the treaty states: "The tomb of Suleiman Shah, the grandfather of the Sultan Osman, founder of the Ottoman Dynasty (the tomb known under the name of Turk Mezarı), situated at Jaber Kalesi [Castle], shall remain, with its appurtenances, the property of Turkey, who may appoint guardians for it and may hoist the Turkish flag there."

This agreement was renewed after Syria gained independence in 1936, and two years later, on May 30, 1938, an outpost was built at the castle for the Turkish army to guard the tomb. A Turkish flag flies over the tomb, and a small garrison of around 25 troops is permanently stationed there. Therefore, any direct or indirect attack on the castle would be viewed as an attack on Turkey's sovereign rights.

Turkey beefed up the security in and around Jaber Castle when the Syrian crisis erupted three years ago and warned the Bashar al-Assad regime not to attack the castle or suffer the consequences. Two Turkish F-16 fighter jets are on standby and ready to be scrambled at a moment's notice to protect the tomb from an attack either from forces of the Syrian regime or extremist groups. Assad, who knows the sensitivity of the location for Turkish people, has stayed away from committing any type of provocation against the castle and does not want to give Erdoğan a boost in public opinion. It does not make any sense for the Syrian government now to revisit that policy, given that the regime has gained the upper hand over the opposition militarily and politically. Neither will Assad jeopardize the international support he has picked up for a political solution to the crisis by an escalation in the tension with Turkey, a NATO member.

Therefore, the provocation must come from a third party, possibly an extremist faction acting as a contractor or triggerman. The rumor has it that Turkish intelligence, under secret orders from the prime minister, may have already contracted an armed faction within Syria to commit sabotage on Jaber Castle in order to create the pretext for a limited military operation into Syria. Last week, clashes between opposition groups the Free Syrian Army (FSA) and the Islamic State of Iraq and the Levant (ISIL) reportedly intensified in the region, raising the specter of such a contingency. The news that the al-Qaeda-affiliated ISIL had taken control of a town near Jaber Castle prompted immediate reactions from Turkish officials.

Foreign Minister Ahmet Davutoğlu said Turkey had the right to take all precautions necessary to protect the tomb following clashes around the shrine. "As of now, there has been no [move on] our soldiers or our land there. But in the event of such a threat, we are ready to take all sorts of precautions," Davutoğlu told reporters in the eastern province of Van on March 14. His remarks stand in sharp contrast to earlier comments he made during a dinner with Turkish dailies' Ankara bureau chiefs in Ankara in July 2012. I remember distinctly how he had pleaded with journalists not to bring up the issue of Jaber Castle in their reports, citing the sensitivity of the issue for the Turkish people.

Now, not only Davutoğlu but also a handful of other Cabinet ministers seem eager to raise that issue publicly, ready to come out with guns blazing. What has changed? Perhaps under the pressure of the massive corruption scandal and looming elections that may indicate a significant drop in support for the governing party, Erdoğan desperately needs a crisis. A day after Davutoğlu's remarks, Defense Minister İsmet Yılmaz escalated the belligerent tone, warning that the world should have no doubts about Turkey's intentions in case of such an attack. Yılmaz said Turkey would treat any attack against Jaber Castle as if the attack had targeted Turkish territory. "Those who take Turkey for an enemy will have no right to live in this region," he vowed.

This possible plot the Erdoğan government might orchestrate involving Jaber Castle in order to distract the Turkish public has prompted concern among the opposition parties. In an interview with the Samanyolu News channel on March 19, main opposition Republican People's Party (CHP) leader Kemal Kılıçdaroğlu called on Chief of General Staff Gen. Necdet Özel "not to embark on the adventure" of a military intervention in Syria to protect the tomb of Süleyman Şah as the March 30 local elections approach.

"He [Erdoğan] could decide to move the army into Syria before the elections. I'd like to address the chief of general staff: Don't send Turkey on an adventure. Especially when there is a suspect prime minister in charge," Kılıçdaroğlu said. He argued that no Syrian group had attacked the tomb, but that "a provocation might happen." He said he had received "some unconfirmed information" and warned that "everyone should be very careful."

The warning from the main opposition leader apparently made the Turkish government uneasy. Responding to Kılıçdaroğlu, Energy Minister Taner Yıldız told reporters on March 20: "The tomb of Süleyman Şah is a special place, which is Turkish land outside of Turkey's borders. There is no difference between the tomb and Ankara or Sinop. The soil on which it is located is Turkish soil. Our armed forces are ensuring its security and protecting it." He then asked: "Does Kılıçdaroğlu or anybody else for that matter want us to be indifferent if there is an attack there? Is he saying, 'Act as if nothing has happened'?"

Surprisingly, the Turkish energy minister elaborated on the scale of an operation, saying that any operation to protect the tomb would be a limited and targeted attack. "I can say clearly that there will be no [operation] if there is not an attack there. But if it is needed to defend our own land, we will do it. An operation in that place may be in question if necessary, but it won't be a wide-scale operation," Yıldız explained.

The increasing chatter on a possible military operation among Cabinet members indicates that the Erdoğan government is seriously contemplating such a military operation. What I hear in the Turkish capital is that the military is not enthusiastic about such an adventure and that the Erdoğan government's pulse-reading efforts have not elicited a strong response from the chief of general staff. The Turkish military's restrained military response, if it is in fact true, is good news, but that may not be enough by itself to curb the enthusiasm on the part of Erdoğan's government to engage in a "false flag" operation.

Recalling how the Imia/Kardak crisis in the Aegean quickly escalated within a 24-hour news broadcasting cycle, forcing government officials on both sides to issue harsh remarks and mobilize their forces to the brink of war, the Turkish military will find it hard to resist government and public pressure in the case of a possible provocation against Jaber Castle. As the US had to intervene to ease the crisis in the Aegean, perhaps a third interlocutor may be needed now to prevent such a provocation from happening in the first place—or to stabilize it quickly if it happens.

Troubles Spill over the Border[36]

The Twitter and YouTube ban in Turkey confirmed the arbitrariness of justice and the suspension of the rule of law, because there was no court judgment ordering a complete shutdown on access to those social media sites. The ruling Justice and Development Party (AKP) government under strongman Prime Minister Recep Tayyip Erdoğan did not even enforce the court ruling that had been won by lawyers representing Twitter. Hence, the government's claim that Twitter had not complied with several court judgments asking for the removal of specific offensive content was defeated by Erdoğan's own failure to enforce the court judgment that ordered the suspension of the ban. It was the Constitutional Court, in the end, that came out and saved the day by unanimously deciding that the ban was illegal. The government reluctantly had to implement the ruling, albeit with some delay, as Erdoğan slammed the court for disregarding the national interest and protecting an American company.

Let's stop beating around the bush. The Erdoğan government has no interest in sorting out this issue, or any other issue for that matter, through legal arguments. He is bullying Twitter and YouTube, just as he has been trying to do with practically every person, group, or business in Turkey that has not yielded to his authoritarian rule. Even senior officials in the ruling party expressed their displeasure with the top court's decision on Twitter, as the pro-Erdoğan media plastered pictures of top judges across their pages. Since Turkish society is vibrant, dynamic, and diverse, with an aspiring young population and a flourishing middle class, Erdoğan is frustrated to see that he has failed to create a country in his own image. Despite the victory in the local elec-

---

[36] First appeared in *Today's Zaman* daily on Apr. 04, 2014

tions, which gave him 43 percent support, he has to deal with the fact that the majority in Turkey did not agree with his policies or harsh, bitter rhetoric. He was hoping to top the 50 percent of the vote he had scored in the 2011 elections, but he lost 7 percent despite a rise in the number of young voters.

One way or another, the law will catch up with Erdoğan eventually, just as it has with others in the past. Therefore, sorting out today's seemingly intractable issues from a legal point of view will offer us guidelines on how events will unfold in Turkey. For one, the Turkish government will scare foreign investors who are sensitive about freedom of speech and press in a country where they are investing. Respect for the rule of law and trust in the home country's justice system are paramount for the security of investments.

Secondly, since Twitter and YouTube are US companies, Erdoğan's singling out of these companies and drawing a bull's eye on their back will irk the US administration, which is sensitive about its companies' reputation and investment portfolios. Therefore, Erdoğan will be butting heads with US President Barack Obama, who is already feeling the heat from the US Congress, business lobbies, and advocacy groups about freedom of speech and the right to free enterprise.

Erdoğan may act with impunity at home for now, albeit temporarily, but he will not be able to stop the legal challenges altogether. What's more, if the legal issues are not sorted out here in Turkey, it will spill over to other countries and international platforms. I think Turkey's Constitutional Court has realized that danger and put a stop to the illegal Twitter ban. Thanks to the right to file individual petitions with the top court for violations of fundamental human rights, which was established with the 2010 public referendum, Turkey's Constitutional Court has positioned itself as the ultimate arbiter in the rule of law, basic rights, and liberties. As such, it needs to keep its reputation and protect valuable relations with its interlocutors abroad, especially the European Court of Human Rights (ECtHR), whose judgments are binding. Turkey's top court knows that if it does not act as an arbiter in these violations through this new remedy offered to Turkish citizens, the complaints will move on to the Strasbourg-based ECtHR.

I think the ECtHR's final ruling on March 18, 2013, on the case of Yıldırım vs Turkey, in which the applicant won the case against the Turkish government over the local court's order for the Telecommunications Directorate (TİB) to block access to Google Sites, was in the minds of the judges in the Constitutional Court ruling that announced the illegality of the ban on Twitter. In this case, the ECtHR ruled that the Turkish government had violated Article 10 of the European Convention on Human Rights (ECHR), which protects the right to freedom of expression. Recalling its earlier ruling in Times Newspapers Ltd v. the United Kingdom, the ECtHR said, "In light of its accessibility and its capacity to store and communicate vast amounts of information, the Internet plays an important role in enhancing the public's access to news and facilitating the dissemination of information generally."

Likewise, the Strasbourg-based court ruled in Observer and Guardian v. the United Kingdom in November, 1991 that Article 10 guarantees not only the right to impart information but also the right of the public to receive it. When the issue involves the press, the court is more sensitive, because it recognizes that "news is a perishable commodity and to delay its publication, even for a short period, may well deprive it of all its value and interest." Since all these rulings are also binding for Turkish courts, and because they should act as precedent and guidance for future cases, the Erdoğan government is fighting a losing battle on legal grounds. Even if the government finds friendly judges and prosecutors to crack down on freedom of speech and press domestically, it will be reprimanded by the ECtHR when these cases land in Strasbourg.

The Yıldırım case, which was about the collateral damage caused by the Internet block, was the first time the question of freedom of expression on Web 2.0-based platforms was put to test by the ECtHR. Its ruling is a landmark one and should serve as a guideline for future cases. The Court highlighted the devastating impact of a complete ban on access and labeled it a "collateral effect of a preventive measure adopted in the context of judicial proceedings." The Court ruled that the measure adopted by the government amounted to interference by a public authority in the applicant's right to freedom of expression, of which the freedom to receive and impart information and ideas is an integral part. The Court concluded that the interference resulting from the application of the Internet Law did not satisfy the foreseeability requirement under the Convention and did not afford the applicant the degree of protection to which he was entitled by the rule of law in a democratic society.

Not only has the Erdoğan government violated ECtHR case law, but it is also is in breach of a number of international obligations. For one, Turkey infringed upon the Council of Europe's (COE) declarations, resolutions, and conventions on freedom of expression on the Internet. If any of these measures adopted by Erdoğan's government are challenged at the ECtHR, I'm sure the court will ask the Turkish government to amend the legislation in line with the standards set out above. So far, it seems the Constitutional Court is doing its job and is not burdening the Strasbourg-based court. But if Erdoğan puts pressure on the top court and attempts to prevent it from functioning, let's say by not enforcing the judgments, the ECtHR may be forced to intervene when a complaint is filed.

Now there is a more serious threat brewing in Turkey that targets private networks used by individual companies, especially the press. Internet servers and websites used by critical media in Turkey have been under sustained cyber-attack since a couple of days before the local elections held on Sunday, and this has been going on until today. The cyber-attack has allegedly been launched by circles close to or controlled by the Erdoğan government and has targeted private networks used by individual companies. The whistleblower Twitter user @fuatavni claimed on Thursday that Turk Telekom, partially owned by the Treasury and controlled by businesspeople close to the government, has even asked Chinese telecom giant Huawei, a solution provider company that Turk Telekom has partnered with on occasions, to limit the Internet speed in Turkey and went ahead with limiting the bandwidth in spite of Chinese objections.

The Cihan news agency, which has become a well-known brand in Turkey by delivering election results quickly, was exposed to a severe cyber-attack on election night. Cihan's subscriber web sites, which include national print and broadcast media, were also targeted in the attack. The web servers for Turkey's largest dailies, *Zaman* and *Today's Zaman*, as well as the critical liberal daily *Taraf*'s website, were attacked, making pages inaccessible to readers from time to time. The critical Samanyolu News channel's Internet access was completely severed on Thursday, while malicious software generating a forged document was implanted into its network of computers. All these point to a pattern whereby the critical press has been targeted in a systematic campaign of sabotage against its infrastructure, thereby preventing the dissemination of information to its audience at home and abroad.

This is a perfect case in which the articles of the Convention on Cybercrime, which entered into force on July 1, 2004, have been violated. The convention deals with various types of offenses in the sphere of cybercrime, which includes action directed against the confidentiality, integrity, and availability of computer data and systems, computer-related forgery and fraud, and content-related offenses. Likewise, the 2005 Declaration of the Committee of Ministers of the CoE, the European Union's recommendation that was adopted by the European Parliament (EP) on March 26, 2009, and the United Nations Human Rights Committee's (UNHRC) in July, 2011, comment on the International Covenant on Civil and Political Rights (ICCPR); they all state that restrictions on the Internet must be limited and justified on sound legal grounds.

In today's highly interconnected age, where information networks spread easily across national boundaries, placing undue restrictions on the Internet and dealing a blow to the domestic communication infrastructure in order to disrupt the services of private companies may have serious repercussions abroad and give rise to claims that the Turkish government has breached its commitments. Even though Erdoğan said he does not care what the international community might think about his restrictive moves on the Internet, he will have to face the bitter reality and confront growing criticism, resentment, and even a backlash from Turkey's allies and partners.

EU Commissioner Duped[37]

Having scrambled to derail a huge corruption investigation that was exposed on Dec. 17, 2013, along with any other probes into the increasingly authoritarian government of Recep Tayyip Erdoğan, all of a sudden the ruling AKP-dominated Parliament has been turned into a "law-factory" to produce legislation that would empower Erdoğan to squeeze what is left of the rule of law and fundamental rights in the European Union candidate country.

It seems there is no end to the rushed bills pushed through Parliament by the ruling AKP government in the last five months, with each controversial bill sparking a huge outcry among the opposition parties, media, jurists, and civil society. This pattern of behavior has also raised eyebrows abroad, especially in the Council of Europe and the European Union, where Turkey is a full member in the former and in accession talks in the latter. Yet Erdoğan does not seem to be looking out for the 57 percent of Turks who did not vote for him in the last elections or what his allies and partners abroad would think of him. The government's new bill that was sent to Parliament, which will seriously hinder internet journalism if passed, is a testament to the erratic behavior of his party.

The bill comes on top of the already-approved controversial Internet law in February that severely curtailed freedom of expression online and gave the government agency, the Telecommunications Authority (TİB), the power to shut down websites without obtaining a court order first. On face value, the Internet journalism bill is supposed to acknowledge the growth of online journalism, especially news portals, in Turkey by granting them legal recognition and allowing them access into the lucrative official advertisement market, something that online journalists have been demanding for some time. The draft was sitting in the Office of the Prime Minister for the last two years without any action on it. Against the background of the corruption scandal that has rattled the government and incriminated the prime minister, his family members, and his close associates, the government suddenly decided to send the draft to Parliament with some last-minute changes.

---

[37] First appeared in *Today's Zaman* daily on May 19, 2014

This unexpected rush, after a hiatus on the draft, raises the specter of further clamping down on online news portals because most of the voice recordings had originally leaked to the Internet through Twitter and YouTube, prompting the government to sever access to social media sites, without a legal basis, on the eve of elections.

The Constitutional Court canceled the government's illegal decision to shut down Twitter and is considering the application on lifting the ban on YouTube as well. Hence, the motivation on sending this new bill may have nothing to do with what online journalists actually want, but rather is related to further cracking down on freedom of expression under the guise of granting recognition for online news portals.

The draft was prepared by the Directorate General of Press and Information (BYEGM), a government body overseeing the media, with the orders from Prime Minister Erdoğan and his deputy, Bülent Arınç; it was prepared three years ago, when the government was in full swing with EU-oriented reforms. After a series of meetings with different stakeholders, the BYEGM came up with a draft in a year and sent it to the Office of the Prime Minister. Having sat on it for two years, the Prime Ministry suddenly decided to take up the draft in March and sent it to the Parliament Speaker's Office on March 12. On April 4, the bill was forwarded to three relevant commissions for review before being forwarded to the general floor for likely approval.

The original draft was revamped by the Prime Minister's Office; however, this took place after a Cabinet discussion on the issue which came right after the controversial Internet Law No. 5651 that severely restricted freedom of expression on the Internet. The draft is not a stand-alone bill but rather lumps a series of amendments to the existing laws, especially the one that deals with the press (Press Labor Law no. 5953). Although the bill does not require all online news portals to register their services with the government agency, those who shy away from registering officially will neither be provided with official press cards nor allowed to receive advertising from the government. For those who register, the government perks will come with liabilities as well. In other words, the government employs a carrot-and-stick approach to tame online news portals.

The government also did not seek the advice of experts employed at the Ministry of European Union Affairs during the drafting stage to determine whether or not the bill is in compliance with EU standards and norms. The opinion on the bill was delivered by an expert from the EU Affairs Ministry only at the EU Harmonization Commission meeting in Parliament on April 24. Given that the Justice Commission is the main body tasked to move the bill to the floor, a few concerns raised by the expert sent by the EU Affairs Ministry did not even matter for the ruling AKP deputies, who have been instructed to push it from the floor at any cost. It is also mind-boggling that despite serious flaws in the bill, the EU Affairs Ministry's expert testified in the commission that the bill is not in violation of EU acquis.

This is also a clear violation of a promise made by EU Affairs Minister Mevlüt Çavuşoğlu, who pledged to the European Union's top enlargement official, Stefan Füle, during a meeting in Brussels a couple of months ago that Turkey will consult the EU on upcoming bills during the drafting stages.

The agreement was reached after a flurry of criticism from EU officials on what was seen as regression on major accomplishments in the rule of law and fundamental rights in a candidate country. Füle suggested that the consultation must be made in advance to prevent public criticism and Çavuşoğlu agreed.

Yet the deal was not honored at all. Forget about discussing drafts with Brussels in advance; the Erdoğan government did not even seek the opinion of its own EU Affairs Ministry on the possible repercussions of drafts on the EU accession process before the draft came to Parliament.

Fearing that the Erdoğan government just wanted to buy some time to weather domestic troubles and prevent further criticism from Brussels, Füle revealed this private deal he had reached with Çavuşoğlu to the public on April 10 during his address at the EU-Turkey Joint Parliamentary Committee meeting in the European Parliament in Brussels. Without going into much detail, he said: "I believe we already need to change the way in which we cooperate as regards the accession negotiations. This is particularly important for the areas of the rule of law and fundamental rights. We need to intensify our dialogue at all phases of policy and law-making on these issues which are at the very center of the accession process." Adding to this, he vowed, "They must be treated as an absolute priority."

The bill amending laws to define Internet media in Turkey has ramifications with regard to Chapter 10 on information society and media as well as Chapter 23 on the judiciary and fundamental rights. It may also give rise to legal challenges at the European Court of Human Rights (ECtHR) on Article 10 of the European Convention on Human Rights that protects freedom of expression. In its current form, Article 7 of the bill gives the government agency, TİB, the power to cancel journalists' press cards during an investigation and can also use investigations as a reason to cut off official advertisements—paid for by the state—in online portals, disregarding the principle of the presumption of innocence.

There is no judicial review in advance for these administrative penalties rendered by a political body. What is more, the government envisages harsh measures for online news media that are not applicable to traditional print and audio media. These measures are in clear conflict with the EU acquis as well as the Council of Europe (CoE) benchmarks, especially the ECtHR case law.

Another controversial issue is seen in Article 8 of the draft that requires online news portals to maintain storage of content for six months and provide it when requested by authorities. Considering that the European Court of Justice, on April 8, canceled the Data Retention Directive 2006/24/EC which allowed member states to store citizens' telecommunications data for a minimum of six months and at most 24 months, a similar provision in the Turkish draft also violates the principle of proportionality, and rights to privacy, data protection, and freedom of expression.

The draft, which cleared the sub-commission of the parliamentary Justice Commission without any significant change, is expected to be adopted in Parliament. The fact is that seven advocacy groups on online journalism and Internet media did not even bother to show up at the EU.

The Harmonization Commission meeting on April 24 indicates civil society groups have given up on their hopes to impact the law-making process. They know that whatever they say won't matter at all because the government is simply trying to hush up leaks on corruption and other damaging investigations that are published on online news portals. Since the secondary regulation to map out the implementation of the law, if adopted, is left to the government, there will be more limitations there as well.

The Erdoğan government will use this law to suffocate online journalism, just as it has done with print and broadcast media, and will suppress critical outlets while supporting pro-government news portals. There are already too many hate-disseminating web portals, allegedly operated with implicit support from the government and its notorious intelligence agency, attacking Erdoğan opponents. The critical news portals, however, are under constant threat of an access ban from TİB, which was given enormous powers with the recent Internet law. The bill on Internet journalism will provide new tools for the government to crack down on what is left of the critical media landscape in Turkey. It appears Füle has been duped by Turkey once again.

Erdoğan: Divider-in-Chief[38]

After exporting the divisive themes in Turkish society to some 3 million expats living in Germany a month ago with his controversial visit ahead of the presidential election, Turkey's divider-in-chief, Prime Minister Recep Tayyip Erdoğan, did the same in Austria and France this week, raking up sensitive issues to polarize Turks living abroad.

Understandably, the countries hosting the Turkish prime minister were uneasy. On the one hand, they did not want to upset their relations with an important country, but they also loathe Erdoğan's bitter discourse, which may very well disturb immigrant groups, upset the social balance and provoke xenophobic and extremist movements. It is clear that Erdoğan has chalked up a plan that is predicated upon inflicting fear, creating division and stirring resentment by any means necessary in order to distract Turks from debating real issues so that he can sustain his rule and survive political and legal challenges.

---

[38] First appeared in *Today's Zaman* daily on Jun. 20, 2014

Turkey's partners and allies simply do not want to get caught up in the Turkish prime minister's personal battle with liberals, secularists, social democrats, nationalists, and the moderate conservative groups that are not supportive of his government. It seems millions of Alevis who shied away from voting for Erdoğan have felt the brunt of Erdoğan's wrath, just as millions who follow Islamic scholar Fethullah Gülen, who has been preaching interfaith and intercultural dialogue to bridge the divides in Turkish society for decades, have also felt it. To put it simply, Erdoğan is keen to amass personal power and wealth by enflaming a divisive climate. He does not seem to have the best interests of his people and his nation at heart.

The prime minister's tactic of widening the divide among those beyond Turkey's borders is not limited to Europe, home to millions of immigrants of Turkish descent. He has done the same in the Middle East in recent years. His favoritism toward Hamas against al-Fatah deepened the rift in Palestine for some time. Working with Qatar on a number of regional issues without taking into account of the rest of Gulf countries helped contribute to the breakup of unity among the Gulf Cooperation Council (GCC) states. His exploitation of Egyptian developments for his domestic political campaign after the ouster from power of former Egyptian President Mohammed Morsi effectively severed Turkey's ties with the most populous Arab nation.

By the way, I do not think Erdoğan is enamored with the Muslim Brotherhood (MB) or interested in protecting its interests. Otherwise, he would have engaged with Egyptian rulers and worked closely with them to help achieve a national reconciliation that would bring the MB into the political process. It was the Erdoğan government that encouraged Morsi to defy warnings from the military and the opposition, precipitating the fall of Egypt's first democratically elected president from power.

This is an anecdotal story shared with me recently in a first-hand eyewitness account, but it sheds light onto Erdoğan's thinking when it comes to the brotherhood. It was Sept. 15, 2011, and Erdoğan was very late to a dinner gathering in Cairo after delivering a fiery speech at Cairo University during his visit to Egypt amid the so-called Arab Spring events. Some guests had grown frustrated and left the dinner before Erdoğan arrived, but those who stuck around were about to witness a surprising comment from the Turkish prime minister.

While speaking to people around the table through a translator sitting on his right, he mentioned that Turkey had successfully experimented with secularism and that he hoped to see Egypt adopt the same principles during its transition. Turkish Foreign Minister Ahmet Davutoğlu, sitting on Erdoğan's left, quickly leaned backwards and whispered to the translator to use the word "civil" (*madani*) for "secular" rather than "ilmanniyya," which has a meaning closer to "irreligiousness" in Arabic. The translator did what Davutoğlu asked, but was immediately rebuked by Erdoğan, who said he should translate it as he said it. The members of Muslim Brotherhood were furious and not a single one of them showed up at the airport to see him leave the country next day.

Although Erdoğan later said his words were misunderstood because of a translation mistake, this story indicates that his remarks were deliberate and designed to stir up resentment among Egyptians, who are highly sensitive about the concept of secularism. He sowed similar discord when he raised the sensitive integration issue at a rally held in May in the German city of Cologne as the crowd booed German Chancellor Angela Merkel. He defied common sense and ignored pleas for restraint from both Turkish and German politicians. His remarks not only didn't help the perception of the millions of Turks in Germany, but raised questions about those Turks' loyalty to Germany, as well.

Cem Özdemir, the co-chair of Germany's Greens Party who is of Turkish descent, said Erdoğan has lost the support of "100 percent of Germany." "When the crowd booed Merkel, it made a very bad impression; it was an ugly scene. It will remain in the minds [of Germans]. We will pay the price for it," he lamented. "You [Turks] are living here, making a living here, paying your taxes and sending your children to school here and taking advantage of the social state here. But you boo this country's chancellor," he noted. The same thing happened in Austria this week, helping neither Turkish expats nor Turkey's relations with Austria.

All these rallies overseas did, however, serve Erdoğan's primary purpose of maintaining the divide among Turks. He has the political machine and the finances to fuel this divide. A forest of straw men lured with money, position, power, and privileges have been helping Erdoğan run this campaign of fear. His advisers never question the wisdom or rationale of Erdoğan's decision to keep the war on vulnerable groups in Turkey going. They think broadening social programs, offering amnesty to tax evaders, and giving contracts and tenders to government lackeys will create more beneficiaries and, in turn, more supporters for the ruling Justice and Development Party (AKP).

There are fundamental flaws in Erdoğan's strategy of divide and rule, however. For one thing, his credibility with voters has begun to erode as the ratcheted-up rhetoric has reached its limit. A fatigue factor has already kicked in with regard to Erdoğan's relentless conspiracy campaign and it will become increasingly difficult to shake the lethargy growing among his supporters. The fact of the matter is that Erdoğan is fighting a losing battle and he knows it. He already lost some traction in the last elections and he is not sure he will win the presidency—if he ever runs. That is why he appears to be angry all the time.

Secondly, the opposition smartened up by developing some tactics to defeat his bellicose discourse. Main opposition Republican Peoples' Party (CHP) leader Kemal Kılıçdaroğlu, an Alevi himself, helped keep millions of Alevis from pouring into streets in order to prevent provocation and clashes that would likely be derailed by the intelligence organization run by Erdoğan's confidante. For similar reasons, the Nationalist Movement Party (MHP) leader held the nationalist youth back from rising up in protests against Erdoğan. Both leaders realize the violent clashes and mass protests will only allow Erdoğan to play the victim card and help him win mainstream supporters who fear instability and chaos.

Fielding a joint candidate for the presidential race was the latest smart move made by the opposition parties to defeat Erdoğan's divisive tactics. Ekmeleddin İhsanoğlu, former secretary-general of the Organization of the Islamic Cooperation (OIC) and a well-respected intellectual, represents the opposite of Erdoğan's character. His soft-spoken style, his emphasis on compromise, and his well-earned international reputation as a uniter and a healer is a counterbalance to Erdoğan's hardline and divisive posturing that has alienated him from much of the world.

Without a doubt, the road ahead will be a bumpy one. Turkey's divider-in-chief will likely turn up the volume on hate speech, deepen divisions, provoke clashes, run smear campaigns, and apply pressure on his opponents by abusing state powers, including the criminal justice system, with measures like phony lawsuits. Going against him with similar tactics would only add fuel to the fire and inflict irreparable damage on the nation. As has been proven time and again, the truth, patience, and endurance will eventually prevail as we forge ahead to develop Turkey. Erdoğan's scaremongering tactics making this wonderful country a battlefield are doomed to fail.

Backlash against Turks Abroad[39]

The blatant interference of Turkey's top political Islamist, Recep Tayyip Erdoğan, into other country's affairs comes with a hefty price tag, which his countrymen will have to pay irrespective of whether citizens care about the reputation of their leader globally and respond with disapproval, praise, or mere indifference to his belligerent discourse.

In Europe, Erdoğan's harsh narrative helped inflame xenophobia, undermined the difficult battle with Islamophobia, and annoyed, if not antagonized, governments in places such as Germany and Austria, which have invested a great over the years in tackling integration issues. In the Middle East, his open support for the Muslim Brotherhood at the expense of other groups, coupled with Erdoğan's relentless bashing of Egyptian leaders, cast a long shadow on the perception of Turkey in Arab nations. Countries in Central Asia and South Asia continue to harbor their well-deserved suspicions towards Erdoğan, who they suspect may be encouraging Islamists in their own regions.

The result of such ill-advised and partisan foreign policy is the escalation of risks that Turkish citizens face when they settle in other countries for business, investment, or education activities, or when they simply travel abroad for leisure or professional purposes. The kidnapping of Turkish citizens in Syria, Ukraine, Lebanon, Libya, Iraq, Afghanistan, and other places in recent years exposed that threat.

---

[39] First appeared in *Today's Zaman* daily on Jun. 30, 2014

Yet we do not see encouraging signals that the Erdoğan government will revise its foreign policy choices or fine-tune policies with tweaks here and there to reduce the risks facing citizens abroad. On the contrary, political Islamists dominating the government attempt to spin the victimization of Turks and Muslims abroad, hoping to pick up points in domestic politics.

The case in point is Erdoğan's recent journey to a few European countries. Despite pleas for common sense and wisdom, Erdoğan's insistence on polarizing and divisive discourse during major rallies held in Germany, Austria, and France for his presidential bid—in Turkey—indicates he does not care much for the well-being of Turks in Europe. Just as immigrant communities have increasingly become targets of extremist parties that politicize the issue of migration to shift European countries' economic and social problems to others, Erdoğan is hijacking the legitimate concerns of expats residing in Europe for his domestic political purposes. He may have effectively added more fuel to the election campaigns of far-right political parties that present migrants as a threat to and burden on society.

In fact, German Greens Co-chair Cem Özdemir, who was heavily criticized by the Turkish prime minister for being critical of his controversial visit to Cologne in late May, said Erdoğan's appearance brought more tension to Germany and that Turks in Germany will "pay the price" for booing German Chancellor Angela Merkel at Erdoğan's rally in the German city. He also said Erdoğan is destroying his formerly positive image among Germans and that he has lost the support of his advocates in Germany.

I think the key operative words to focus on in Özdemir's comments are that Turks will have to "pay the price" for what Erdoğan did at the Cologne rally. Erdoğan lashed out at a German politician who is of Turkish descent by saying that "you don't have the right to speak about the prime minister of a country that you belong to considering your [ethnic] origin." He called Özdemir a "so-called Turk" and indicated that he does not want him in Turkey. Erdoğan's attack on the German politician strained ties between Turkey and Germany as the German Foreign Ministry summoned the Turkish ambassador to Germany to express Berlin's displeasure over Erdoğan's harsh remarks.

Erdoğan's fiery and divisive rhetoric also received a strong rebuke from Austria early in June when Austrian officials became worried that the Turkish prime minister would stir up trouble in their country. "I expressly warn Premier Erdoğan: He cannot drive a wedge into Austrian society. Integration is touchy and sometimes difficult. The wrong speech can set us back and poison the climate," Austrian Foreign Minister Sebastian Kurz said in advance of Erdoğan's visit. He also noted that if Erdoğan were to make a statement similar to the one he had earlier made in Germany, the Turkish population in Vienna would be harmed more than anyone else. Yet Erdoğan did not refrain from using inflammatory language and a marginalizing narrative during his speech in Vienna.

The issue was brought to the agenda last week during the summer session of the Parliamentary Assembly of the Council of Europe (PACE) by Austrian politician Stefan Schennach, who is from the Social Democratic Party of Austria (SPÖ). After thanking the Turkish workers who first came to Austria in 1964 and helped the country become one of the eight richest countries in the world, the Austrian politician said: "The things that the Turkish prime minister has said in Germany and Austria are poison to integration. We are trying to achieve integration, but then somebody turns up and gives an electoral campaign speech that destroys the tiny seedling of integration. We need to say that this is poison. What Mr. Erdoğan did in Austria a few days ago was very deleterious. We will suffer for years from what he took two hours to say."

It is not just Turks who live in European countries that Erdoğan's polarizing tongue disturbs; Turks living in the Middle East also suffer from Erdoğan's exploitation of foreign policy issues for domestic political purposes. Turkish businesses naturally fear backlash from host governments over Ankara's policies as they try to navigate carefully through a difficult period. The lives of Turkish citizens have also been put at risk. Almost 300 Turks have been kidnapped in Middle Eastern and Central Asian countries since 2002, mostly in Iraq, Afghanistan, and Yemen, and many of them in the last couple of years. Just last week, in eastern Libya,

Turks were declared persona non grata by a renegade general and two Turkish workers were kidnapped by unidentified people. Two Turkish pilots were kidnapped by militants in Lebanon in August last year before they were finally freed in October with the efforts of the Palestinian ambassador in Ankara. Some 50 Turks, including consulate staff, are still being held hostage by terrorist group the Islamic State of Iraq and the Levant (ISIL) in Iraq.

Unfortunately, Erdoğan risks turning the Turkish communities living abroad, once valuable assets, into liabilities for their host countries. No matter how well integrated these communities are, Erdoğan's attempt to export divisions raises questions for host governments. Instead of capitalizing on the vital bridge these communities offer in terms of social, economic and cultural connections, Erdoğan divides and polarizes communities in order to survive Turkish politics back at home.

This also hampers the exchange of values in developing a positive framework between Turkey and its partners simply because Erdoğan's parochial vision commands absolute compliance with political Islam. The fact that he keeps dividing Turkish society along sectarian and ideological lines instead of reaching out and striving to achieve reconciliation is not just a worry for Turks at home, but also a serious challenge for Turkey's partners, who are keen to prevent the spillover of that threat. After all, there are growing indications that Erdoğan desires to export that world vision to other countries as well.

Chapter 8

Muzzling the Free Press

Battle Plan against Free Press[40]

T he massive corruption investigations that broke on Dec. 17, 2013—even though they suffered a temporary setback with the government-orchestrated reshuffle of prosecutors and judges—exposed a major scheme by Prime Minister Recep Tayyip Erdoğan to create a media landscape in his image through lucrative contracts, tenders, and state funding. The multi-billion dollar deals have generated a huge hoard of funds for Erdoğan to buy off some media outlets through proxies, hire new sets of journalists to defend his government line, and even convert critical analysts with fat checks to prod them to the other side of the aisle.

In the second graft investigation that implicated prominent businesspeople close to Erdoğan, the case file alleges that businesses were asked to contribute to a pool of funds from shares they had received from mega projects and contracts. This fund was to be used to purchase a big media group, entrusted to someone loyal to Erdoğan, to support the government's policies, especially during the election period. In the first graft case, investigators have discovered that a top editor at a pro-government newspaper asked the general manager of state lender Halkbank, now in pre-trial detention, to wire TL 2 million right away in exchange for counterfeit advertisement invoices. Many state-funded companies are illegally ordered to put their ads in pro-government newspapers even though their circulation is very low in

---

[40] First appeared in *Today's Zaman* daily on Jan. 17, 2014

Turkey. In a sense, the corruption investigations have helped lift the curtain on how the government has been engineering a government-friendly press in Turkey, although much of it was known to media professionals.

Now Erdoğan seems to have set his eyes on squeezing the critical media further with the legal, financial, and even social instruments at his disposal. He knows he has lost the legal battle, judging from the formidable evidence of wrongdoing in the government, and is trying everything to stall the investigations. He has also lost the fight for public opinion, where the perception of how deeply the government is involved in these corruption scandals was further bolstered by panicked moves by Erdoğan. With pressure on the judiciary and even open interference in the ranks of prosecutors and judges, as well as non-enforcement of judgments and summons, he may have succeeded in delaying the trials temporarily. But the public has already passed judgment on these cases and found Erdoğan guilty of all charges thanks to the continued existence of a free and fair media in Turkey.

Erdoğan will do his best to reverse that perception by feeding the pro-government media's international conspiracy theories with more garbage every day while intimidating the critical media. Since he does not care much about freedom of expression and information in the media as an essential requirement of democracy, and hates public participation in the democratic decision-making process, Erdoğan will likely wage an unprecedented war on the critical media. So, the battle for the soul of democracy in Turkey will not be fought only in the courtrooms and ballot boxes, but also in the media landscape as well.

First, he will try to use his parliamentary majority to curb the right to a free press and freedom of speech with new national legislation. The recent law on the Internet, ostensibly made in the name of protecting the right to privacy and buried in a large omnibus bill, brings new restrictions on digital media. Second, he will launch a series of defamation lawsuits to protect himself against criticism and slander in a way that gives him greater defenses than ordinary people enjoy. Politically motivated cases based on defamation charges will be used to silence legitimate criticism. Erdoğan has already sued one of our reporters for tweeting comments about him.

Third, he will make extensive use of the penal codes covering such offenses as incitement to hatred and endangering the public order and national security to prosecute journalists, without caring much about the requirements for necessity and proportionality in the application of restrictions on freedom of expression. Investigative reporter Mehmet Baransu, who exposed the government's massive profiling of unsuspecting citizens, including members of the opposition parties, in a Watergate-type scandal, was charged by the government for revealing a confidential document drafted by the National Intelligence Organization (MİT). The prosecutor, following a government complaint, is now demanding a 12-year sentence for him for exposing the government's dirty laundry.

Fourth, the government will subject journalists to undue requirements and new rules of accreditation to make their work unnecessarily difficult. The government will limit openness in the government and restrict reporters' access to resources in government agencies, dealing a blow to public control and democratic scrutiny. For example, Foreign Minister Ahmet Davutoğlu instructed all ambassadors not to speak to the press during an annual convention in Ankara this week, as opposed to the past practice of encouraging them to engage with the media. The politically friendly media will be granted preferential treatment in a discriminatory way. During Erdoğan's last overseas trip to Southeast Asia, major media outlets—including *Zaman*, the most-circulated paper in the nation—were barred from assigning reporters to accompany the official delegation.

Fifth, Erdoğan's government will guide taxpayer-funded public news and broadcasting agencies in its favor by granting its people senior management positions there. Since state news agency Anadolu and public broadcasting station the Turkish Radio and Television Corporation (TRT) will be government mouthpieces from now on, the government will not see a problem in granting exclusive reporting rights for major events of public interest and excluding private media from coverage. It is also no surprise to see an increasing number of partisan and ruling party-affiliated people in high management positions in the private pro-government media.

The sixth step in Erdoğan's plan relates to ongoing legal cases, in which the government has already started a campaign to limit the flow of information because of damaging charges implicating senior members of the government. The government has imposed an unprecedented ban on police reporters' access to the premises of police departments, despite a court decision that such a ban is illegal. This drastic measure was not even seen in the military coup eras in Turkey. The government has also launched a series of aggressive criminal investigations against those who leaked information to the media. Erdoğan defies the general standard in such cases, where the media should be free to report on the functioning of the criminal justice system, especially matters of public concern, as part of the public right to receive information. The established practice that reporters must have access to both police officers and judicial authorities in order to obtain truthful information is blatantly disregarded.

The government will use the secret nature of investigations to go after critical media for covering the ongoing investigations into corruption and the al-Qaeda terrorist organization. Although the European Court of Human Rights (ECtHR) recognizes such restrictions and values the principle of the presumption of innocence, it also underlines that, as in its Du Roy and Malaurie judgment of Oct. 3, 2000, the absolute secrecy of criminal investigations is compatible with Article 10 of the European Convention on Human Rights (ECHR), which talks about the right to freedom of expression. Erdoğan seems to take only the part that suits him while disregarding the rest in a very important standard set by the case law of the court.

Seventh, the Erdoğan government is not expected to draw up legislation that will make the lives of journalists easier in Turkey any time soon, despite past pledges made in the ruling Justice and Development Party's (AKP) official program and election manifestos. For example, the bill on the protection of private data will likely never be raised in Parliament, even though it became part of the Constitution in 2010 and the government promised to create legislation on that amendment to put it into practice. Given that the government has been profiling unsuspecting citizens of this country based on their ideological, religious, or ethnic affiliations, I do not think Erdoğan has any interest in a bill that would put a stop to this illegal profiling in the foreseeable future.

What is more, he needs the intelligence agency to do his dirty work, finding skeletons in his opponents' closets while invading the private lives of journalists and civic activists in order to intimidate them. I would rather expect Erdoğan to strengthen the laws on state secrets and intelligence in order to reinforce the government's prerogatives at the expense of fundamental rights and freedoms. Another bill to guarantee the confidentiality of journalists' sources of information or whistleblower-type legislation won't be brought up, either, despite the fact that these rights are recognized by the ECHR under Article 10.

The eighth step in his plan is to exert social pressure on the critical media in Turkey with his relentless public campaign that is bashing the national media for its critical coverage of the corruption cases. He has accused the media of conspiring with international groups, a veiled reference to the US, the European Union, and Israel, in order to topple his government and suppress the national will. His reference to specific news headlines on the same day that he held rallies singles out the critical media as a target to be attacked by his supporters. This public lynching reached a worrying level when it resulted in protests in front of the buildings of government-critical media. I'm not sure how the government will deal with the increasing physical threats against journalists, as the Erdoğan government has even removed manpower from the security detail provided for the now-removed graft prosecutors.

The last step in this deplorable scheme is to use the regulatory authorities to pressure the media into muzzling criticism. The ruling party-dominated Radio and Television Supreme Council (RTÜK), a broadcasting watchdog agency, has recently fined some channels for airing details of the investigation files on the four ex-ministers who were charged with taking large bribes in exchange for favors. The government unsuccessfully tried to seize a bank through the Banking Regulation and Supervision Agency (BDDK) with a staged run on the bank in order to suppress criticism from media groups believed to be close to the Hizmet Movement. There are other worrying examples.

In the final analysis, I don't think this battle plan will work, given the vibrant and dynamic media landscape in Turkey. Social media and online news portals have changed the equation dramatically in an Internet-savvy and mostly young Turkish society. Every night, hundreds of thousands of Turks have been flocking to Twitter to protest the government with a new hashtag for the last two months, and these hashtags have quickly climbed to the top of the chart, not only in Turkey, but also around the world. Erdoğan has launched an aggressive campaign to counter this protest movement with a generously funded army of Twitter users, including illegally signing up government employees to perform political campaigning. Yet he has still failed to overcome what is a volunteer-driven Twitter campaign against the Erdoğan government's policies.

Sub Judice Rule[41]

One of the points Turkey's embattled Prime Minister Recep Tayyip Erdoğan often invokes to defend himself against damaging revelations that have implicated senior members of his ruling Justice and Development Party (AKP) government, as well as his son and prominent businesspeople close to him, is the "secret nature of investigations." His reasoning is based on two frequently exploited articles of the Turkish Penal Code (TCK). One is Article 285, which criminalizes the "violation of confidentiality," and the other is Article 288, which criminalizes "attempting to influence the impartiality of the judiciary."

It is not difficult to obtain a gag order from a judge based on these articles, and that is what happened in the second corruption and money laundering investigation that was revealed on Dec. 25, 2013, and implicated Erdoğan's son Bilal Erdoğan, as well as some close business associates. The government abuses these articles to suppress national debate on matters of great public interest, and in fact it violates the cardinal rule balancing secrecy against the public's right to know what is going

---

[41] First appeared in *Today's Zaman* daily on Jan. 20, 2014

on in the government. The argument about secrecy allows the government to avoid discussing the substance of the allegations and enables Erdoğan to hide behind this protection of secrecy.

Although it is understandable that Erdoğan would resort to this line of defense when he faces serious charges threatening his rule, he seems to forget that the principles of the confidentiality of judicial investigations and the presumption of innocence are not absolute. They must be weighed against the right to freedom of expression and cannot be used to violate the public's right to know, especially in high-profile cases that generate a lot of attention. Since Turkey accepts the judgments of the European Court of Human Rights (ECtHR) and considers the Strasbourg-based court's jurisdiction binding, the ECtHR's case law sheds light on how to balance these seemingly contradictory rules of secrecy and freedom of the press.

In a landmark ruling on the Du Roy and Malaurie case on Oct. 3, 2000, the court found the French government guilty of violating Article 10 of the European Convention on Human Rights (ECHR), which says, "Everyone has the right to freedom of expression." It said the French journalists' conviction amounted to "interference" in the exercise of their right to freedom of expression and rejected government arguments that the interference was intended to protect the reputation and rights of others and maintain the authority and impartiality of the judiciary. What's more, the court underlined that the conviction of journalists for reporting criminal proceedings was a measure that was not reasonably proportionate to the legitimate aims pursued. It said priority must be given to the interest of a democratic society in ensuring and maintaining press freedom at the expense of the protection of others' reputation or the secrecy of judicial proceedings.

In the massive corruption cases that have forced four ministers to resign from the government so far and landed dozens in pre-trial detention, with many others waiting to be questioned, there is a huge public interest in knowing the details. The sweeping al-Qaeda investigations that imprisoned 13 suspects who were charged with sending arms to al-Qaeda groups in Syria, kidnapping a journalist, planning to assassinate US President Barack Obama, and laying out plans to bomb high-profile targets in urban centers have attracted public interest as well. The Erdoğan government gives the impression that it wants to sweep the dirt under the carpet and will try to prevent the media from reporting the details of these investigations at all, if possible. It uses both administrative and judicial instruments to prevent reporters from accessing the case files. For example, the government has banned police reporters from entering police department premises altogether and did not even enforce the court ruling on the suspension of the ban when an advocacy group won the case in a court of law. A gag order was obtained for the second graft case to prevent reporting as well as to prepare the groundwork for the filing of lawsuits to harass those journalists who still dare to report.

Not only the ECtHR but also the 47-member Council of Europe's (CoE) advisory body, the Venice Commission, provides important benchmarks on how to deal with the delicate balance between the presumption of innocence and freedom of expression. In a report issued by the commission in March 2010 on judicial independence, the advisory body said, "In order to shield the judicial process from undue pressure, one should consider the application of the principle of 'sub judice', which should be carefully defined, so that an appropriate balance is struck between the need to protect the judicial process on the one hand and freedom of the press and open discussion of matters of public interest on the other."

A more liberal interpretation of the rule of "sub judice," which means "under judgment" in Latin, in the last couple of decades and its application in Turkey through the case law of the ECtHR has provided a healthy framework for further debate in Turkish society. The rule refers to pending or ongoing judicial processes in which comment or conduct may cause prejudice in the case and be considered a criminal offense and contempt of court. We saw this rule tested time and again during the landmark Ergenekon and Balyoz (Sledgehammer) cases, where the public interest was huge, and the media reported extensively from the case file during the investigation stages of the police and prosecutors, as well as in the trial.

The Turkish judiciary's record on the sub judice rule was quite different in the period before the 2010 public referendum on the restructuring of Turkey's key judicial council, the Supreme Board of Judges and Prosecutors (HSYK). There were thousands of cases launched against media groups and reporters—either in the prosecutorial stages or in the trial phase—for reporting on ongoing cases. When the HSYK turned into a more democratic and pluralistic structure after the Venice Commission and European Union-endorsed changes in 2010, most of these cases were thrown out of court by judges, and investigations were dropped by prosecutors. Prosecutors and judges started to value the right to freedom over the right to confidentiality. They should have done this a long time ago, just by taking the precedents of the ECtHR into account, but they simply chose to ignore the judgments of the Strasbourg court despite the fact that the articles of the ECHR carry the force of constitutional articles in Turkey.

Now, with the government-endorsed bill approved by the Justice Commission last week, which will be debated in Parliament this week before its likely approval, we will probably see a regression on the sub judice rule, because the HSYK will be subordinated to the justice minister who, as a government appointee, will decide on disciplinary investigations and the reassignment and dismissal of all judges and prosecutors in Turkey. Therefore, judges and prosecutors will pay more attention to political sensitivities, and the government can easily intimidate journalists with frivolous cases to harass the free media. On gag orders, reporters will be more likely to be found in contempt of court in government-launched cases, and secrecy will prevail over freedom of information. This is a major concern for the media and freedom advocacy groups.

We have more guidelines from other institutions, such as the Consultative Council of European Judges (CCJE), another advisory body of the CoE on issues related to the independence, impartiality, and competence of judges, which also affect this issue. In its 2001 opinion, the CCJE underlines the difficulty "in striking an appropriate balance between for example the need to protect the judicial process against distortion and pressure, whether from political, press or other sources, and the interests of open discussion of matters of public interest in public life and in a free press." It notes that judges are public figures and refers to the ECtHR rulings on relevant cases for guidance and therefore tilting more towards freedom of information.

In another landmark judgment, on the De Haes and Gijsels v. Belgium judgment of Feb. 24, 1997, the Strasbourg court ruled in favor of Belgian journalists and underlined that the press plays an essential role in a democratic society. "Although it must not overstep certain bounds, in particular in respect of the reputation and rights of others and the need to prevent the disclosure of confidential information, its duty is nevertheless to impart – in a manner consistent with its obligations and responsibilities – information and ideas on all matters of public interest," the judgment said. Therefore, we have sufficient guidelines to make reporters' lives easier in Turkey, if the Turkish government cares to pay any attention to them at all.

If Erdoğan gets his way in Turkey by completely overhauling the judiciary to his liking, he will not be much concerned about ECtHR case law, nor will he worry about whether Turkey will have a lot of cases pending against the government on its press freedom woes in Strasbourg. The only thing he will be paying close attention to is his reputation and the government's image in the eyes of the public. For that, Erdoğan will extensively use the sub judice rule to drag Turkish reporters to court, in a campaign to compel them to be silent about massive corruption or any other scandals involving his government.

Right to Dissent[42]

No doubt that the right to dissent and differ is far from treasonous— and it is actually more patriotic than just going along with everything else the Recep Tayyip Erdoğan government in Turkey stands for. The primary reason why members of Hizmet (Service), a faith-inspired social movement inspired by Islamic scholar Fethullah Gülen, have been attacked, vilified, and stigmatized by a government that is dominated by overzealous political Islamists and pro-Iranian sympathizers is that

---

[42] First appeared in *Today's Zaman* daily on Apr. 07, 2014

Gülen is standing up to the increasingly authoritarian powers of Erdoğan, who has seized control of the republic's institutions—including the judiciary—leading to increased polarization and tension in Turkish society. The vitriolic accusations and slanderous campaign run by Erdoğan and his loyalists—backed by their mouthpieces in the pro-government media—against their opponents aim to crush dissent, muzzle criticism, and intimidate the independent press amid massive corruption scandals.

In an op-ed piece he wrote for the Financial Times on March 10, Gülen described the predicament the country is facing by saying that "a small group within the government's executive branch is holding to ransom the entire country's progress." In fact, Gülen's diagnosis of the key problem that has tarnished democratic credentials and dealt a blow to accountability, rule of law, and fundamental rights and freedoms in the governance of the country confirmed similar accounts of many insiders who had served as Cabinet members and senior ruling party officials alongside the Turkish prime minister. The series of leaked audio files in the past three months has exposed this oligarchic cadre led by Erdoğan that has collectively plotted to eliminate opponents, buy off the press, and collect their share from those that wanted to do business with the government.

During the March 30 local elections, Erdoğan bought some time to sustain his rule when the governing Justice and Development Party (AKP) won 43 percent of the vote in the last elections, albeit with a 7 percent drop from the 2011 elections. His plans to consolidate his rule were thrown into disarray, nonetheless, when he realized the risks of running for the presidential office as his popularity numbers are not enough to clear the first round. What is more worrisome, Erdoğan must take care of lingering legal troubles stemming from a series of charges ranging from corruption to money laundering, and from influence-peddling to abuse of power. Just as the great Roman historian and orator Publius Tacitus maintained, "The more corrupt the state, the more numerous the laws." The Erdoğan government will have to push a series of laws through Parliament in order to bring immunities and reduced sentences for the prime minister and others implicated in the corruption.

In the meantime, Gülen and others who stood up against Erdoğan's abuses of power will continue to be scorned and ridiculed in conspiracy-laden campaigns in a pathetic attempt by Erdoğan and company to discredit their opponents. Perhaps that is the price the nation must pay to consolidate its fledgling democracy. The unconstitutional profiling of unsuspecting citizens and illegal wiretaps and surveillance programs against Erdoğan's critics will likely pick up speed. Since the Turkish prime minister commands total obedience, he will not hesitate to use scare tactics, wide-scale deception, and massive corruption practices to oppress people, groups, and businesses that are not cowed. In the meantime, the divide between true democrats and Machiavellian-type bureaucrats, intellectuals, academics, and politicians will become crystal-clear.

The oft-used word "traitor" by Erdoğan and his company to smear opposition in Turkey is an important indicator of how Turkish democracy is far from a full-fledged democracy and leaning fast towards authoritarianism. Not only members of the Hizmet Movement but also other critics of Erdoğan have been quickly accused of treachery by government officials. Muharrem Yılmaz, president of the Turkish Industrialists and Businessmen's Association (TÜSİAD), the wealthiest and most powerful business group in the country, was accused of treason by Erdoğan in a public rally when in fact Yılmaz simply warned the government that foreign investment will not be made in a country in which there is no respect for the rule of law, where legal codes conflict with European Union rules, public procurement laws have been amended dozens of times, and companies are unfairly pressured through tax fines. Such a harsh accusation should not be expressed by an elected leader without strong evidence and solid legal grounds. Yet Erdoğan, acting as prosecutor, judge, and jury, has lately been leveling treason charges against anyone with an opposing stance, from business organizations to journalists, from political opposition parties to members of the judiciary.

Equating criticism with treason by the country's highest political leadership fuels a climate of "spy-mania" in Turkey and raises the specter of a country in which dissidents and critics are summarily prosecuted and persecuted under "treason, anti-government activities, espionage, and secrecy" charges. The Erdoğan government's expanding campaign to pressure legitimate political opposition as well as clamping down on dissent and criticism by business lobbies, advocacy groups, and civic movements continues to spin out of control in Turkey. That unfortunately has the impact of poisoning politics and threatening the social fabric of the country.

Now the government's extensive efforts to spin the conspiracy stories with its own twists and turns in order to water down the corruption scandals implicating Erdoğan and his family members have engulfed the Turkish diaspora as well. The Turkish prime minister deliberately escalated his fight against Hizmet overseas, trying to drag Turkey's partners into a domestic dispute. He even misquoted a phone conversation he had with the US President Barack Obama before the local elections and lied, saying that his grievances over Gülen were accepted by Obama, drawing an unprecedented rebuke on his distorted remarks from the White House.

Picking up after his boss, Foreign Minister Ahmet Davutoğlu, the architect of fundamentally shortsighted foreign policies in Syria and Egypt, mobilized Turkish diplomats in exporting domestic divisions to expat communities abroad. Davutoğlu openly accused Hizmet of treachery and attacked the critical media for questioning incidents on the Syrian border and for criticizing the content of a security leak that exposed an alleged staging of a conflict with Syria over a false-flag operation. The Turkish foreign minister, who had been praising Turkish schools and visiting them until a year ago, suddenly had a change of heart because Hizmet did not support his ideology-driven foreign policy choices in the Middle East at the expense of Turkey's traditional approach that valued its ties with transatlantic partners and allies.

Erdoğan, who had characterized his many meetings with the Hizmet community in diaspora as an effort to attract attention from foreign leaders and marshal political support at home, now portrays Hizmet as an enemy and lobbies his interlocutors abroad to crack down on their schools just as he has been trying to do in Turkey—albeit with limited success. Despite the fact that these volunteer-driven and non-partisan schools do not receive any funding from the Turkish government and that they are successful educational institutions perfectly in compliance with the host country laws and regulations, the Erdoğan government's demonizing efforts will eventually boomerang on the Turkish government itself as this would be seen as meddling into other countries' affairs. The fact that these schools are among some of the best-achieving educational institutions in the countries in which they were established, and that they actively maintain outreach activities, belies the slanders and smears run by the Erdoğan government.

Erdoğan's war against Hizmet, while not based on any sound policy advice, is mainly motivated by personal anger and bitterness over his loss of a major endorsement by an important group as well as his huge embarrassment over the corruption scandals. He treats the slightest dissent as treason—as displayed in numerous incidents where Erdoğan publicly slammed journalists for expressing views that are deemed to be critical of the government. If the new draft intelligence bill that gives sweeping powers to the government gets enacted in Parliament, the Erdoğan government will have a broader driftnet in its hands to round up practically anybody who creates an inconvenience for the government. This witch-hunt, already unleashed by the Erdoğan government against opponents, aims to smother criticism and stifle dissent, first and foremost.

The concern expressed by some Turkish NGOs abroad has nothing to do with a partisan political issue but rather a genuine worry about the future direction of Turkish democracy regardless of what Erdoğan and Davutoğlu think of it. Criticism will not be limited to the political arena, either. The Erdoğan government will surely face a series of legal challenges both in Turkey and abroad including the Strasbourg-based European Court of Human Rights. The embattled Erdoğan's enlisted allies abroad, if any, will also be pulled into this quagmire where politically motivated prosecution on trumped-up charges of treason and espionage will prompt a huge outcry in Turkish society and in the international community.

War against Arts and Culture[43]

As the authoritarian tendencies of the ruling Justice and Development Party (AKP) government under the divisive political leadership of Recep Tayyip Erdoğan become more visible, with fresh evidence of intolerance over the right to dissent revealed practically every day, the government's relentless campaign to stifle freedom of expression is not just limited to freedom of the press anymore, but has now engulfed artistic and cultural expression as well. A draft bill prepared by the Erdoğan government—without actually consulting the arts community in Turkey—will bring state-funded artistic and cultural activities under tight government control.

Many suspect the bill, ostensibly aimed at overhauling decades-old institutions managing art and cultural works, will serve as an important tool for the government to crack down on free expression of artistic work, creativity, and cultural themes. It will eliminate the relative autonomy the arts community has been enjoying for decades in Turkey. The government's notorious record in controlling the independent judiciary and clamping down on free press with severe restrictions on print, broadcast, and Internet media portals have raised a similar specter of pressure on the arts community. Given that the government, heavily dominated by political Islamists, has shaped educational, scientific research and social policies to cater to its own narrow constituency, Turks may very well witness a radical shift in government priorities in steering the arts and culture with an overemphasis on Islamist ideological inklings.

The bill, kept secret until recently, prompted a huge outcry in the arts community when it was leaked, which in turn led to a hasty decision to organize a workshop with bureaucrats from the Ministry of Culture and Tourism. It failed to allay concerns expressed by the arts community, unions, and civic groups, however. The bill envisages the establishment of the Turkey Arts Council (TÜSAK), which will oversee the disbursement of state funds to artists and organizations that offer artistic and theatrical events in Turkey. At face value, it tackles a long

---

[43] First appeared in *Today's Zaman* daily on Apr. 11, 2014

overdue reform. Yet in practice, it gives the government the absolute power to shape the arts and culture through an 11-member Arts Council, all of whom are appointed by the Cabinet chaired by Erdoğan on the recommendation of the culture and tourism minister. Only six members are required to have a degree or credentials in art branches, which the government subsidizes. This board will decide on the development of opera, ballet, dance, theaters, symphony concerts, art exhibitions, children's plays, and artistic activities which are rarely able to survive on their own without government financing.

Judging by how the AKP has politicized other government agencies with partisan appointments, the composition of the board and the selection and appointment of its members spells danger for Turkey's arts community. Media regulator Radio and Television Supreme Council (RTÜK), in which most members are appointed by the AKP-dominated Parliament, acts as though it is the ruling party's branch, cracking down on critical TV stations both during the Gezi protests and the election campaign period in the last three months. In TÜSAK, all members are selected directly by the government, which means the council may risk becoming a puppet at the hands of the AKP. This raises questions on the capabilities of the council, which may be less equipped to allow funding to be used efficiently and to be responsive to the needs of the artistic community.

Another problem with the bill is that all subsidy and funds disbursement for artistic and theater programs across the county will be decided by the council itself through a procedure that is not transparent. The bill does not have an oversight function to check whether TÜSAK's decisions are in line with the needs of the arts community and whether funds are distributed equally. Considering that the Ministry of Culture and Tourism, in cooperation with the Ministry of EU Affairs, funded approximately 3,500 cultural projects valued from TL 150,000 to as high as TL 6.5 million in the form of grants and interest-free loans between 2003 and 2011, the financing of arts and culture programs must follow transparent procedures which are rigorously checked by an independent board. Since the final word on all art-related projects in Turkey will lie with this new council, there is the increased likelihood that funding will go to people and companies that are close to the government.

Section four of the draft bill is also problematic in that the council will fund only half of the budget needed by the applicants and the ratio will increase or decrease depending on the quality of the project. The council can also decide to entirely support the costs related to exhibition catalogues or writing projects. This is open to political jockeying for influence peddling and will work against new artists and cultural performers because they may lack the adequate financing to come up with 50 percent of the budget. It also dissolves positions for the current cadre of artists employed by the state when the bill becomes law, encouraging them to retire or move to other positions. According to artists employed by the state, the bill will result in the closure of 55 state institutions and turn artists into unqualified or subcontracted workers.

The government defends the bill as being necessary to decentralize the arts community, drawing an example from the British experience of an "arm's length principle" to establish a buffer between politics and the arts. The first article in the bill specifies that "while this institution is doing its job, it is to be independent and no organ, office, specific position or person shall be allowed to influence its decisions…" This will remain true only on paper as we have seen based on similar examples in other government agencies. TÜSAK's composition and its member selection defeat the purpose of liberating the arts community from political interference. In Turkey, the political culture under the authoritarian Erdoğan government has already dealt a huge blow to the independence of regulatory agencies, turning them into proxies for the government to intimidate and harass opponents.

The bill also sees the commercialization of the arts, citing costly and money-losing programs heavily subsidized by the government. It practically does away with state-funded performing arts institutions in the country, including the Turkish State Theaters (DT) and the State Opera and Ballet (DOB) under the guise of restructuring them, forcing them to survive on their own means with limited funding from the state. This has its own fallacies in Turkey. There is no strong tradition in Turkey where philanthropic donations, be it individual or corporate, can sustain artistic activities that are unable to draw in big crowds. Some may survive on revenues generated at the box office, but others, such as opera, ballet, and symphonic orchestras, cannot survive without subsidies, be they sponsorships, donations, or other means.

The real danger is that the Erdoğan government may be starting to bring culture and the arts in line with political Islamist ideology. There is already increased supervision and regulation of the arts community since 2011, when the AKP won 50 percent of the vote in national elections. There were criticisms that funding was directed to the arts industry to perpetuate political Islamist values, which the Erdoğan government wants to embed in Turkish society. It will not only be funding, but also policy decisions on the arts and culture which will be directed through this council. In a way, the AKP government sees arts and cultural activities as another way of disseminating political Islamist symbols and encouraging ideological indoctrination. This will inevitably lead to the suppression of other forms of critical artistic productions that are deemed to be inappropriate for the nation based on political considerations.

Even before the draft bill becomes law, we have started seeing how the Erdoğan government, dominated by political Islamists and pro-Iranian sympathizers, became partisan and ideological in its attempts to obstruct the Turkish Culture and Language Olympiad, mostly funded by private donors. While slamming the Turkish Olympiad in election rallies, Erdoğan threatened to refuse to even grant a location to the event's organizers. The Ministry of Education, the Ministry of Culture and Tourism, the Turkish Cooperation and Development Agency (TİKA), and Turkish Airlines (THY) had all supported the Olympics for the last 12 years. But because of Erdoğan's fallout with Hizmet, a movement inspired by Islamic scholar Fethullah Gülen and critical of corruption in the government, the AKP government has dropped its support for this very important activity which brings together thousands of students from some 150 countries annually and is attended by millions in Turkey. Interestingly enough, the Erdoğan government is supporting a similar competition to be held in Tehran in August. Go figure.

The bill defines the council's function as such that it can directly support any national or international project aimed at promoting the country as well as the creation of such projects. Perhaps this should be read as promoting the Erdoğan government's own parochial interest and political Islamist ideology. It would not be surprising to see TÜSAK acting as a partisan branch and propaganda machine for culture and art-related activities for the Erdoğan government when the draft bill becomes law in the AKP-dominated Parliament.

Parliamentary Opposition Restricted[44]

Hampering the democratic functioning of Parliament under the abuse of the majority represented in Parliament by the ruling Justice and Development Party (AKP) has been a worrying development, one that has aggravated press freedom woes in Turkey and that has gone largely unnoticed. If the functioning of the national Parliament in overseeing the executive branch was rendered ineffective because of obstructions by the majority, the role of the media in serving as a public interest body to watch over any excesses of government authority has also been dealt a significant blow.

Unfortunately, that has been the case in Turkey under chief political Islamist Recep Tayyip Erdoğan's government, which sees Parliament as a simple "law factory" that produces the bills that help him govern the country in the way he sees fit, disregarding decades-long traditions in parliamentary rules and procedures as well as universally accepted democratic principles. The opposition parties were not given enough opportunity to express their views on bills and motions tabled by the ruling party's parliamentary group and endorsed by the government.

The Parliament speaker, a deputy from the ruling AKP, has often resorted to formal rules in order to set aside democratic principles and traditions such as limiting the broadcast of debates in Parliament by public TV and thereby preventing citizens from following the activities of Parliament. The parliamentary debate on setting up a commission

---

[44] First appeared in *Today's Zaman* daily on May 09, 2014

to investigate graft allegations that forced four Cabinet ministers to resign was not aired on public TV with the decision of Speaker Cemil Çiçek. Private broadcast stations were not allowed to set up a link to the floor, either.

Moreover, access to public radio or television by opposition deputies is severely restricted under the Erdoğan government, especially during election periods. This is quite unprecedented and in fact goes against the rules and regulations that are supposed to secure the fair and well-balanced coverage by the public broadcaster of political debate in Turkey. According to the Radio and Television Supreme Council (RTÜK), the broadcast regulatory authority, public broadcaster the Turkish Radio and Television Corporation (TRT) allocated 13 hours and 32 minutes of campaign coverage time to the ruling AKP, but a total of only 95 minutes to the three opposition parties represented in Parliament in a 12-day period between Feb. 22 and March 2.

The governing party also abuses the working hours and timetable of meetings in Parliament, giving the opposition little or no time to prepare themselves for a debate on upcoming bills and resolutions. Since Erdoğan commands the majority in Parliament, he is the one who sets the agenda in Parliament, killing the oppositions' motions with unfair rules of procedure. The democratic quality of Parliament has been significantly reduced because of limited means available to the opposition to perform its duty of oversight, criticism, and prevention of misuse and dysfunction in government agencies.

This dramatic departure from democratic accountability in governance and transparency in public decision in fact represents another dimension of an authoritarian tendency that has been a dominant feature in the Erdoğan government in recent years. The opposition in Parliament is stripped of means to play an effective, responsible, and constructive role. In most cases, the opposition deputies do not enjoy the same treatment and privileges given to ruling AKP deputies. For instance, independent Istanbul deputy Muhammed Çetin, who recently resigned from the ruling AKP, was discriminated against and blacklisted by national flag carrier, Turkish Airlines (THY).

The opposition was also shorted-changed by the Erdoğan government when its right to receive auditing information from the Court of Accounts was violated, citing a new revision in the law for the last three years. Parliament's oversight role was not properly functioning when the opposition did not have any informed opinion on budgetary, auditing, and finance matters. Without comprehensive reports and reliable sources of information on government expenditures, the opposition could not fulfill its duty of monitoring the government.

The leaked audio that was posted on YouTube in March revealed how the government was afraid of auditing reports coming to Parliament for review. The audio, purportedly belonging to the ruling party's parliamentary group deputy chairman, Nurettin Canikli, and Prime Minister Erdoğan's personal secretary, Hasan Doğan, shows the men complaining about auditing reports, and blasting the Court of Accounts for tightening the screws around the ministries by auditing their public spending. Canikli is heard saying in the voice recording that "thankfully" the 2012 audit reports, which he described as "terrible," had not come to Parliament. The court was prevented from fully auditing government institutions and ministries for 2012 due to a lack of cooperation from the relevant institutions.

The political opposition has also faced physical threats in Parliament, which is dominated by ruling party deputies. During discussion of controversial bills either in the commissions or on the floor, ruling party deputies who have resorted to fist fights to intimidate the opposition have not been harshly censured by Erdoğan. In fact, rumor has it that Erdoğan privately encourages and appreciates deputies who initiate brawls in Parliament. Confrontations with frequent outbursts of anger and physical fights have erupted over corruption allegations, the situation in Syria, education reform, and the Kurdish settlement. The ruling party, instead of showing political maturity and respect, often uses arm-wrestling to get what it wants from Parliament.

The watering down of the right to information to which the opposition is entitled in Parliament has exacerbated the terrible state of press freedom in the Turkish media. Turkish media outlets are accustomed to sourcing their information based on official responses provided by the government or from inquiry motions filed by the opposition deputies. Since this information represents official accounts by the government, it is supposed to give reliable and authoritative responses for the public, including the press. Unfortunately, the exercise of this right to ask written and oral questions, and to receive reasonable replies to these questions, has been hampered a great deal by the Erdoğan government.

The government in most cases refuses to respond to parliamentary questions submitted by opposition parties on a variety of issues in order to save itself from oversight of its actions. What is more, when it responds, the government provides totally irrelevant answers, giving rise to claims that it is seeking unlimited authority and power by blocking all means of auditing its actions. For example, Özcan Yeniçeri, who has directed 4,162 parliamentary questions to the government, the highest-ever number for one deputy, has said the government has not given satisfactory answers to 80 percent of his inquiries. The pro-Kurdish Peoples' Democratic Party (HDP) deputy Altan Tan, who has directed 855 parliamentary questions to the government, says 95 percent of his questions on financial issues, foreign policy, and domestic security have been left unanswered by the government.

The rate of parliamentary written questions answered on time by the 26-member Cabinet, including Prime Minister Erdoğan, is 18 percent. The rules require the government to respond to questions within two weeks. The rate of parliamentary questions answered by ministers, including those that have been answered late, is 37 percent. Interior Minister Efkan Ala is the worst performer in terms of answering parliamentary questions. He did not respond to any of the 971 written parliamentary questions on time that have been sent to him since Dec. 26, 2013, when he was appointed interior minister. In fact, he has answered only six written parliamentary questions in total.

What is most shocking is that two ministers, whose portfolio covers Turkey's relations with other countries and should have set an example by respecting the parliamentary oversight role, have performed terribly. One is the European Union Affairs Minister Mevlüt Çavuşoğlu who responded to only 1 percent of questions on time. Considering that

Çavuşoğlu had served as the president of the Parliamentary Assembly of the Council of Europe (PACE) for two years between 2010 and 2012, he should have been ashamed for blatantly disregarding Parliament's role of scrutiny. The other is the foreign minister, who responded to only 79 questions on time out of 850 inquiries submitted by the opposition, corresponding to 9 percent overall.

Prime Minister Erdoğan is also among the Cabinet members whose rate of answering written parliamentary questions on time is below 18 percent. Erdoğan has been sent 8,055 parliamentary questions through the Parliament Speaker's Office, but the prime minister has answered only 1,398 of them on time.

All in all, the Erdoğan government has severely restricted the opposition's right to exercise scrutiny in Parliament, risking formation of an opposition outside of Parliament, which may not necessarily be peaceful. The weakened opposition in Parliament is an important gauge in measuring the maturity of democracy in Turkey. Erdoğan, who has been more assertive in displaying his political Islamist ideology in recent years and started building a country in his own image, is now the main driver in reversing hard-earned democratic gains that this country has been able to achieve after a painstaking process and many turbulent decades.

Chapter 9

Post-Erdoğan Era

Erdoğan Becomes a Liability[45]

There are worrying signs that Turkey's beleaguered Prime Minister Recep Tayyip Erdoğan, who faces major legal troubles originating from massive corruption investigations that implicate his son and people very close to him, has been burning bridges to save himself and his family from the looming threat of prosecution. He declared an open war on the judiciary, accusing it of "betraying the nation" while constantly bashing critical media as "treacherous." He has effectively suspended the rule of law in the country as the police will no longer enforce court judgments or prosecutors' summons. Those who do enforce judicial rulings face the wrath of Erdoğan and are replaced immediately. Now, with controversial bills he has submitted to Parliament, he wants to legalize his flagrant breach of rules and laws while usurping the powers of the judiciary.

Erdoğan's blow to the credibility of the Turkish justice system will have indirect results on an economy that is already facing external challenges from the US Federal Reserve's tapering, just like all other emerging countries, as well as domestic problems like the burgeoning current account deficit, weakening currency, and slow growth. There is no doubt this will have a chilling impact on foreign investment in Turkey. Two recent cases lead me to believe that Erdoğan's egregious actions will not just result in collateral damage, but, more disturbingly, will shake the very fundamentals of the Turkish economy with direct impacts.

---

[45] First appeared in *Today's Zaman* daily on Jan. 13, 2014

The government-orchestrated attack on Bank Asya—Turkey's largest participation bank, owned mostly by Hizmet (Gülen) Movement sympathizers—with the hope that the pro-Gülen media would be forced to remain silent on the corruption cases is just a hair-raising development.

The government deliberately tried to provoke a run on the bank with the abrupt withdrawal of deposits owned by government agencies as well as pressuring major clients of the bank to break off their business with the bank. The move was bolstered by a defamation campaign run by pro-government media outlets for weeks after the corruption scandal exposed the government's dirty laundry. The government even lobbied regulators at the Banking Regulation and Supervision Agency (BDDK) to seize the bank, whose balance sheet was dealt a blow overnight. Yet the bank quickly recovered from the shake-up, thanks to the campaigning of citizens and new investors who rushed to aid the bank with fresh capital. The regulators have been left with no justification to seize the bank, a move that was also reportedly opposed by the economy czar, Deputy Prime Minister Ali Babacan.

This is an unbelievable scandal which might have put the whole banking and financial industry in Turkey in jeopardy, triggering a domino effect on other institutions. Trying to force a bank that is publicly traded on the stock market into bankruptcy has no justification whatsoever and no sensible leader would sign on to this devious campaign to shut down the nation's largest participation bank, which has international obligations as well as big domestic depositors. This clearly shows how far Erdoğan is willing to go to save himself. He does not seem to care about the national economy, much less the country's reputation.

The second example is the gold mining company Koza Altın A.Ş., a 100 percent Turkish-owned company that also has interests in print and visual media outlets. Because the editorial side of the business has been providing critical coverage of corruption cases, the Erdoğan government shut down the company's operations in the Çukuralan gold mine, near İzmir, citing problems in the licensing paperwork. The company won the court case after an appeal for a stay on the stoppage of work and resumed its operations some 10 days later. In the meantime, however, the company lost money from the work cessation and lost market-share value. The government's attempt to punish a company that is the third private firm on the list of top performers in terms of corporate taxes and one which employs thousands of workers is another strong indication that Erdoğan does not care much about the economy at this stage.

There are other examples, too, such as Turkey's largest conglomerate Koç, which Erdoğan is not happy with and which his government constantly harasses with tax audits. On top of all these worries, Erdoğan's problems raise the specter of unrestrained populist spending on the eve of elections because he has so much at stake at the ballot box. He believes that if his government gets a strong mandate in the elections, he will have the upper hand politically to fight his legal challenges and that he will be able to overcome most of his problems.

The economy and the rule of law are not the only causalities of Erdoğan's strong survival instincts. He may deliberately damage the social cohesion in an already very polarized society, which may impact stability in the governance of the country for years to come. I'm not the only one who is concerned that the government could provoke incidents across the country during protest rallies about corruption. The leader of the Grand Unity Party (BBP), Mustafa Destici, who has the benefit of being privy to confidential information thanks to the party's network in the state apparatus, recently hinted that the government may try to derail the massive corruption investigation by staging deliberately violent demonstrations in several places. He thinks the government wants to benefit from corruption protests the same way it did with the Gezi protests by provoking violence at the rallies to sow fear among the Turkish public.

Moreover, the political discontent over corruption may have a new and perhaps even more dangerous flavor this time around because of the amplified emphasis on the symbolism of political Islamist ideology, which has the apparent backing of the government. Last month, a group of young men from the youth branch of the ruling Justice and Development Party (AKP) in Trabzon wore shrouds to show their support for Erdoğan with banners reading "to the death." The prime minister has resorted to similar tactics whenever his government found itself in hot water. During the Gezi Park protests, a large crowd of AKP supporters welcomed Erdoğan at the airport upon his return from North Africa in June at the height of the demonstrations, chanting "Give us the way, we will crush Taksim," in a reference to protesters at Taksim Square in Istanbul.

Erdoğan's deputies and aides have been openly making threatening remarks to those critical of the government, with one deputy from İzmir hinting that the now-removed lead graft prosecutor, Zekeriya Öz, may end up like another prosecutor who was suspiciously found dead at his home. Foreign Minister Ahmet Davutoğlu reportedly recalled at a Paris meeting that Turks have a state tradition of even sons being sacrificed for the good of the state in Ottoman times. When Erdoğan openly attacks the media at public rallies and singles out those who are critical of his handling of the corruption cases, we suddenly see a group of what look like radical people chanting extremist slogans in front of media buildings. My colleagues and I have been receiving threats every day. This is not surprising, given that Davutoğlu openly says on live TV that we represent the "crusaders' mentality" in our homeland. Considering that Turkey boasts a young population and that there is a major civil war going on right on our southern border in Syria, where some young Turkish kids were pulled in to fight on the side of radical groups, Turkey may be facing a new set of domestic threats that are quite worrisome.

Just like under any authoritarian leader, Turkish foreign policy is likely to fall victim to Erdoğan's troubles, as he will want to exploit those issues to distract public attention from his troubles at home. The once-powerful generals used to escalate tension with Greece using dog fights over the Aegean and maritime disputes to maintain their privileged position in Turkey. They used to maintain a low-intensity battle with the outlawed Kurdistan Workers' Party (PKK) terrorists without having the intention of actually defeating it. Erdoğan may also want to employ similar tactics by picking a fight with the Syrian regime and then passing the hot potato on to NATO under Article 4 of the NATO charter, which provides for consultations when a member state feels its territorial integrity, political independence, or security is under threat.

Who can guarantee that the provocation would not trigger even the invocation of the collective defense clause, Article 5? Erdoğan said in the past that "NATO has responsibilities to protect the Turkish border according to Article 5."

Overall, things will get worse before they get any better. What the nation is facing during these uncertain times is a question of how much harm Turkey will sustain before Erdoğan realizes it is too late for damage control with xenophobic and nationalistic discourse. Looking at the dynamics of Turkish society, the country certainly has what it takes to overcome these problems eventually. In the short run, however, the nation will have to pay the price as Erdoğan hopelessly tries to hedge against the judiciary with everything he's got. He will not hesitate to politicize any issue he thinks will benefit him. That makes Erdoğan a huge liability, not only for Turkey but for Turkey's allies and partners, as well. As he is frantically searching for new allies to enlist in his survival game amid the worst legal woes of his life, the country will further descend into uncertainty and unpredictability. Turks have to prepare themselves for a long restoration period in the post-Erdoğan era because putting the monsters Erdoğan has unleashed back into the box once this is over will be a formidable task. But in the final analysis, despite Erdoğan, Turks will achieve a better democracy with strong checks and balances in place.

Truth and Reconciliation[46]

Given that a slow-motion civilian coup has been taking place in a European Union candidate country where the rule of law has been suspended, the principle of the separation of powers has been discarded, human rights abuses have become rampant, and a vast shield of immunity has been awarded to government agencies that are tasked only to do Prime Minister Recep Tayyip Erdoğan's own bidding, perhaps the only way for Turkey to get out of this debacle is to look forward to an era of reconciliation in a post-Erdoğan period.

---

[46] First appeared in *Today's Zaman* daily on Feb. 07, 2014

One way to repair the damage dealt by the Erdoğan government in the last couple of years and to provide some form of closure for the dark period of Erdoğan's third term in government is to set up a truth and reconciliation commission. Without discounting the role of the criminal justice system, a truth commission can be utilized in a complementary role to help citizens move on with their lives in Turkey after colossal wrongdoings by the government.

We know that many public officials are not comfortable with the way the Erdoğan government has been ransacking the bureaucracy and Parliament with blatant disregard for traditions, rules, regulations, laws, and even constitutional articles. Yet, they are powerless to stop the excesses of the government as the judiciary and Parliament were rendered ineffective when the government simply stopped enforcing laws and constitutional articles.

The mass culling season orchestrated by the government in purging public workers and reassigning them en masse has even reached clerks, maintenance workers, receptionists, and guards in government agencies. In the private field, the government exerts all forms of pressure to get people fired from their positions, mainly in the media, simply because it does not like the way they express their opinions. It abuses the government's power to shut down companies with thousands of workers, intimidate them with tax audits, license suspensions, and executive fines.

There is no doubt this era will be over sooner rather than later. But the wounds sustained during this period—especially in social unity and cohesion—will not be easy to patch up. In the post-Erdoğan era, all these violations have to be accounted for and a redress must be provided. The judicial system, after having been dealt so many blows by the current government, may not be competent enough to cope with the huge challenges. Therefore, establishing a truth and reconciliation committee may be the only viable solution allowing Turks to close this dark chapter in the recent history of the republic.

This does not mean of course that the key culprits will be let go with impunity as the criminal justice system must function to hold those political figures that held ultimate authority in directing McCarthyism in Turkey accountable in a court of law. This has been the common approach in the European continental system and Turks will adopt that course as well. During the landmark Ergenekon and Sledgehammer trials, we saw the criminal justice system deal with meddlesome generals and pushed the military back into their barracks. But that came with a hefty price of increased polarization in Turkish society.

Therefore, making use of a truth and reconciliation commission can play a role in reducing tension while helping Turks address past human rights violations as well as identify root causes of mistakes. It can promote the necessary reforms, including stronger checks and balances, in order to prevent similar tragic events from being repeated in the future. It will encourage victims to move forward while low-ranking civil employees will be emboldened to provide a comprehensive picture of how wrongdoings in the government bureaucracy were committed.

It has become apparent that Erdoğan and his loyalists have no problems instituting social exclusion on a mass scale for diverse groups in Turkey. Aziz Babuşçu, the powerful chairman of the Istanbul branch of the ruling Justice and Development Party (AKP) and Erdoğan's point man for all public tenders and property redevelopment schemes in the city, said last year that the party was parting ways with Turkey's liberals. "The Turkey that we will construct, the future that we will bring about, is not going to be a future that they will be able to accept," he told party supporters in a meeting.

On Jan. 30, Babuşçu also admitted on live TV that the elimination of Hizmet Movement sympathizers from state institutions started long before the breaking of a graft investigation on Dec. 17 of last year, which the government claims was an attempt to destabilize it with the help of the Hizmet Movement. Therefore, it is not only liberals but moderate conservatives—all of whom are not aligned with the political Islamist ideology Erdoğan represents—who are being excluded in Turkey.

When you add nationalists, Alevis, and social democrats to the list, according to leaked confidential profiling documents by the government, social cohesion in Turkey under the current government is at risk of collapsing. A truth commission will help reconstitute the sense of civic membership for these alienated and stigmatized groups while helping them to finally gain recognition and redress the injustice suffered.

A truth commission, which has been experimented with by some 30 countries in the world so far, is not a foreign concept in Turkey. It was done in Parliament in a different format and under customary names. In 2012, a Coup and Memorandum Investigation Commission was set up in Parliament and later gave a very comprehensive report after listening to hundreds of witnesses from the public and private sectors.

Similarly, the terrorism sub-commission of the parliamentary Human Rights Investigation Commission was also very helpful in providing a comprehensive picture of the toll of terrorism, mainly by Kurdistan Workers' Party (PKK) militants in Turkey. The main difference between these and a truth commission is that parliamentary commissions have not included any civil society organizations in Turkey, although representatives from CSOs were heard in the parliamentary commissions.

The parliamentary Corruption Investigation Commission in 2003 had issued a 200-page report detailing the wrongdoings in previous governments' eras. Therefore, Turks can tailor a truth commission to their own unique set of traditions, drawing on past experiences and adding new characteristics to the commission's mandate to make a Turkish-style model. The commission needs more credibility in order to restore the sense of justice in society and to reconcile the nation with itself.

The common features of various types of truth commissions should be applied to the Turkish model as well. For example, the focus must be on the past in order to free the current political atmosphere from being held hostage to past events and the goal is to identify patterns rather than dwelling on individual cases. There should be a deadline to wrap up the work although extensions may be obtained. The post-Erdoğan government must stand by the commission to provide credibility, access to information, and draw lessons in formulating new reforms. The final report to be issued by the truth commission will be important in formulating new reforms. Those who will follow up on the recommendation must be clearly identified in advance to prevent the report from being shelved on dusty racks, just like many other reports.

Erdoğan's hateful speeches, repeated over and over again in public rallies, have inflicted deep wounds in Turkish society, pitting people against each other. Thank God this tension has not spilled over into violence yet, but there are growing signs that it could happen anytime. The harsh anti-riot police response to several protests over corruption indicate that Erdoğan will not shy away from picking a fight with the opposition, no matter what the eventual cost will be.

Hence we can anticipate that the social bill from the government's oppressive and authoritarian rule will only grow on the eve of elections. The last straw by Erdoğan is to generate a series of pieces of legislation in Parliament to provide immunity from current and future prosecution, similar to how military rulers granted themselves immunity from prosecution before handing power over to civilian rule. This is yet another piece of evidence that we are nearing the end of the line. Things will get worse before they get better. But it will definitely improve as Erdoğan's way of handling government affairs is no longer sustainable.

But whatever happens, Turks have to learn to let go of the past in order to save their future. Instead of adopting an adversarial position, they need to practice a compromise-seeking approach that would be better suited to governing a large country like Turkey with diverse ethnic, ideological, and religious groups. A truth commission, among others, may help the nation achieve that balance. This is the only way to restore democracy, the rule of law and respect for human rights in Turkey.

Battle Won, War Lost[47]

The results of Sunday's local elections—which became a vote of confidence for the governing party—have verified one crucial diagnosis many have been suggesting for some time: The ruling Justice and Development Party (AKP) under Prime Minister Recep Tayyip Erdoğan has lost its bearing and its main electoral appeal as a progressive party. Voters decided to stick with the least bad of all the bad options among existing parties, despite massive corruption scandals and a social media ban. The defiant Erdoğan has won the battle in the local elections, but the

---

[47] First appeared in *Today's Zaman* daily on Mar. 31, 2014

collateral damage he has suffered by polarizing Turkish society, alienating and stigmatizing large swaths of societal groups and upsetting the balance among state institutions will eventually cost him the war. As his armor of confidence was dented, Erdoğan's long-time strategy of becoming a strong man of Turkey has collapsed even though the results might have given him fresh hope.

Judging from his victory speech at the balcony of the party headquarters building in Ankara, Erdoğan does not seem to comprehend the fact that the election results suggest an urgent retooling for the ruling AKP to get its balance back in order to stop bleeding the party's popularity. Instead, he exploited the victory moment to present his family members as if the results cleared the serious legal troubles his family members were involved in. His tone was belligerent and his speech was indicative of further polarization in Turkish society. Erdoğan may find the results encouraging in his drive to drag the country down an anti-democratic path by further suspending the rule of law, curbing fundamental rights, reining in the judiciary, and acting with impunity.

There was significant damage to the AKP's baseline at the center and center-right, suggesting that there are growing numbers of disenchanted voters that pine for an alternative but have not yet been fully capitalized on by existing political parties. Perhaps the need for a new party to tap into this growing frustration has become more evident as the established parties are still struggling to bridge the trust gap with voters. This will embolden new challengers against the ruling AKP, pushing Erdoğan to play defense all the time. Erdoğan, who has provided guidance for the deputies in the AKP, has nothing to offer except further assault on freedoms, the rule of law, and democracy. That will not be sustainable in today's Turkey, no matter how strong a mandate he was awarded in the local elections.

Now Erdoğan faces two significant challenges: One is time, which is running out fast as the looming presidential election in August 2014 approaches—to be followed by national elections in 2015 with the possibility of an early election. Second, Erdoğan has lost the political momentum to drive his own agenda and it will be very difficult for him to gain traction in the face of very controversial election results. The very close margins in victories the AKP claimed in Istanbul and Ankara will certainly have a chilling impact on politics beyond mere votes. The baseline support by itself is not enough to carry Erdoğan to the presidency and he needs new allies to achieve his dream of becoming president.

The bitter election campaign period, during which Erdoğan abused all state powers to create unfair conditions for the opposition—including banning Twitter and YouTube without court judgments—has cast a long shadow on the results of the local elections. Citizens' access to free and fair reporting was thwarted by increased pressure on the media, while Erdoğan used the media he built to promote conspiracy-loaded messages that his government was under attack by international forces and domestic collaborators. The AKP used its unmatched financial resources to buy ads on TV, in print media, and on billboards, and mobilized state resources to help its candidates beat their competitors. Changing the electoral law to redistrict some 30 municipalities worked to the advantage of the ruling AKP in many cases.

Now that the elections are over, the lingering questions on the fairness of the race must be addressed. The entire electorate in Turkey needs closure that can be only achieved if both the ruling and opposition parties come to a common understanding on the final results. That seems unlikely, however, considering the diverging positions by the government and the opposition that were expressed in the aftermath of the elections. If Erdoğan continues to pursue the hostile attitude toward the larger electorate that he adopted in the campaign trail, Turkey may even see violent protests and street clashes. If the widespread allegations of fraud in elections are not properly addressed in court challenges and people strongly feel they are being cheated by the government, street demonstrations may be unavoidable. Erdoğan must reach out and bolster the conviction among Turks that democratic channels for people to express themselves are still open and strong.

Since the Peace and Democracy Party (BDP), the political wing of the Kurdistan Workers' Party (PKK), made significant inroads in the southeastern and eastern provinces at the expense of the AKP, Erdoğan will start feeling more heat from the electorate in the rest of the country. With its murky settlement process, which only factored the terrorist PKK and its jailed leader, Abdullah Öcalan, into the resolution of the Kurdish problem, disregarding other actors in Kurdish politics, the Erdoğan government helped the BDP monopolize the issue. The threat and intimidation campaign by the PKK, which went unchecked because of the Erdoğan government's specific order for the police and military forces to stand down in the face of assaults, threats, and provocations, left the larger Kurdish electorate at the mercy of the armed, militant, and terrorist group, dealing a blow to free and fair elections in predominantly Kurdish southeastern Turkey. What's more, the AKP fielded low-key candidates in southeastern provinces in exchange for support from BDP-affiliated Kurds in Istanbul. The simmering resentment among Turks may take a toll on Erdoğan's government in the future on the Kurdish issue.

This was in fact one of the main reasons why the Nationalist Movement Party (MHP) gained some support in local elections despite a lackluster campaign run by its leader Devlet Bahçeli. Turks have been increasingly uneasy about the wrongly configured settlement process, which has emboldened militant leaders who used harsh rhetoric, and this was reflected in a jump in MHP votes in many provinces. My earlier projection of a "credibility gap with voters" for the Republican People's Party (CHP) was verified with this election. Although the CHP certainly stopped its decay and started gaining ground on the center-left and even made inroads into the conservative voters' block, it will need some time to build trust with voters. The CHP needs to consistently play that "reaching out" message to voters that were traditionally skeptical of the CHP because of its past record.

Erdoğan, once touted as a formidable politician who may hold his grip on power until 2023, when the centennial of the establishment of the republic will be celebrated, has been really shaken up in the past three months in the aftermath of the corruption scandals. He has lost some ground in these elections in contrast to the 2011 elections, in which one in every two voters supported him. Before the anti-government Gezi Park events of May-June last year and the corruption scandals that were exposed on Dec. 17, 2013, Erdoğan was proudly boasting that his party's support had reached 60 percent. If he had been faithful to his legacy as a democratic reformer, he could have scored much better in the local elections. Now he will be remembered as an authoritarian leader who did not hesitate to pull out all the stops to make sure he got a comfortable majority in the local elections. Nobody will remember election percentages 10 or 20 years from now, but they will recall how the country slid down a path on which Twitter and YouTube were blocked and journalists, businesspeople, and vulnerable groups were profiled and targeted.

Unfortunately, Sunday's elections have not settled outstanding issues in Turkey, and the government does not seem ready for any soul-searching to draw lessons from them either. That means the nation is heading into a more turbulent period than ever before. Erdoğan may have won the first round at great damage to himself, his party, and the country, but he may not possess enough energy to maintain his strength for the remaining rounds of the fight against the background of significant challenges Turkey is facing in terms of politics, the economy, and security.

Stability[48]

Turkey will likely enter a new transitional period when beleaguered Prime Minister Recep Tayyip Erdoğan, who has now become a major drag on his ruling Justice and Development Party (AKP) amid massive corruption scandals, realizes he is done with governing. Erdoğan, the most canny and savvy politician of recent times, simply cannot survive the current political, legal, and social challenges he brought upon himself when he grew into an overconfident and overbearing authoritarian leader. The power he has amassed in the past decade corrupted him so much that he thought he had become untouchable, committing a series of mistakes. He let himself get involved in a massive corruption scheme with commissions that paid for his role in managing state contracts, tenders, money laundering, and influence-peddling schemes. The magic spell of impunity for Erdoğan was broken on Dec. 17, 2013, when the corruption operation by prosecutors was made public.

---

[48] First appeared in *Today's Zaman* daily on Mar. 14, 2014

Now the question is, who will usher Turkey into a new era and lead the transformation of the country that is a crucial NATO ally, EU candidate, and important regional power with significant assets at its disposal to make things better or worse for its partners? How will Turkey look in the post-Erdoğan era—will there be a gap in the transition that may be filled with unaccountable power brokers? Assessing what direction developments may take, I would say there is no doubt that whoever gets the mandate to run the country in free and fair elections will form a representative government. There is no going back on that long-held tradition as the democratic functioning of state structures, with all its shortcomings, is still a sine qua non for Turks.

The recent crises with the Erdoğan government—which effectively suspended the rule of law—dealt a blow to the independent judiciary, cowed most media into silence, and alienated a large swath of society. These crises have taught Turks a valuable lesson by shedding light on what they want for their future. That includes preventing one person (or state branch) from consolidating too much power, shoring up weak accountability and transparency rules, strengthening parliamentary oversight functions, restoring respect to the rule of law, fundamental rights and liberties, establishing an independent and impartial judiciary, and doing away with a presidency that rubberstamps what comes to his/her desk.

On the political landscape, the map will change. For one, the ruling AKP under Erdoğan is finished. The only way for the AKP to survive is to get rid of corrupt leadership and bring a new one to make a fresh start. That seems unlikely as Erdoğan will fight to the death with loyal delegates as foot soldiers at his side. That means a new party on the center right will branch out from the AKP to appeal to the masses, which are clustered mainly in the mainstream and are largely conservative. It will be an umbrella party with liberals, moderate conservatives, and social democrats. In contrast to the AKP's start-up years in the early 2000s, political Islamists, who have inflicted so much damage on Turkey's national interests with ideologically-motivated wrong choices, will have no place in the composition of the new party, at least not substantially. The party will be led by a new breed of politician rather than risk-averse dinosaurs that succumb to petty interests. Perhaps the leadership will be shaped by collective bargaining rather than mobilizing around one single man.

The main opposition Republican People's Party (CHP) still needs some time to establish trust and credibility with voters. It has a huge gap with women voters, small and medium-sized business owners, the younger generation and the conservative bloc—attributed to wasted years campaigning on ideological divisions that did not bring a significant vote. It appears the CHP has decided to become a truly social democrat party, but it needs to play a progressive message consistently and over time, not just during election campaign periods. Still, there is a drag on the party from neo-nationalist, ultra-secularist, and Kemalist factions that makes mainstream and conservative voters uneasy. It needs to trade off increasingly marginalized groups with new voters for a broader appeal. Given enough time, the CHP will eventually be able to overcome the trust gap and present itself as a credible alternative.

The Nationalist Movement Party (MHP) is the one that gained more from the recent upheavals in Turkish politics, despite the fact that it has no clear party programs or mass appeal. But since it is not a xenophobic or racist party, unlike its peers in Europe, the MHP will be able to tap into voters' growing frustration with the ruling AKP, especially among conservatives. It will not be a strong challenger in Turkey, however, especially under the current leadership.

The Peace and Democracy Party (BDP) will be confined to the Southeast, where predominantly Kurds live, and it will survive as long as the terrorist Kurdistan Workers' Party (PKK) holds voters ransom through pressure, intimidation, and threats. When the PKK is neutralized and a secure environment is restored, the BDP will have to compete with new challengers. More diversified and pluralistic Kurdish politics will emerge in Turkey. The BDP will grab more votes in upcoming elections, but will not be able to sustain that support for long unless it radically transforms itself.

Three non-political actors will play a significant role in the future of Turkey. One is the military. Given that Turkey is in a tough neighborhood where political and sectarian crises have been unfolding, the country will need a stronger military. That naturally gives the military undue influence over politics, usually exercised through the National Security Council (MGK). Battered badly by the Ergenekon and Sledge-hammer cases where the anti-government junta in the military was tried and convicted, the military has distanced itself from reckless and interfering generals. It deliberately kept a low profile to prevent its reputation from being further tarnished by the fallout from court cases. The current leadership in the Turkish military is not comfortable with the release of detainees in the Ergenekon terror network whose shady figures apparently made a deal with the embattled Erdoğan. It will neither support the failing government that was swamped by the corruption scandal nor allow the junta to gather its strength in the military.

For the moment, the military seems to have adopted a wait-and-see policy while trying to differentiate itself from Erdoğan, albeit quietly. It wants to see the results of the March 30 elections before making a bigger noise. It knows it will be recalled for duty to tackle the impending PKK threat in the Southeast, radicalization along the Syrian border, spillover from the Iraqi and Ukrainian crises, and troubling signs in the eastern Mediterranean. Hence, it will have a vital interest in supporting stability in the governance on the domestic front but not with Erdoğan's AKP, which has become a destabilizing force by itself. I think the military will make its peace with the long-alienated conservatives in this country when it transforms the institution to be more inclusive and representative of society. Otherwise, the military's position becomes untenable in the country.

The other actor is the Hizmet Movement, inspired by Muslim scholar Fethullah Gülen, who has publicly explained in detail his vision of the future Turkey. In a BBC interview aired in late February, he once again spelled out the most important challenges for Turkey: establishing unity among diverse groups that include Alevis, Kurds, and others; boosting educational opportunities for the young population; and tackling the long-running poverty problem in Turkey. He offered his own views on a variety of issues and reaffirmed his support for the settlement process with caveats, criticized the government on corruption, and expressed concern over polarization and the lack of consensus and dialogue in society. Later in an article he penned for the Financial Times earlier this week, Gülen urged Turkey to write an entirely new constitution as a way to save its democracy. In other words, he was referring to a new social contract to start addressing the country's chronic problems.

Many wonder: then why does the Gülen-inspired movement persistently avoid establishing a political party to channel its views to the government? First, the movement knows that if it establishes a political party, it will lose its broad appeal. It fundamentally defines itself as a faith-inspired civic movement with a huge emphasis on education, dialogue, and social activities that require constant efforts to reach out to people from all walks of life. It knows it can only win the hearts and minds of people from the diverse ideological, racial, and religious make-up that is the social fabric in Turkey and retain its credibility abroad if it stays a non-political actor. This is a vital for the movement and not a luxury it can afford to lose. That is how it survived a decades-long history of political parties failing in Turkey, and that is why it picked up support in over 150 countries where it has established schools, performed charity work, and opened dialogue institutions.

But that does not mean the movement will stay idle in the face of the political transformation that is taking place in Turkey, the birthplace of the movement. As it did in the past, it will lend its support to political parties that represent ideals it has been defending for a very long time: the rule of law, democracy, fundamental rights, accountability, transparency, inclusiveness, and ownership. This is not only for the benefit of the country but also for the movement itself, which can only flourish under stable, transparent, and democratic governance. Therefore, it won't be surprising to see people affiliated with the movement actively working in politics and in various parties. This is the richness the movement has gained and how it has established public trust. It simply will not squander those hard-earned assets by investing everything in a single basket. In the meantime, it is only natural for movement sympathizers to enter into public employment—from the judiciary to the police, from the military to the foreign services—based on merit and qualifications.

The last group that will be a major actor in Turkey's future is the millions of Alevis who have been shunned by successive governments for decades. Although the group is very diverse, they overwhelmingly vote for the CHP. Just like members of Hizmet, conservative groups, and Kurds, Alevis have also been profiled and denied government jobs for years, despite the fact they are citizens and taxpayers of this country. Gülen's efforts to reach out to Alevis, as he has done with Kurds and non-Muslim minority groups for decades, have paid off in establishing mutual trust and reducing tension in Turkish society. This consensus will be an important asset in the post-Erdoğan restoration era during which citizens' interests and views should be taken into consideration in an inclusive manner on reforms, draft bills, and policy decisions.

As for foreign policy orientation, I don't think Turkey will turn away from the trans-Atlantic direction that has benefited the country immensely for so long. This alliance has in fact been valuable for Turkey in developing ties with new partners in Africa, Southeast Asia, and Latin America. That does not mean, however, that diversification, especially in trade and investment, will be discarded. Turkey's appetite to open up to other markets will only grow stronger and in fact will be better facilitated when the political Islamist agenda is dropped from the mix of Ankara's motives. As a result, Turkey will be more stable, more democratic, and more predictable. There is no need for Turkey's allies and partners to worry about the future of this nation.